Robert Apthorp Boit

Eustis

A Novel

Robert Apthorp Bolt

Eustis
A Novel

ISBN/EAN: 9783337028367

Printed in Europe, USA, Canada, Australia, Japan

Cover: Foto ©Thomas Meinert / pixelio.de

More available books at **www.hansebooks.com**

EUSTIS

A NOVEL

BY

ROBERT APTHORP BOIT

BOSTON
JAMES R. OSGOOD AND COMPANY
1884

CONTENTS.

CHAPTER.   PAGE.

     I. Southward Bound 5
    II. Captain Lee 14
   III. The Southeaster 26
   IV. At Anchor 34
    V. The Eustises 45
   VI. At the Polls 50
  VII. Madge 74
 VIII. The Oaks 82
   IX. The Dinner 97
    X. Deer-Hunting 113
   XI. Home-life and the New Regime . . . 136
  XII. Mr. Brown's views of Florida . . . 151
 XIII. At School 158
 XIV. Confidences 171
  XV. Christmas—"The Point" 179
 XVI. The Old Nurse 187
XVII. The Ball 198
XVIII. An Evening Call 217
 XIX. A Ride 235
  XX Colonel Richard Shorter 247
 XXI. On the Porch 260
XXII. Advice 270
XXIII. An Encounter 281
XXIV. An Explanation 292
 XXV. Midnight 303
XXVI. Morning 315
XXVII. Leave-takings 328
XXVIII. Down the River—Beachgrove—Epilogue . 339

EUSTIS

CHAPTER I.

IN the autumn of 1868 I was called home from Europe, where I had been travelling in search of pleasure, by the sudden death of my mother. She had lived for many years with my only sister and her children, at our old family place in the neighborhood of one of the pleasantest of New England cities.

My father, Henry Strong, after whom I was named, had died when I was a mere lad, and the settlement of a large estate, left in trust to my mother during her lifetime, devolved upon me at her death.

The whirl of business into which I was at once plunged, and for which I was entirely unprepared by experience, served an excellent purpose in distracting my mind at a distressing time.

But although I succeeded, with the assistance of my brother-in-law, in arranging our affairs more or less to my satisfaction, I developed no taste for

work of this nature, and was very glad to be able
at last to leave my interests in his hands and shake
myself free from business.

As good fortune would have it, just at this time,
and in the autumn of the second year after my
return to America, I received a cordial letter from
my old classmate, James Eustis, asking me to pass
the winter with him in the South. The invitation
could not have come more opportunely. I seized
upon the idea with delight, and made my preparations for a speedy departure.

According to the old custom of the Southerners,
Eustis had been educated at the North. We had
first become schoolmates at fourteen, and soon such a
strong intimacy grew up between us, that when we
entered college we became "chums," and lived together as long as he remained at the university.
But, when the civil war broke out, our pleasant companionship came to an end, for Eustis felt obliged
to return to the South, where, shortly afterwards,
he entered the Confederate army.

In our schooldays, my sister Alice had been very
fond of Jim, who seemed, indeed, almost like a
second son in my mother's house; and now she
heartily rejoiced with me at the thought of our
meeting again. Yet, at the same time, if I remember aright, she did not abstain from mingling her
sisterly farewells and messages to the Eustises with
certain admonitions against the wiles of southern
women, whom, for reasons best known to herself,
she appeared to regard with considerable distrust.

I left home early in November, and having engaged my passage by a steamer that was to sail from New York, I was obliged to stop there overnight, and in the morning, after a late breakfast at one of the best restaurants in the world, and with still an hour or so to spare, I took a carriage for the pier.

As I drove down the principal thoroughfare of the city, watching with interest the endless flow of vehicles and humanity on either side, my reflections upon this turbulent river of life were arrested by the sudden stoppage of my carriage. At the same time, I heard an unintelligible volley of shouts and oaths, and on looking out of the window for the cause of the disturbance, found that the street was blocked, and that all the vehicles near me were wedged hopelessly together, and had, like my own, come to a standstill.

Just in front of me, and where the torrents of Billingsgate rained fiercest, I saw a carriage that had been struck and half upset by a heavily loaded dray. Its occupants, who were evidently travellers, were clambering out to the sidewalk, as best they could, with their shawls, umbrellas, and portmanteaus.

As there seemed no immediate prospect of the block giving way, I got out, and, led by curiosity, pushed my way through the crowd to where the unfortunate party now stood, looking helplessly at the wreck. In the centre of the group was an elderly and distinguished looking man. He was stout, erect, and somewhat above the average height. His features were clear cut, and his complexion ruddy. His eyes and eyebrows were black, in striking contrast to his long gray moustache.

The faces of the two ladies with him were concealed by heavy veils; but their general air and similarity of dress and figure seemed to suggest that they were mother and daughter. Behind them stood a negro maid, weighed down with their many wraps.

As I drew near, I heard the gentleman say,—

"Well, my dear, we seem to be in a rather unfortunate predicament. The steamer sails in half an hour, and I see no chance of getting another carriage in time to catch it; so we must make the best of it and remain here for another week, unless you can be induced to go by rail."

"No," replied the elder of the two ladies, rather fretfully, "I do not feel equal to the fatigue of the journey by land. But I should think *something* might be done. It is too provoking to be stopped in this way!"

I listened for a few moments to their discussion, and then, agreeing with the lady that the case was a hard one, I stepped slightly forward and said to the gentleman,—

"Excuse me, sir, for intruding upon you, but my carriage is just at hand, and I should be most happy to have you use it. It will not put me to the least inconvenience."

After considerable hesitation on his part, and

many assurances on mine, he finally transferred his traps to my carriage, and by that time the police had succeeded in extricating the vehicles from their confusion, and the noisy stream was again in motion.

As the gentleman was about to enter the carriage, into which I had already helped the ladies, he stopped and said,—

"By the way, sir, will you kindly favor me with your card? I should be much pleased to know to whom I am indebted for this kindness," and at the same time he handed me his own.

I did as he requested, and, as I closed the door of the carriage after him, the younger lady raised her veil, and, for an instant before they drove away, gave me a glimpse of an attractive face.

I had not a moment to spare, so I hailed the first stage that would take me to the neighborhood of the pier from which the steamer was to sail, and succeeded in reaching it just in time, for I had scarcely gained her deck before the hawsers were cast off, and the vessel backed slowly out into the stream.

With some anxiety as to whether my luggage had arrived—which I had forwarded before breakfast from the hotel—I went at once to my stateroom, where I was relieved to find it all safely packed away as I had ordered.

After a hasty survey of my narrow and rather unsavory quarters, I lighted a cigar and strolled up on deck to enjoy the sail down that beautiful bay with which I was not altogether unfamiliar. It was a perfect November noon; the air as clear as a bell.

The sails and rigging of the vessels, and the outlines of the forts and headlands, stood out sharp and
well-defined against the deep blue sky, that gave its
color to the water; and the little waves glittered
and danced, as they rose to the northwest wind.

I had been standing for some time by the rail on
the quarter-deck, lost in the scene about me, when I
heard a voice at my shoulder say, with an exclamation of surprise, " Why, Harry Strong! you here?"
and turning, I discovered it to be that of Frederick
Brown, an old schoolmate of mine, but a man whom
I had seldom met of late years. He had been born
and bred in the village near our country place, and,
although we had never been intimate, I had known
him all my life.

" Well, this is good luck!" he said; "I was
afraid I should find no one I knew on board. As
soon as I arrived I went to the passenger list to read
the names, and I wondered if the "H. Strong"
might not possibly be you; so I was on the lookout
for you, and I thought I saw all the people come up
the plank, but somehow I missed you. When did
you come? Where are you going?" Upon my explaining the cause of my arrival at the last moment,
he went on. " Well, that's the reason, then, for
when the bell rang I went to look after my things ;
I was afraid, you know, some one might run ashore
with them just as the steamer was leaving. So you
are going to———? Well, I am also, if this old
craft ever manages to get there, for I don't think
she looks very new and strong, do you?"

"To tell you the truth," I answered, "I have not thought much about it. I should judge, however, that she is seaworthy enough."

"Well," he replied, "I must say I don't much like her looks. Then the staterooms and the berths are so small, and it smells so downstairs! But that does not so much matter, for I shall pass most of my time on deck. This is my first experience of the sea, you know, and, in fact, I was never before even inside of one of these steamers. I almost wish now, I had gone by land, but I wanted to try the life, you see; and, besides, the doctor thought the sea air might do me good. It was the doctor, you know, who ordered me to go South, or I never should have done it, for I don't like either the country or the people—to be sure I have met very few Southerners—but, then, I understand just what they are."

"Perhaps," I put in, as he paused to take breath, "perhaps, you will change your mind when you come to know them better."

"O no, I shan't," he replied. "I know them through and through. I haven't read the papers for the last ten years for nothing! Still, I intend to judge for myself and entirely without prejudice, and I expect to take very careful notes of all I see and hear. I hope I shall have the good fortune to meet some rebel generals, for I should like so much to hear what they have to say about our march to the sea, and our taking of Vicksburg and Richmond! I think they cannot fail to have a certain amount of admiration and respect for both Sherman and Grant,

don't you? Halloo! we're almost out to sea, aren't
we? I say, Strong, do you suppose it will rock a
great deal more than this, when we get out of sight
of land? I don't believe I shall be sick, though, do
you? Why, I have been out rowing sometimes
when it was really very rough, and I didn't mind it
in the least. I think I'll go downstairs now, and
look for my pipe, but I'll be back in a few minutes."
And so my loquacious friend left me.

Fred Brown was a man of about my own age;
tall and slight, and with rather sloping shoulders.
His complexion, hair, and moustache were all of a
like neutral yellow tint; his forehead was high,
but narrow; his features sharp; and the eyeglasses,
that he habitually wore, added to his general air of
inquisitiveness. He and I had gone to the same
school when we were boys, but in early life our
paths had separated, and now I suspected that there
must be as little sympathy between us in our thoughts
and tastes, as there had been similarity in our lives
and surroundings.

Fred, after graduating with honors from our
Normal School, had obtained a good position as
teacher at an Academy in one of the neighboring
towns; but, as I learned from him afterwards, the
sedentary life had undermined his naturally somewhat weak constitution, until his doctor had insisted upon the necessity of rest and a winter in a
milder climate. Thus his days had been passed,
until now, in a small provincial circle, and his mind
had had every opportunity to sink deeper and deeper
into its narrow ruts.

He had always been a hard worker, and when a boy at school had often, at trying times, helped me with my arithmetic, in which I was backward for my age. I had not forgotten it, and still felt a certain sense of gratitude towards him, for having saved me from many an hour of confinement after school, and more than one sound flogging.

CHAPTER II.

CAPTAIN LEE.

IN the mean time we had left far astern the last
points of land that guarded the harbor's mouth, and
were racing with the following waves and winds for
the open sea. The foresail was set to speed the vessel on; and she rose and fell with easy motion to the
ground-swell that rolled in from the eastward, possibly the forerunner of a storm.

When at length I arose from my seat to stroll
about the deck, I recognized at a distance the
gentleman to whom, in the morning, I had given
my carriage. He was standing near the wheelhouse,
looking out over the vast plain that stretched away
to the southward and eastward. I was not surprised to see him, for, without giving it much
thought, I had felt instinctively that we should
meet again.

When we parted I had been so much absorbed in
the idea of making my own connections, that I had
thrust his card hastily into my pocket, and now, with
a slight feeling of curiosity, I drew it out to look at
it. It read, Captain George Lee—and the name did
not sound unfamiliar, though at the moment I could
not remember where I had heard it.

Meanwhile, the captain had turned from his con-

templation of the sea, and came towards me. When
he drew near, he recognized me at once, and stopped
to speak.

" Well, sir " he said with pleasant dignity, " I am
surprised and pleased to meet my good Samaritan
so soon again, and to have the opportunity of
thanking him for his kindness this morning ! "

" Don't mention it " I replied, " I am happy to have
been of service to you."

" I see by your card," he continued, "that your
name is Henry Strong. Is it possible you are the
son of Harry Strong of Ingleside ? "

Upon my answering in the affirmative, his face
lighted up with unfeigned interest.

" Well, then, I am truly delighted to meet you.
Your father and I were great friends some thirty or
forty years ago. I was a young lieutenant in the navy
and stationed at Washington, where, as you know,
he passed several years in his official capacity. We
saw much of each other and became fast friends.
He was one of the best fellows, and most honorable
gentlemen, I ever met. Why, did you never hear
him speak of me ? "

" My father died when I was very young, I said,
" perhaps you did not hear of it ? "

" O yes, I did, poor fellow, but time flies by on
such swift wings with us old people, that I did not
realize it could have been so many years ago. He
was about your age, or younger, when I first knew
him, and a fine manly looking fellow. You may
well be proud, sir, to have inherited something of his

expression and figure, though, perhaps, not his perfect regularity of feature," and the old gentleman looked at me so critically and gravely, that I felt somewhat abashed. " He was a great favorite among us naval officers, and was equally favored by the ladies. We were both young and unmarried then, you know. Perhaps you never heard that I acted as his second in that little difficulty of his with Labouchere, of New Orleans. No? Duelling was not common even then among Northerners, and I am glad to think it is going out of fashion everywhere in these days. But there may be circumstances under which it is unavoidable, and if ever a man acted with honor and dignity your father did, sir! The young lady, however, was much to blame, as is so often the case! Ah, there's the loud tocsin sounding the alarm! We must secure our places at the table. It will give me great pleasure, after dinner, to present you to Mrs. Lee and my daughter." So we separated at the foot of the staircase, the captain going in search of his ladies, and I to my stateroom.

The captain's face and manner had greatly prepossessed me. I felt much interested in his conversation, as in everything that touched my father and his life, whose memory I had from boyhood interwoven with virtue and honor, and every manly grace, and now my feelings warmed towards the man whose affectionate reminiscences tallied in a measure with my ideal.

After dinner, I went again on deck in search of my new friend. I espied Brown leaning over the rail near the gangway, watching the mate counting the knots as the sailors drew in the log-line, and was not sorry to escape his notice!

I soon found Captain Lee and his party, comfortably seated in wraps and sea-chairs. When he saw me, he got up and introduced me to his wife and daughter, and drawing to his side a vacant chair bade me to be seated.

" This is our friend of the morning, Mrs Lee, and as good luck would have it, the son of Henry Strong, of whom you so often have heard me speak. Sit down and let me offer you a cigar. The ladies are quite used to it, I assure you. In fact, they like it."

I always do smoke at sea, and though the after-dinner cigar is the pleasantest of the day, on this occasion I denied myself the luxury, whether from politeness, or the desire of making a good impression on the ladies, I am not prepared to say.

Mrs. Lee was an aristocratic looking woman; with regular features that showed signs of beauty in her youth. Her eyes were good and her smile, though rare, was pleasant and disclosed a set of white and perfect teeth. But there were careworn wrinkles about her face, and its expression in repose was reserved and melancholy.

As to her daughter, how shall I describe her? I cannot with justice. Her eyes were brown and fringed with long dark lashes; her nose was straight and delicate; and her mouth well shaped, not small, but ever varying in its expression. Her complexion was almost that of a brunette, but the brown in her

cheeks changed softly to a snowy white at throat
and temples. Her hair, too, was brown, and fell in
waves above her broad white forehead. She was
above the average height, and her figure, rather
slight than stout, was simply perfect; well developed, but still having lost nothing of its childish
grace.

After the usual commonplaces that follow an introduction, giving time for that first survey of face,
dress, voice, and attitude, from which deductions of
character are often so erroneously drawn, Mrs. Lee
said,—

"I suppose, Mr. Strong, you are going to Florida
for the winter. It is becoming more popular with
Northerners every year."

"So I have heard," I answered, "and perhaps I
shall get a chance to run down there for a while, but
now I am on my way to———, I expect to pass the
winter with a friend of mine who has a rice plantation
near there,—James Eustis, perhaps you may have
heard of him?"

"Jim Eustis!" exclaimed the captain, "why, his
plantation is next to ours, in Churchill County.
Know Jim! We have all known him from the
cradle up, haven't we Mary?"

"Well, hardly that," answered Miss Lee smiling.

"Jim and I are great friends," continued the
captain, " he is one of the best fellows that ever lived.
Many's the good hunt we have had together, and will
have still, I hope. Do you remember, Mary, that magnificent buck we brought home last Christmas morn-

ing?—O no! I forgot, you were away at school—but your mother remembers. It was one of the largest ever shot in the county. It weighed, dressed, forty pounds to the quarter. His antlers were perfect. Why, when Jim and I hauled him by a rope up into a tree, to keep him from the hounds till the cart came, he looked as large as one of our native cows; and we shot him, too, within half a mile of The Oaks! He came out of the thicket within twenty yards of me, right in the 'open'—and I gave him a regular broadside! He bounded away like a shot from a cannon and did not fall till just after passing Jim; but, bless you! I couldn't have missed him! Jim didn't say so—but I saw he thought he did the killing! However, he is, perhaps, just the least trifle conceited about his shooting! It's natural enough, you know! He's young, and certainly an excellent shot! Well, sir, if you are fond of sport, we will give you some fine hunting and fishing before you leave us."

I expressed my liking for sport of all kinds, but, at the same time, my doubts as to the result of my inexperience in an unfamiliar country; and on this and kindred subjects, the captain and I talked for half an hour or more. Sport was evidently a theme he loved, but I judged from his conversation, that, although an ardent, he had not been an altogether successful huntsman.

At length we were interrupted by Mrs. Lee, who claimed the captain's services to unlock a refractory trunk and they left us, having first asked me to

arrange a blanket shawl which they insisted their
daughter must add to the burden of her wraps.
The task was not an unpleasant one, and in retaliation for a little laugh on her part, at my clumsiness,
I securely pinioned both her hands and feet in its
generous folds.

"You have indeed made me your prisoner," she
said, looking up at me with a smile.

"Then I should, no doubt, consider myself very
fortunate," I answered lightly. Her smile vanished
as I spoke, and fearing that she thought my remark
impertinent, I added soberly,—

"I will set you free at once, if you wish me to."

"Oh, no!" she replied, "I am very comfortable.
Is not the sunset lovely?"

"Yes," I said, looking at the brilliant tints in sea
and sky. "It seems to me at this moment that I
never before saw a more beautiful one; but within
a month I shall, no doubt, think the same of half a
dozen others, and the colors in the sky to-night will
be forgotten."

"Do they make so little impression upon you?"

"No, they delight me while the colors last, but I
cannot remember them, even for their beauty, if
that is all! The thoughts and feelings with which
they are in unison, or contrast, alone impress them
upon my mind. Free from associations, like songs
without words, though perhaps beautiful in themselves, I soon forget them!"

"You are very poetical!" she said, turning from
the sky and glancing mischievously at me.

"No," I replied, a little disconcerted, "I have no aspirations in that direction."

"Ah! then I was mistaken?" she said softly, as she turned to the sky again.

I felt provoked, as one does when the expression of a sober thought meets suspected ridicule, although I was aware that I had laid myself open to it.

Neither spoke for a few moments. At length she said,—

"So this is your first visit to the South, Mr. Strong?"

"Yes; and I have looked forward to it with the greatest pleasure. It will have all the novelty of a visit to a foreign country, with the additional advantage of being able to use one's own tongue."

"I suppose you expect to find a land of barbarians?"

"Oh, no!" I said laughing. "Some of my best friends have been Southerners, and they were much like the rest of the civilized world. I suppose I shall find many customs and peculiarities that may or may not please me; but then, you see, whatever I like I shall call American, and what I disapprove, Southern!"

"Then I shall always look for compliments in your disapprobation," she answered, smiling at me over the top of her blanket shawl.

"Of course you will never merit it," I said.

"Which?" she asked quickly, "the compliments or the disapprobation? With your assistance I will leave you now. Will you carry some

of these things below for me? Thank you," she
said, as I unwound the shawl and she arose. "I
shall have to trouble you to give me your arm, the
vessel is rolling so!" And with steps worthy of
Bacchanals we crossed the deck to the companion-
way.

"I know you will be very glad to leave me," she
added, as we parted at the foot of the staircase.
"Now you can smoke your cigar in peace, and you
have just time before tea. I suppose," she continued, hesitating for a moment, "you could not
get a seat at the captain's table?"

"I shall certainly do my best to secure one to-
night," I replied, feeling flattered by her apparent
interest.

" Yes, do," she said, " and please take the seat
just opposite mine, for a German sat there at
dinner, and distressed me by trying to commit
suicide with his knife!" and with an amused smile
she left me.

I lighted my cigar and went on deck again, to
think over my new friends. My thoughts centred
on the youngest of the party, and I found myself
dwelling upon the fulness of her voice and the
sweetness of her southern accent. Her ease of
manner and her grace, struck me as strange in a
young girl, and there was a touch of satire, or
coquetry, perhaps, in her words that piqued and at
the same time interested me.

After much idle speculation, I concluded that I
should find no pleasanter occupation for the next

few days, than to study this new and beautiful
creation. How many have spent the best years of
their lives far less distractingly, and to as little purpose!

That evening, although the German's seat was
empty, I did not avail myself of the opportunity,
but took my place at the lower end of the saloon.

Outside of my few friends, the ship's company
was not an interesting one, composed chiefly of
German Jews, travelling salesmen, and consumptives in every stage of the disease, in search of that
which many of them had never lost, and few would
ever find. Nor was the ship's "cuisine" out of
keeping with her company. There was no lack in
the number of the dishes, but they were unsavory
to the palate, as unappetizing to the eye.

After supper, I returned to the upper deck. It
was a starlight night with scarce a breath of air
stirring. The steamer rolled lazily along, leaving a
snowy wake on the black surface of the water. As
I strolled about the deck, smoking, I saw Brown in
the wheelhouse, immersed in the charts or compasses.
I left him undisturbed, and having caught a glimpse,
in the darkness, of my Southern friends sitting near
the stern I joined them.

The Captain did his full share of the talking that
night, for the rest of our little party was in a quiet
mood, induced by the starlight overhead, and the
easy sway of the vessel. I enjoyed listening to his
many stories of adventure. How narrowly he had
escaped in the dead of night, in swift blockade

runners, through the ironclad fleets that guarded the Southern coast, and how once, in broad daylight, on finding a squadron stationed at the mouth of the harbor which he was about to enter, he had hoisted the Union Jack, put on a full head of steam, made straight for the Flag Ship, run close under her port guns, " And, by jove, sir ! you would hardly believe it, but I had passed into the harbor and reached the cover of the forts, before they had sufficiently recovered from their surprise to give me a parting shot ! "

It needed only an occasional word to lead him on, and this I was ever ready to supply.

At length, however, as the night wore on and the deck was deserted by all but ourselves, the Captain said, turning to his daughter,—

"Now, Mary dear, give us a little song before we turn in for the night."

"Perhaps Mr. Strong does not care for singing, papa," she replied.

"Try me," I said, "and see if I am not a good listener."

She did not answer, but shortly after began to sing, in a full mellow mezzo-soprano voice,—

" When stars are in the quiet sky."

It was an old song, familiar to me from childhood, but I had never before heard it sung so sweetly. When she had finished, I waited a moment, and then said, " I am very fond of those old-time songs. Won't you sing again ? "

"Certainly, if you wish it," she answered simply, and again her sweet voice filled the night air. This time she sang the old love song,—

"I do not love thee ! No, I do not love thee !
  But yet when thou art absent—I am sad,
And envy e'en the bright blue sky above thee,
  Whose quiet stars may see thee—and be glad.

"I do not love thee ! Yet, when thou art gone,
  I hate the sound, though those who speak be dear,
That breaks the lingering echo of the tone
  Thy voice of music leaves upon mine ear !

"I do not love thee ! Yet, I know not why,
  Whate'er thou dost seems still well done to me,
And often in my solitude I sigh,
  That those I do love—are not more like thee !"

Her voice was not, perhaps, very highly cultivated, but rich and sympathetic ; one that once heard could not be easily forgotten.

"Bravo, Mary !" said the Captain, "you sing almost as well as your mother did at your age! Come, now, we must all go below or we shall have to get to bed in the dark, for they turn the lights out at 'five bells.'"

Little else was said. I helped them with their shawls down the companion-way, and retired to my stateroom with the music still ringing in my ears !

CHAPTER III.

THE SOUTHEASTER.

I PASSED many hours of the next day with my new acquaintances, and by sunset we had become almost like old friends, such, at least, was the case with the Captain and myself. As it is so apt to be with officers of the navy, he was genial and talkative, and with a large fund of general information gathered from experience and ready observation. His anecdotes and reminiscences, and his broad views, the result of a long and varied intercourse with men and countries, made him an agreeable companion.

Mrs. Lee I found it difficult to know, as she was quiet and reserved, but Mary and I rapidly established ourselves upon a friendly footing, as young people so naturally do when thrown together on shipboard. She had left school the previous spring, and had passed the summer travelling about the North. The coming winter was to be her first in society, and she was full of girlish anticipations.

Thus far our passage had been smooth, with light following winds, but during the second night we doubled Cape Hatteras, and came into the teeth of a southeaster. The good ship plunged fearlessly on, rocking and pitching greatly to the discomfort of her passengers; and late on the following morning I found Fred Brown still in his berth. He had not "turned out," though it was nearly noontime, and was in a most pitiable and helpless condition. What little it was possible to do for him, I did, and promising to return again in the course of an hour or so, I went in search of the Lees.

Mrs. Lee was in her stateroom, with the Captain in attendance, from whom I learned that Mary was on deck. Thinking that it might be of use I took from my stateroom a double blanket shawl, and went to find her. The vessel was rolling heavily as I made my way along the slippery deck to the leeward of the wheelhouse where Miss Lee was sitting alone, watching the gray sky and the foaming waves as they rushed past. Excitement had heightened the color in her cheeks, and the smoke of the south-easter had gathered in tiny drops upon the waving hair above her forehead. At times the jealous wind swept in among her shawls as if determined to tear them from her; but she only clasped them more tightly about her, and, with lips compressed, looked defiantly into the storm.

"You are having quite a little battle with the elements this morning. You are very brave," I said, when I reached her side. She had been too busily engaged to see me coming, but when I spoke she turned to me with a quick smile,—"You must use my shawl," I continued. "You are not properly protected from these blasts of wind and rain," and I began to wind it around her.

"I will not take it all, Mr. Strong, you must use the rest, I insist upon it," she expostulated, before I had done. I did not require to be urged, and drawing up a chair I sat down beside her, and held the rejected end about me. After all a storm at sea may have its bright side. What a pleasant talk we had! The wildness of the elements quieted us both, and our conversation took that meditative tone that seems to draw people near together. I caught little glimpses of her inner life and mind, and feared lest some inadvertent word might break the gentle current of her thoughts. At length she said in a low voice,—

"Were you very bitter against the South during the war?"

"How could I have been, with some of my best friends in the Southern army? No, I supposed it a social crisis that sooner or later must inevitably be reached. I deprecated the causes that led to it, and forced the settlement to one of arms. But when arbitration was no longer possible, I naturally desired the success of the Northern armies. The whole thing was terribly sad to me, and the South fighting as they did, or thought themselves to be, for their homes and constitutional rights, were never without my sympathy. We both have much to forgive, but your part is far the hardest!"

"Perhaps, then, after all we can be friends," she said quietly.

"Why do you doubt it for a moment?"

"I have always said I could never like a Northerner, and those that have come among us since the war have not lessened my prejudices."

"Believe me," I answered warmly, and with a touch of satire, "there are many good and conscientious gentlemen north of Mason and Dixon's line!"

"I do not doubt it, but their ideas and education are so different from ours, that we seem to have no common ground to stand upon."

"We have at least the common ground of all humanity, truth and honor! and what is more, the same religion, and the same blood!"

"Yes, but when I remember all the sufferings of our people, I find it hard to believe there can be anything good in those who brought them upon us!"

"Well," I said, turning it off with a smile, "let us not discuss it. It is useless. Forget that I am a Northerner; or, if that is asking too much, try to think that one of them, at least, may not be so very horrid and wicked. Will you not promise to try to be my friend?"

"No, I shall make no rash promises—I shall treat you simply as you deserve."

"Then I am confident you will become very fond of me before the winter is over!" said I laughing.

"You take altogether too much for granted!" she answered with some spirit.

"Not at all, for whether I deserve it or not, you shall like me before the winter is over, if I wish you to!" I replied with quiet impertinence.

"Your present tone, certainly, is not likely to increase my admiration!"

"Then the simple truth is distasteful to you!" I coolly answered.

"No, I like to hear the truth when I can recognize it as such, but your presumption is most disagreeable!"

I saw the rising flush upon her cheek but could not resist the temptation to continue,—

"You are unjustly severe. I simply said——"

"I do not wish to hear what you said; it was not worthy of repetition!"

"There again you are unjust, for I am certain it was no presumption on my part to say, that if I wished, I could make you like me! I really have hardly tried to make myself agreeable yet, you know, and still I think already you rather fancy me!"

"I hate you!" she exclaimed, turning upon me with flashing eyes, and at the same time trying to rise from her seat.

"Wait a moment" I said with imperturbable gravity and slowly freeing my end of the shawl, "I hope you will give me full credit for my gallantry in releasing you!"

"I shall give you full credit for your impertinence, sir, you may be sure!" she answered, drawing herself up with angry dignity, "I am ashamed of having listened to you so long. No I thank you" she added, rejecting my proffered arm, "I can manage very well for myself," and with hesitating, unsteady steps, she started towards the companionway. I followed near at hand, but without speaking. She had almost reached it when the vessel gave a sudden lurch, and in an instant she had lost her balance. I sprung forward, and bracing myself as best I could, caught her in my arms, saving her from an ugly fall against the bulwarks. For a moment her face was close to mine, and her hair touched my cheek! She hurriedly disengaged herself and regained her feet.

"I suppose I must say thank you," she said turning her flushed face towards me, and with a look in her eyes that spoke of anything but thanks.

"Don't mention it." I answered "it must be so very disagreeable to feel under an obligation to a man you hate!"

"It is, I assure you," she said with much asperity. "I would infinitely rather have fallen!"

Her eyes were brimming with tears of indignation as she spoke.

"Very well, on the next occasion I will be more considerate of your feelings," I answered as she turned away. We had now reached the companion-way and there we parted without another word.

When left to my own reflections I was not particularly proud of the part I had acted; in fact, I went so far as to call myself names. Yet, still, there lurked within, that certain satisfaction which the evil-minded feel on having been successfully aggravating. Then, too, her beauty in her anger harmonized so well with the grandeur of the angry

sea! However, what had it profited me? The dislike
of an attractive woman; the loss of an agreeable
companion, and much introspection not altogether
flattering to my self-esteem.

In penance I passed the remainder of the day in
the lugubrious company of my friend Brown, who
had not sufficiently recovered to leave his stateroom,
and I was rewarded before nightfall by drawing him
into a talkative and cheerful frame of mind.

"By the way, Strong," he asked, "who are those
people I have seen you with so much?"

"Well," he continued after my reply, "the Captain
is a fine looking man and his daughter is certainly a
beauty; but they all look awfully proud; did they
own slaves? Two or three hundred! I wonder if
they used to sell them and divide up their families
like a herd of cattle? It is really dreadful to think
how they treated those poor creatures, breaking up
their homes and domestic ties without pity; selling
their wives and daughters naked in the market-
place; and separating the fathers and mothers from
their children, just as if they had no human affections. I should be much obliged if you would introduce me to Captain Lee. I should like to ask
him a few questions about slavery. If he is a man
of sense, I think I could persuade him how bad the
system was and how fortunate it was for the honor
of the country that the North took the cause of
the persecuted negro in hand."

"I think, perhaps, you would waste your sympathy, on those that belonged to the Captain, at

least, for he tells me nearly all his old slaves are still with him."

"Then it is only because they were brought up in too much ignorance to appreciate liberty when they got it."

"Perhaps, on the other hand, it was because they had sufficient sense to appreciate the comforts of their old home, and the kindness of their master."

"I doubt it," said Brown, with a sagacious shake of his yellow head.

"Well, I will give you a chance to talk the matter over with the Captain to-morrow, if I can get you on your feet again, and now the best thing for you is a long night's rest. The wind is going down, and I hope for fair weather by sunrise."

"I trust you are right, for they say to-morrow evening we may get in. I would not, for anything, miss seeing the coast and harbor, and especially the old fort at its mouth. They say our batteries just knocked it all to pieces."

"Good night. I will look in in the morning and see how you are getting on. Don't try to read any more to-night. Sleep is the medicine you need, and the bigger the dose the better."

That evening Miss Lee did not appear on deck. The Captain told me she was not feeling well, and insisted upon sitting with her mother. He, too, turned in early, and as the solitude of the dark night and wet decks depressed me, I, soon after, flung my damp cigar into the phosphorescent sea and betook myself to a land of disquieting dreams.

CHAPTER IV.

AT ANCHOR.

ON the following morning the sun rose in a clear sky, as I had hoped. There were more stragglers on deck than during the previous day, but the sea was still too rough to tempt the timid from below.

The seagulls followed us, now high in air and again swooping down into our smooth wake.

I was standing well aft, with several other men, watching their graceful flight, when Brown suggested shooting at them ; so I offered them the use of my rifle, and brought it from my stateroom.

There was much joking and laughing over the frequent failures of the party, till at last Brown, who had missed a gull that was floating very near us on the water, said, handing the rifle to me with an expression of disgust,—

"Come, Strong, take your old gun and show us how to use it."

Now I was, or thought myself, a good shot, and this was my pet Winchester, so taking it with some confidence, I said,—

"Very well, gentlemen, I'll wager the cigars that I can bring down that large dark fellow, flying just above the others ! "

"Taken!" exclaimed two or three voices at once.

I threw the rifle to my shoulder and was on the point of firing, when I was stopped by a light touch upon my arm and a woman's voice saying,—

"Please don't, Mr. Strong."

"Certainly not, if you object," I answered, at once lowering my rifle, as I recognized Miss Lee, and before I could say more, she had thanked me quickly and crossed the deck, to where she and her mother had been sitting unobserved.

My companions, disconcerted at this sudden interruption of their sport, stood gazing rather blankly and in silence at each other and the gulls. "Well, gentlemen," I said, laughing, "I certainly owe you the cigars," and after a few words more I left the group, to return the ill-used Winchester to its case.

When I was going below, Brown reminded me of my promise to introduce him to Captain Lee, and added,—

"I say, Strong, why do you suppose Miss Lee stopped our shooting?"

"I have no idea," I replied, "but perhaps you will have a chance to ask her yourself this afternoon."

So, after dinner, as I happened to see the Lees sitting together, I hunted up Brown and having warned him not to be too severe in his comments on the past, I gave him, with some misgivings, the introduction he desired.

The captain shook Brown cordially by the hand,

and said he was glad to meet any friend of mine. The ladies too received him kindly.

I felt doubtful how Miss Lee would treat me after yesterday's little passage at arms, and, thinking it best to be on the safe side, I conferred the pleasure of her society upon Brown, and tried to give my own attention to her parents.

However, after awhile, I could not help listening to the talk of the younger people and I heard Brown say,—" Well, Miss Lee you spoiled some good shooting this morning."

" Did I? " she answered smiling, " I really was not aware of it."

" You are undoubtedly right," he replied, "if you judge only by the results. But two of those men are regular out-and-out sportsmen. Really their stories of hunting experiences are awfully interesting. They tell me they have shot no end of buffaloes, and that sort of thing, out West."

" Probably they were not used to such small game as that of to-day ! "

" I guess you must be right," he answered reflectively, and added, " I suppose you don't approve of sport ! "

" O yes, I do, my father is a devoted sportsman. I have grown up in the midst of it."

" Then, why did you stop us this morning ? "

" O I do not consider that sport at all, simply to kill for diversion, with no hope or desire of recovering your game ! "

" Then, I suppose, you take the ground that noth·

ing should be killed unless for self-protection or for food," he answered, waxing argumentative, " now I think I can show you there are other politico-economical reasons, even stronger than those you have mentioned."

" Pardon me, Mr. Brown," she said, laughing good-humoredly, "I mentioned no reason. In fact, I doubt if I have any. I am not at all logical, but some things strike me instinctively as cruel. I will grant that I am entirely wrong and unreasonable, rather than argue the point. I feel certain I should have the worst of it, and you know when women are argued down they become very dangerous and fly to their only safe refuge,—personalities."

" Certainly we won't discuss it, if you don't wish to, but I heard a very interesting lecture on that subject, and thought I might give you one or two rather good hints about it."

" Well hints have never been good friends of mine—for, do you know, whenever I have felt inclined to give them, I have found the mind that provokes the hint is incapable of understanding it."

" Yes, I think I agree with you," he replied.

" And few hints, on any subject, are of themselves of value, only the mind that diligently pursues the subject can make good use of them as stepping-stones or signposts. Without previous education the hint falls on the sterile mind, like seed upon stony ground."

" Yes, undoubtedly," she answered, with a twinkle of amusement in her eye, " and by the way,

Mr. Brown, speaking of signposts, it is time our sign-post, the lightship off the shoals, should be in sight, is it not?"

"O I had forgotten about it! Why, yes," looking at his watch, "it ought, by the purser's time, to have been in sight for the last half hour. Please excuse me," he added, rising hastily. "I must go and see about it at once!" And with an air of importance that augured ill for the keeper of the lightship if he did not bring his vessel in sight at the appointed time, he bustled away towards the wheelhouse.

At the same time, the Captain and Mrs. Lee went forward to watch a pilot boat that was bearing down upon us, and Mary and I were left alone together. I felt heartily ashamed of my yesterday's conduct and would gladly have begged forgiveness, if I had not feared my overtures might be repulsed. Thus for a few minutes we sat in silence, Mary looking down into her lap, and I gazing absently out over the water.

At length I turned towards her, and blushing and smiling she raised her eyes to mine. In a moment I had moved my chair to her side, and had besought the forgiveness that I knew was mine without the asking.

It is rather pleasant to abase ourselves at times, if only for the sake of being told that we really are not quite so bad as we choose to paint ourselves, and especially is this the case, when a pretty and forgiving woman consents to raise us from humiliation to the level of our usual self-esteem ! However, it is a pastime on no account to be indulged in, without sufficiently strong grounds for thinking that the helping hand will indeed be offered, and that we shall not be left to brush off, unaided, the mud with which we have bespattered ourselves.

At length I said, " Will you give me your hand in pledge of your friendship ? "

" Yes," she answered, holding it out frankly.

I took the little outstretched hand in mine. It was so white and perfect, that I could not resist bending hurriedly down, and pressing it to my lips.

She drew it hastily away, and with flushed face and sparkling eyes, said, " Why will you always say or do something disagreeable at the very time I think I almost like you ? "

" If your hand itself is not excuse sufficient, I have none to offer. Indeed," I added, " you must not make me unhappy. Do not be angry with me so soon again. I meant no harm, but it struck me as a very fitting seal for our compact of amity. Now, you see, it is signed, sealed and delivered, and all in your own hand ! "

" Very well," she said, smiling again ; " I will try you once more, but I have very grave doubts as to how long our friendship will last. You are too changeable, I fear. I like to have my friends always the same, and at the very least consistently polite."

" I promise from this moment to be everything you desire. Never disagreeable, provoking, nor

angry, always placid and even-tempered, and while
you favor me by watching this glorious transforma-
tion, you may, at the same time, attribute it all to
your own unvarying example ! " I answered.

By this time the sun was setting, and the low
coast line was clearly visible on our starboard bow.

Captain Lee, passing in his perambulations, told
us we should make the river's mouth by eight
o'clock, but owing to the tide could not run up to
the city before morning. Though he seemed annoyed at the necessity of passing another night
on board, I could not respond very heartily to his re-
grets. In fact, it would not have worried me to
have been told our voyage must last another week.

As Mary and I sat in the twilight, I asked her
many questions about our mutual friend, Eustis, and
his family.

"You will not find him changed," she said. "He
is the same bright, energetic, merry fellow he has
always been. I am sure, after you have been with
him an hour you will feel as if he left you only yesterday." Then she added thoughtfully, after a moment's pause, "He is so kind and good to his sisters ! "

"His elder sister, Kate, is a widow, is she not?"
I asked.

"Yes, and both she and Margaret have lived with
him ever since their father and mother died. To be
sure, Mrs. Jackson has a house in the city, but she
passes most of her time at the plantation. Madge
is just my own age. She is an intimate friend of

mine. How strange you should know Jim so well, and yet never have met his sisters! "

" I did know Mrs. Jackson years ago," I answered. " While Jim and I were at school together, she stayed with my sister one winter. I only recollect that she was very lively and full of fun. They said she was a great belle, and received no end of attention. Two or three men were supposed to be heartbroken when she left us. But Jim and I were too much absorbed in our own pursuits, then, to take much interest in such things. What a fine manly fellow he was! "

This seemed to be a pleasant subject to us both, and I recounted many of our youthful escapades, in which Jim was always the leader. There was nothing too daring and venturesome for his high spirits and youthful prowess. Quick and hot-tempered, but always ready to repent and ask forgiveness, or accept apology. Warm in manner, and true at heart!

And as we sat there talking, how vividly I recalled the scenes of the night before he left us! A dozen or more friends had met together in our college rooms to bid him good-by, and, in honor of the occasion, a supper was spread that, to our not over fastidious appetites, seemed worthy of Epicurus and his disciples! Their wines might have been purer, but they did not have our Jim to mix and sweeten them into that insidious punch, pronounced by all the crowning effort of his life. That night he was, as ever, the brightest and liveliest of our party.

How merrily the jests went round! Followed, perhaps, by gloomy speculations of what the war might
bring, to be in their turn banished by the wild joke
and ringing laugh!

The next day, in the gray morning, I went to the
railway station to see him off, and we had never
met again. Occasionally we had heard from one
another, and after the close of the war had kept up
a desultory correspondence. But friendship may
live, though correspondence dies, and my affection
for his warm-hearted, impulsive nature remained as
strong as when we parted.

At the expected time the steamer entered the
river's mouth, and dropped anchor in the quiet bay
to await the returning tide.

The few hours left were precious to me; and,
after supper, Mary and I went on deck again, to
walk up and down in the starlight. The absence
of the sound of paddle-wheels and engine, which
for the last few days had been incessantly thudding
in our ears, intensified the stillness of the night.
There was scarce a ripple on the surface of the bay,
and the great beacon on the headland threw its
path of yellow light across the water to our feet.
The silence was unbroken, save by an occasional
bugle call from the fort hard by, or the cry of the
sentinel marsh-hen warning her fellows of our
late and mysterious arrival.

We talked long and low, not wishing to break
the spell of the quiet night, and once more in semi-
confidential utterances, dangerous to one's peace

of mind at all times, but oh! how much more so, when nature encourages the folly with her most seductive influences.

The time flew by unheeded, and it was nearly twelve before Captain Lee came to remind us of the hour. But when he left us, with Mary's promise to go below, we still lingered for a little while. It seemed a pity that the moonlight should be wasted upon the deserted decks.

At length she arose to go, and I said, half jestingly, "This is the pleasantest voyage I ever made. I wish it had never begun or might last a lifetime."

"Unless the lifetime were very short indeed, I fear you would tire of it," she answered, handing me her shawl to carry.

"I hardly think so," I replied, "though, of course, you may be right. However, you should have too much confidence in yourself to say so!"

"O no," she said, as we walked slowly along, "it is not that, but because I have so little confidence in man."

"I should hardly think your experience could have been exhaustive," I answered.

"Perhaps not—and yet," she added seriously, after a little pause, "I have little faith in their constancy to anything, except to themselves? Their professions are too ready and profuse to be sincere!"

"If you were forty, single, and soured, your doubts might be natural enough," I answered, as we reached the companion-way, "but as it is they must arise simply from wilfulness or inexperience! Ah! what a lovely night," I added, looking out over the sparkling water, "will you not give me something to remember it by? you know my memory is very poor, and I should like to remember to-night!"

"Yes," she answered, "I will, though you are not flattering! But you must promise to return it to me, if I ever ask for it," and unfastening a little confederate coin from her watch chain, she handed it to me, "you must not lose it," she continued, as I attached it to mine, "I have had it for years and years."

"I shall not lose it until I lose your friendship. When you ask me to give it back, I shall know that you have ceased to be my friend! How long shall I keep it?"

"No doubt longer than you deserve!" she answered, holding out her hand, and bidding me good night.

After she left me I stayed on deck to smoke a last cigar. I felt unaccountably cheerful and happy, notwithstanding the pleasant voyage was at an end. I did not care to scrutinize my feelings too closely—content to leave the future to itself.

CHAPTER V.

WHEN in the morning I made my rather tardy appearance, everything on board was in a state of great disorder. The saloon was blockaded with traps and luggage of every description, disgorged from the adjoining staterooms.

The passengers, many of whom I had not seen during the voyage, were rushing aimlessly about, calling to one another and the waiters, or sitting bewildered in the midst of the confusion.

I made my way, as best I could, to the upper deck and just in time to see the Lees to their carriage on the wharf.

" Well, Strong," said the Captain, as he bade me good-by " is there anything I can do for you ? "

" Nothing, thank you," I replied, " I suppose Jim will come to town in the course of the day, and look me up. I shall wait for him at the hotel."

" Won't you come and breakfast with us," he asked, " and let him follow if he makes his appearance ? "

" Thank you," I answered, glancing at Mary for a word of encouragement, but as she said nothing, I continued, " I have so many things to attend to, it will be impossible this morning."

"Well, I am sorry," he said, "but we shall soon meet again. We are going out to the plantation in a few days. Good-by! Tell Jim not to make any plans for hunting, without consulting me. Now Moses, drive on!" and with a smile but not a word from Mary they were gone!

As I stood watching the unfamiliar scene about me, Fred Brown came rushing past, with more luggage than he could well manage. "Halloo, Brown!" I called after him. "What's your hurry? Let me take some of that burden from your overtaxed shoulders! Where are you going at such a pace? Is it the returning appetite, anxious to make up for its long inaction?"

"Thank you, Strong," he gasped, "If you will just take one or two of these things to the 'bus for me. No, I am off for Florida, and have just time to catch the train. It is a perfect nuisance having to hurry off in this way. I had laid out the entire day to be spent here, but find, what with the boat up the river from Jacksonville and the trains from here, I can't manage it. But I shall be back after a while to spend a month or more. I can't stop now, without wasting my excursion ticket. Jove! I wish you were coming with me to the land of the palm and the crocodile! Good-by!"

There was no object in my waiting idly on the pier after my friends had gone, especially as I had had no breakfast and was growing uncomfortably hungry, so I returned to my stateroom to put up the few things still unpacked. I had just strapped my portmanteau, when there was a knock at the door, and before I could say, "Come in," a great, handsome, black-bearded man rushed in and seized me by both hands. "Halloo, old man! Is it really you, at last? Why it's good for 'sore eyes' to look at you again! And not so very much changed either! Barring moustache, and—'weepers' did we use to call them? and some twenty pounds of flesh, you are just the same dear old fellow I left fifty years ago! By Jove!" he exclaimed, standing back and looking at me with an expression full of happiness and welcome. "This is just the jolliest thing out! But come, let's get out of this spooky hole into the fresh air! Here, David, take Mr. Strong's things to the carriage. I'm glad to see you've not forgotten your guns! There, let me carry this case for you. It feels like a rifle. Winchester is it? Well we'll try to worry up something for you to shoot!"

I was not disappointed. He was just as of old, and, infected with his good spirits, I felt as young again, as when in the spring mornings at home we chased each other through the fields and woods at hare and hounds!

The carriage took us from the street that skirted the quays, where the tall buildings cast their deep cool shade, up through a granite-walled cut in the Bluff to the surface of the plateau upon which the city was built.

It was odd to see the buildings, whose five or six stories towered up so high above the wharves on the river-side, dwindle to rather mean proportions upon the higher level of the broad street on which they faced.

On we went, over the rattling pavement, past endless lines of mule-drawn drays, loaded with cotton, until, leaving the business part of the city behind, we turned into a sandy street whose great shade trees on either side lapped their branches above our heads. On past many picturesque little parks and squares (the "lungs" of the city, Jim called them), each with its flowers, its monument or fountain, its widespreading trees, and groups of children playing in the shade.

"Well, Jim," I said, pointing to the throng of youngsters, "There's apparently little danger of your city's becoming depopulated."

"No," he answered, laughing, "we are doing our best to make up for the ravages of war."

At length we drew up in front of a large white house facing one of the parks. It was not white after the manner of fresh paint, but rather of a soft, grayish color, losing all garishness from the uneven surface of the material with which it was built, called "coquina," and quarried on the Sea Islands near by.

In front of the house, and enclosed by an iron railing from the street, was a garden with well ordered flower beds, and many shrubs whose names I did not know, although, among them I recognized the long drooping leaves of the banana.

The path through the garden, diverging near the

gate, led to the steps on either side of a pillared porch that shaded the front entrance. We passed from the fragrant air up into a marble hall that ran through the centre of the house, and through the open door at the rear I caught sight of still another garden, and a jet of water sparkling in the sun.

"This is Mrs. Jackson's town house, Harry. She is at the plantation, but I thought we had better breakfast here before driving out, as it is twenty miles or so. Bring in breakfast at once, Sam."

It is needless to say I did full justice to the tempting repast that was spread before me. But we had little time to waste, and within an hour were on our way to the plantation in Jim's buggy, and behind a sturdy looking horse.

We drove through the shady streets, past brick and stucco houses, with piazzas often running to the second story, all shut in with green blinds, and with yards surrounded by solid eight-foot walls, useful in old times for imprisoning the slaves after the evening hour, but not ornamental in the eyes of the new civilization; then past clusters of shanties, and plats of stunted grass and sand, the playgrounds of the negro children; past the dirt and squalor that gather on a city's outskirts, to the more open country beyond, where, here and there, white houses with little flower gardens in front, and well kept market farms around them, bespoke much thrifty labor and frugal comfort.

"This old mound," said Jim, "with the stagnant

pool below it, is part of the wall thrown up for the defence of the city. If you look across the fields you will see it rising there at intervals as far as the eye can reach, but the ploughshare has done good work, and before long not a vestige will remain. In old times the forest came pretty well up to where we are, but this half-mile or more was cleared when the city was invested."

Presently we left the open land and entered the shade of the forest which did not again desert us for many a mile, unless at the clearing of some squatter, or some negro hamlet, or at the crossing of some dark river with its adjacent rice-fields diked and ditched in great quadrangles. The dead-level of the country, and the seemingly endless forests, that for an hour at a time enclosed us, gave a welcome charm to the occasional glimpses of broad, sunny marsh that lay along these river banks.

At length we came to an opening in the woods, where, near the roadside, stood a long, low shanty, and before it a team of mules and open wagon in which I recognized my luggage.

"Halloo!" said Jim, "confound that January! He has stopped to get a drink at Isaac's. These Jew grocery stores are the pest of the county. They ruin the negroes with bad whisky! I wish we could run them out of the place! Halloo! January, I say! Halloo there!" and as he shouted an, old darkey hurried out of the shop, climbed to his seat on the wagon, gathered up the reins and started the mules without looking at us.

"Halloo, January!" cried Jim, "what were you up to in there?"

"Halloo, Massa Jim! you thar!" said the negro, turning towards us with well feigned astonishment. "De troof ob de matter is, Massa Jim, de off mule, she seem berry fursty. I jes' done fetch de bucket into de shop. Miss Katie and Miss Margaret gone by heah about free minutes ago!"

"Well, January, you know this is against orders. You promised me last week never to go to Isaac's again. All is, if I catch you at it after this, you'll have to find your meat where you get your drink."

"'Fore de Lord, Massa Jim! I'se nebber touch anudder drop! But de troof is, dat ole gray mule, Massa Jim, she jes' put her hoofs in de san' an' won' go by Isaac's till she ketch her bref!"

"Well, don't waste yours, January, and mind what I say, for I mean it," and he added as we drove on, "Poor old fellow! he can no more help taking in whiskey than the sea the Altamaha! By the way, Harry, do you see those fields of stubble over there? Well, you would be amused at the strange vagaries some of your shrewd fellow-countrymen have indulged in down here, since the war! That was a cotton plantation, and a good one too in its day. It lies next to 'Palmetto Grove,' the Lees' place. It was bought a few years ago by a man named Gore, from your State, who in a couple of seasons exhausted his capital in the experiment of raising cotton under glass! He abandoned the place last year and has returned to his native town very thoroughly disgusted, I am told, with this part of the country. Ah, there are the ladies on the hill near the gate. Don't you see them ? "

And in the distance down the straight road I descried an object or objects, that, to my inexperienced eyes, might have been anything, from a horse to a house.

" Yes, I think I see something. But where's the hill, Jim ? " I said, looking along the dead level before me.

" Why man ! " he answered laughing, " there at the gate of ' The Oaks,' where they are stopping ! Don't you see how the land rises from the hollow yonder ? We are very proud of that hill ! It is the Mont Blanc of the county ! "

We soon reached the gate, and turned into the shady driveway. Through the long vista of oak-trees, whose moss-hung branches were interlaced above us, we could catch a glimpse of the old white house.

These old oaks, which had given the place its name, were magnificent ; their girth of trunk and limb told a tale of sturdy growth through centuries of storm and sunshine.

The place had belonged to the Eustises for more than a hundred years, and this avenue of oaks was their especial pride. Several generations of youth and maiden had passed up together, hand in hand, beneath their cool shade, with all the joyousness of life's maytime ; in turn, at length, to pass down again one by one under the weeping moss on their last solitary journey !

Yet the old oaks lived on in their defiant strength, untouched by time, and gathering to themselves the life of the more ephemeral nature around them, lengthened, year by year, their giant limbs, and pushed out their fresh green leaves with each recurring spring. Behind them, on either side, was a belt of pine woods, and beyond lay open farming land.

It was a grand old avenue; and yet I was glad to leave its spectral looking moss and chilly shade, for the warm sunlight again, as we drew up in front of the picket-fence, that surrounded the garden before the house.

Goats, and poultry of all kinds, were running wild about the half-dozen acres of open land, in the centre of which stood the house and garden; and, under the trees on the outskirts of the clearing, lean, high-backed swine were grubbing in the leaves and underbush.

We heard the hounds baying in their distant kennels at our approach, and as Jim alighted and hitched the horse to a picket of the fence, two or three black and tan-colored pups, with short legs, long bodies and drooping ears, entangled themselves about his feet with whines and awkward demonstrations of affection.

"Well, Harry, my boy!" he said, "here we are at last; and there are the girls waiting for us on the piazza! Down, Jack! down sir, I say! Halloo, Bill!" as a stalwart negro boy came from behind the house, grinning, and touching his brimless hat,

"give Charley a good grooming when you take him
out. Hear? And when January comes, help him
take Mr. Strong's things to his room. Leave the
gun cases in the smoking-room. Hear? Well,
come on, Harry!"

We passed through a garden, full of rose
bushes and japonica trees, and up the steps to a
broad piazza which, supported by brick columns,
ran along the front of the house above the high
brick basement.

Two ladies were sitting there, and, as they arose
to meet us, I saw at a glance that both were pretty,
and that one had the advantage of greater youth
and was the taller of the two.

" Well, girls, we've captured Harry, at last!" exclaimed Jim, as we came up the steps.

"I am delighted to see you again, Harry!" cried
Mrs. Jackson. " It was so nice of you to come to
us. I do not dare to think how many years ago I
stayed with you all at ' Ingleside'! and how is Alice?
and how are the little ones? We drove down to
meet you this evening, but you were later than we
expected. This is my sister Margaret, Harry. I
believe you have never meet."

As I shook the shapely hand, so cordially extended,
I said, " I should have known you anywhere from
your likeness to Jim, although your coloring is so
different."

" Would you like to go at once to your room?"
continued Mrs. Jackson; " or will you sit down and
rest after your long drive? Please move the chairs

to the end of the piazza, Jim; there is a nice breeze there. Now, Harry, take that smoking-chair, and make yourself at home, and tell me all about everything."

" Won't you come and take a little something first, Harry? just to lay the dust," said Jim, coaxingly, and laying his hand on my shoulder, " What say you, now, to a drop of the light wine of the country?"

" No, thank you," I answered, looking up into his handsome sun-browned face, " not just now ; I am altogether too comfortable to move at present."

And thus with easy cordiality they welcomed me. How could I help feeling at home in such cheerful, home-like company? And half reclining in a long, low chair, with swinging canvas seat and back that seemed to afford relief to every muscle, I drank in the odor of the pines, watched the sunlight play with the shadows under the trees, and enjoyed the pleasant consciousness of being a welcome guest.

As we sat talking and laughing, old January with his mule team came slowly up the avenue, and, shortly after, the sound of the dinner bell called me to my room

That evening, when we were sitting together on the piazza, in the breeze and starlight, Jim said,—

" Perhaps you did not know, Harry, that to-morrow is election day? Wouldn't you like to drive down with me in the morning to the 'Corner?' It will give you a chance, by the way, to see the great privilege of the country in the hands of our peers from the rice-fields."

"Yes, thank you," I answered, "I will go with pleasure. But I did not suppose that here, where you held the entire control, the negroes were allowed to vote—at least, not freely."

"O yes!" he replied, "they vote as they please, as you will see to-morrow."

"O, Jim tells me, Harry," said Mrs. Jackson, changing the subject, "that you came out on the steamer with the Lees. Did you like them? I hope so, for we are near neighbors and thrown much together. The Captain is just as nice as he can be, and Mrs. Lee is perfectly lovely, one of the best and sweetest of women; then, you know, she has suffered so much on account of her son's death. He was killed in the war, and in such a sad way, too! And as for Mary! Well, we must ask Jim his opinion of Mary! But, no! I am afraid he is too prejudiced. Have you seen her yet, Jim? What, not seen her, and a whole morning in the same city? Ah! I am afraid you are losing your one redeeming quality of truthfulness! Well, tell me, Harry, what did you think of Mary?"

"I really do not think I know, myself," I answered.

"Nonsense," she exclaimed, "of course you know! Well, did you not think her pretty?"

"Yes, rather," I replied, doubtfully, yet knowing that I thought her the loveliest of women!

"Has she not a sweet voice?" she asked.

"Not so sweet as her mother's at her age," I answered, laughingly, as I recalled the opinion of the Captain.

"Are not her eyes lovely?" she rejoined, "and her figure simply perfect? Well, if you don't admire Mary, you must be very hard to please!"

"But," said I, "perhaps she did not try to please me."

"There! now, I suspect you are coming nearer the truth! Do you know, Mr. Harry, I have a dim suspicion she must have piqued you! You are the first person I ever met, who did not, at least, allow that she was handsome! But she feels exceedingly bitter against the North, and probably something you said annoyed her; and she can be very severe if she likes," she said, half inquiringly.

"O no! we got along very amicably, but then, really, you know, the sea is not famed as a beautifier, beautiful as it is itself!" I answered, hypocrite that I was! For while I spoke, the vision of a face with flashing eyes, and hair sparkling with the sea mist, swept through my mind!

After a moment I added, "I thought them all exceedingly pleasant, and I liked the Captain especially, he seemed so kindly and whole-souled!"

"They are coming out here in a day or two," said Margaret, as she rose to go into the house, "and you shall reverse your opinion of Mary, Mr. Strong."

"Don't call Harry—Mr. Strong—Madge, I won't have it," exclaimed Jim.

"Well, good night, Harry, if you will let me call you so!" she answered, hesitating and smiling as she held out her hand to me. "Come, sister."

And Mrs. Jackson rising bade us good night, and followed her into the house, warning Jim, as she left us, that breakfast would be at eight, and that I required a good night's rest after my journey.

CHAPTER VI.

AT THE POLLS.

I CAME down next morning much refreshed by a good night's sleep, and finding that I had half an hour to spare before breakfast, I concluded to improve the opportunity by becoming better ac-- quainted with my surroundings.

It was a large square house, of the old-fashioned style found so frequently in all parts of our country. The broad piazzas at front and rear, and the wide hall running through the centre of the house, into which opened on either side, the library, draw-ing-room, morning-room and dining-room, might have been copied from a hundred such in our New England villages. The billiard and smoking-rooms were in the high brick basement which was, per-haps, the one exceptional feature of the building.

It was a bright November morning, and when I stepped out upon the back piazza, attracted by the many sounds that reached me, I came upon a scene busy with life. The picket-fence encircling the garden at the front continued its way to the rear of the house, forming there a large enclosure, at the further end of which were half a dozen low wooden buildings occupied by the servants. On my left, and nearer to the house, was a similar building used

as a kitchen, and from its chimney the smoke
floated lazily up into the hazy air. On my right,
and opposite the kitchen, stood the granary, raised
upon brick pillars at its four corners, and the smoke-
house, which completed the little settlement within
the enclosure. Like the main house and fence, all
were painted white, contrasting, not unpleasantly,
with the dark foliage of four great live-oak trees
that cast their shadows over the yard.

Negro children, of all sizes, were playing near
the doorsteps of the cabins. Flocks of ducks,
geese and turkeys were marching and counter-
marching to quack and cackle in ever changing
orders.

A couple of young setters were barking and chasing each other about; now and then, in their awkward gambols, throwing the ranks of the poultry
into wild confusion, or driving them with flapping
wings into the pool near the centre of the
yard; while, just outside the fence, a venerable
sow with snout between the palings, grunted
her disapproval of such levity. Negro men and
women were passing to and fro, with merry
laugh and chatter, in pursuance of their various
avocations, and the whole place seemed instinct
with morning life. As I stood, leaning against
the piazza railing, lost in the diverting scene, Madge's
voice saluted me from the doorway of the hall,—

"Good-morning, Mr. Harry," she said. "You
seem to be an early riser," and as she came forward
and shook me by the hand, she continued, "Won't

you come into the garden, or do you prefer to keep
an eye on the kitchen door? But don't despair,
breakfast will soon be ready, and I should like you
to see some of our last roses. I think they look so
much prettier when the dew is upon them."

She looked very fresh and lovely in her light
morning dress, that fitted to a nicety her tall and
graceful figure.

We passed together through the hall, and out
into the front garden, where the late roses were
still in bloom. She picked a little nosegay while I
held back her skirts from the wet box border that
enclosed the beds.

"There now, let me reward you," she said, select-
ing a bud for me. "If you will keep still a moment,
I'll put it in your buttonhole." And with deft,
slender fingers she fastened it to the lapel of my
coat. Then raising her eyes suddenly to mine, she
asked, "Well, do you like our southern roses?"

"You must remember my experience has been
very brief," I answered. "Those I have thus far
seen appear surpassingly lovely—but I have not yet
felt their thorns. It is one thing to admire, and another to gather!"

She looked into my face a moment longer, as if
to discover whether there was anything implied beyond the simple meaning of my words, then turning
away, she said,—

"To me the risk of being stung adds to the pleasure of gathering them. I think there is little fun in
this world without a spice of danger."

"Well, Miss Madge, when you have arrived at my years of discretion——"

"I hate discretion," she interrupted, "it just spoils everything! The man who had the audacity to couple it with valor, must have been reared in a calculating and unromantic community!"

"Very well," I answered laughing, "you must let me sit at your feet and learn the folly of discretion!"

"Madge, breakfast is ready?" called Mrs. Jackson from the piazza above us, and as we returned to the house in answer to her summons, I said,—

"Now, Miss Madge, pleasure would incline me to remain here with you in the garden, but discretion bids me hasten to the breakfast table!"

"While common sense might possibly suggest," she added gayly, "that you would remain here by yourself."

"Well, Harry," said Jim, after kissing Madge and shaking hands with me, as we entered the breakfast room, "a night's sleep in the piney woods has done you good. Depend upon it, there's nothing like it. Why, you look as fresh as the rose in your buttonhole! Not much of a rose, by the way, though it is Madge's favorite. It does very well in the bud, gives good promise, but does not open up well—all hollow inside. I don't like that style, either in the vegetable or animal kingdom, do you? Though, by the way, that is rather applicable to my own feelings just at present!

"Nero, have 'Buckshot' and the wagon at the

door at nine sharp. Hear?" And turning to me again, he continued, "I suppose you have not changed your mind about going to the polls with me this morning?"

"O no!" I replied, "I am anxious to see the sport!"

"Well, in point of fact," he said, "it amounts to little else, for, of course, you know, most of my negroes vote as I tell them to, and the same with those of the other gentlemen about here. It should be so, for our interests are identical. You might as well take your 'Winchester' along with you, for we may get a crack at an alligator on the way. January told me he saw one at the bridge last night."

After breakfast we lighted our cigars and went to the garden gate, where a spirited looking thoroughbred, harnessed to an open wagon, was waiting for us, with Nero at his restless head. Jim jumped into the wagon and I after him, rifle in hand.

"Now, Nero, give him his head!" cried Jim, and with a rear and a plunge away we sped, out of the sunlight and down the shady avenue at a breakneck pace!

"He's a little lively this morning," said Jim, puffing away complacently at his cigar and without making an effort to restrain his running thoroughbred. His remark hardly seemed to call for a reply; so I said nothing, but clung firmly to the seat, expecting at any moment to be flung into the underbrush at the side of the avenue.

He did, however, check the beast for an instant, with a firm hand, as we swept out of the gate and down the long straight road through the forest.

" He will tire himself out in a couple of miles or so," he said, indifferently, " and be as gentle as a lamb the rest of the morning."

Jim evidently knew his horse, for after another ten minutes of anxiety on my part, he came down, panting, to a quiet trot, and I was free to settle myself in comfort, relight my neglected cigar, and enjoy the coolness and fragrance of the woods.

" This is the place where January saw the alligator," said Jim, at length drawing in his horse, as we neared a wooden bridge, over a small stream ; and through the underbrush on my left, I could see the glinting surface of a boggy-looking pond.

" Now, get your rifle ready, and keep very quiet. By Jove ! there he is ! " whispered Jim, as we stopped at the end of the thicket, next to the bridge.

I followed the direction of his eyes and there upon the black trunk of a tree that had fallen across the swamp some thirty yards away, lay, at full length, the brown monster, basking in the sun.

" Strike him just behind the shoulder," whispered Jim, as I raised my rifle.

I took deliberate aim and fired.

" Bravo, Harry ! well done ! " shouted Eustis, as with a sweep of his great tail, the beast plunged into the black water, and sank out of sight.

" I'm afraid I missed him," I said, feeling rather chagrined at this sudden disappearance.

"Not a bit of it, old fellow! His hunting days are over. Didn't you see him swing his arm up over the water as he went down? That is their way of saying good-by to the world. It's a sure sign the shot was fatal."

"Will he not come to the surface again? I should like to get a nearer view of him; he must have been ten feet long."

"All of that," answered Jim, "he may come up in a couple of hours or so; but we could never reach him through the swamp."

"It seems a pity, though, to leave him to go to pieces so near the road," said I, as we drove on, thinking of the unpleasant probability of passing that way again in the course of a week or two.

"O, no!" replied Jim, as we started on; "the buzzards will soon scent him out and make short work of him."

As we neared the spot where the *vox populi* was about to manifest itself, we passed, from time to time, groups of rough and ragged-looking negroes, plodding quietly along in the same direction as ourselves.

Both in dress and physiognomy, these rice-field negroes were more uncivilized and wretched-looking than any of the race I had hitherto seen, and, as I afterwards learned, it was impossible for one not brought up among them to understand their peculiar jargon. But though a sulky, surly-looking set, I noticed that, with few exceptions, they smiled pleasantly as they touched their hats in answer to

Jim's morning greeting. How he recognized them all, addressing each by name, seemed marvellous to me, in whose eyes they differed only in their dress and size.

At length we came to a white picket-fence, surrounding the poultry yard and kitchen garden of a long, low building with its back towards us, and facing on an opening, where the crossing of two roads gave the Corner its name.

The building, which served for dwelling, post-office, grocery store and polling station was raised from the ground on wooden posts, thereby affording shelter to many swine.

Covered piazzas, with delapidated steps ran the entire length of the building, on the front and rear. Glass and window sashes there were none, but the openings for air and ventilation were protected by wooden shutters against the cold and rain.

We drove up to the end of the fence, where Jim hitched "Buckshot" to one of the palings; and then, after warning me of the light fingers of the negroes, we proceeded with whip and gun in hand, down the road to "the Corner."

On turning the end of the house, what was our astonishment to find ourselves confronted by an encampment of two hundred or more negroes. They were lying about in groups upon the grass, with muskets stacked near by, while here and there fires of fagots were burning, with gipsy kettles hung above them upon tripods.

"What the devil does all this mean?" exclaimed

Jim, as a tall, thin, swarthy, red-nosed man approached us, whose long black hair fell below the collar of his coat.

"They're a bad lot, Mr. Eustis!" answered the man, whom I afterwards found to be the postmaster. "They came over from the next county before day, break and say, they'se going to carry the 'lection to-day, anyhow."

"Why didn't you send the rascals home, Jones, with a couple of loads of buckshot in them?" asked Jim.

"Well, you see," replied our postmaster, in a monotonous drawl, "there's only me and Ned, and they'se rather too many for us, with that man Armstrong to lead um. He'd beat the devil himself! And there's scarce a nigger among um would dare act contrary when he's around! Some of your boys is with um, Mr. Eustis, but mostly they kep' out of the way."

"I'll soon put a stop to that," said Jim excitedly, "Halloo, Sam!" he called to a negro sitting on the steps, near by, "go down among those rascals and tell my boys to go home at once, or I'll cut off their rations from Mr. Jones for the next month, and tell Tom Armstrong I've just a word to say to him!"

Most of the negroes were some little distance from where we were standing, and though, perhaps, they could not catch the words, the sound of Jim's voice raised in excitement, aroused them to sullen watchfulness. They were an unpleasant-looking set, and, feeling that Jim was in no mood to calm

the troubled waters, even if he did not actually
imperil our safety, I suggested quietly that, perhaps,
our best course would be to go home and let the
courts, or other higher authorities see that justice
was done to the county.

He looked up at me with quick suspicion and
said,—

"Very well, Harry, you go back to the wagon
and unhitch the horse. I will not keep you waiting
long."

I did not think it necessary to reply, and stayed
with him to see the issue.

A moment later, a large, powerful-looking negro,
gun in hand, approached us from the crowd. He
came steadily on with a swinging, shuffling gait.
The brim of his felt hat was drawn close down upon
his shaggy brows, and from beneath their ugly
scowl, shone a pair of small, beady black eyes. He
was a shade or two lighter in coloring than most of
his fellows, and his high cheek-bones and comparatively straight nose, suggested a slight admix-
ture of Indian blood. His army-blue trousers,
hung several inches short of his long ankles and
ponderous ill-clad feet. His flannel shirt, half open
to the waist, disclosed a thick, muscular neck and
hirsute breast; and the remnants of an old black
coat, whose sleeves, scarcely reaching below the
elbows, left bare his sinewy wrists and arms, completed his attire. A creature not pleasant to contemplate as a peer and equal; nor one to be chosen
as a companion for a dark night in the forest !

The negroes, who had hitherto been sitting or lying on the grass, now arose, unstacked their arms, and drew a trifle nearer.

" Well, Armstrong," said Jim, when the negro reached us, and stood leaning upon his gun, with both hands crossed upon its muzzle, " What do you mean by bringing a crowd of armed men into the county?"

" What do we mean, Misser Jim?" he retorted, with an insulting sneer, " Why, we mean to carry de 'lection, Misser Jim, dat's what we mean, and we'se gwine to do it, too. We'se gwine to hab our rights!"

I saw the color rising to Jim's face, but he replied with composure.

" Why, Armstrong, this is all nonsense, your votes will amount to nothing here, they will all be thrown out, and you and those poor devils you have brought over with you, will stand in danger of the chain-gang."

" What you took me fo', Misser Jim. You can't come ober dis colored man. Guess we knows our rights. White man wore de breeches long enough! But deys better go home and look arter de chickens, now!"

" Well, you're a fool, Armstrong, and you'd best look out for yourself after this. If you're caught again in this county, it will be as much as your life's worth, and the buzzards will get some poor pickings!" said Jim, turning angrily away.

" Hold on, Misser Jim. Don't try to talk big like

dat. De bottom rail's on top. All de buckra in de county can't keep dis nigger away! I'se like to see um try. I'se not scared o'you or any udder white trash!"

"You black hound!" cried Jim, turning upon him with eyes all ablaze; and quick as a flash he dealt him a stinging blow with his whip, full across the face.

The negro stepped backward with a howl of pain and rage, and in a moment had covered Jim with his musket.

The instant Jim struck the blow, the other negroes, with a wild yell, came rushing down upon us.

It was only the work of a second, and I had knocked up Armstrong's gun and placed the muzzle of my Winchester close against his head.

"Drop your gun or I'll blow your head off, you scoundrel!" I shouted.

The touch of the cold steel upon his cheek seemed to bring him at once to reason, and he obeyed me.

This sudden change in the aspect of affairs, and the somewhat precarious position of their leader, brought the negroes to a standstill within a dozen yards of us, and I succeeded in quieting them still further, by explaining, with such emphasis as I had at command, that besides the ball for Armstrong, there were sixteen more in my rifle for them if they dared to move.

In the mean time Jim had picked up the negroe's discarded blunderbuss, and Jones, who at the first sound of approaching strife had rushed to the house, now returned with his son, Ned, both armed with long, dangerous-looking rifles. With mine still at his head, I ordered Armstrong to move on, while Jim kept a sharp lookout for any movement on the part of the threatening mass of black men in our rear.

In this manner we proceeded to the wagon, and, as we turned the corner of the house, the negroes gave vent to their feelings of anger and defeat in a burst of wild yells and shouts. However, they did not follow us.

We made our burly prisoner seat himself on the floor of the wagon behind us, and, having carried him a mile or more up the road, dropped him by the wayside, after imparting some sound and wholesome advice, which he received in dogged silence.

As we were about to drive on, he raised for an instant his brutal face, and fixing his eyes on Jim, said,—

" You'll hear of me again, Misser Jim ! "

" Yes," Jim answered, " I expect to, right soon, and in the chain-gang. But, mind, Tom, what I told you about coming this side of the river ! " and with that we left him by the roadside, where he stood motionless until we were out of sight.

" Well, Jim, rather a narrow escape," said I to my companion, who had been silent for an unusual length of time.

" Yes," he said, " and if it had not been for you, we should have been carried up under the Oaks, feet foremost to-night." He spoke quietly, and, from his manner, I saw that something was weighing on his mind. Suddenly, he looked up at me, with moist eyes, and, in his impetuous way, went on,—

"By Jove, old fellow! you must forgive my doubting you for one moment. I ought to have known you too well."

"Nonsense, man," I said, interrupting him with a hearty slap on the back. "Mind your horse, or you'll have us both in the ditch."

We said little after this, each being occupied with his own thoughts.

To me this outburst of lawlessness on the part of the blacks was most surprising, for I had read much of their oppression, and how, with an iron hand, they were held in bonds more terrible than those of slavery.

My conversations with Southerners had led me to believe that there was nothing to be feared from the blacks, and I had shared, in a measure, their contempt for them, as physical antagonists. I had thought them an utterly servile race, and here, almost upon our first acquaintance, they had shown themselves free in action, insolent in bearing, and not devoid of courage.

In fact, I found them more unruly and dangerous than I had supposed; and it seemed to me it could be hardly safe to live in these country districts, surrounded by their largely outnumbering population, until they should have reached a higher state of civilization.

Jim dropped me at the gate of the Oaks, and continued on his way to another polling place of the county, where his vote was properly recorded.

When he came home to lunch, he said that after telling of our adventure to the men at the Polls, he had great difficulty in dissuading them from riding down in force to the corner, and driving the negroes over the border.

It will, however, be a matter of satisfaction to my readers to know that the fraudulent vote was, in due course, very properly rejected by the higher powers, and the county returned with an over-whelming white majority!

CHAPTER VII.

MADGE.

JIM had to attend to matters of importance on his plantation that afternoon, and Mrs. Jackson had letters to write, so it was arranged that Madge and I should go to drive.

My companion proved as agreeable as she was pretty. She had much of her brother's liveliness of disposition, and seemed to be fairly brimming over with coquetry; while her naiveté and innocence of speech often betrayed her youth and inexperience.

She was more than pretty, and she naturally knew it. Her face was as changeful as that of the sea on a spring day, when the shadows chase the sunlight over it; one moment grave, and the next smiling mischievously up at you out of her bright gray eyes! Dangerous eyes and a dangerous smile, Miss Madge, for the unwary!

On our return we passed the avenue of Palmetto Grove, and learned from a negro boy who was swinging on the gate, that the Lees were expected home that night.

As we drove on again, Madge said,—

" Now, Harry, you will have a great rival in Jim's

affections! What a pity it is, you did not like·
Mary! It would have been such fun to have seen
you and Jim at swords' points! He would become
perfectly wild if he thought he had a really dangerous rival! What a delightful little romance we
might have had this winter, if you had not taken
this unaccountable prejudice!"

The picture was not a pleasant one, but I did not
think it necessary to set my fair companion right.

Presently she continued, "I believe you have
been abroad for several years, have you not? O
how much I should like to go! Do you know, I
have never been out of this State since I was a
child?"

"And how many years ago was that?" I asked.

"You need not laugh at me, sir!" she answered,
"I am really getting very old. I was eighteen last
May, and my grandmother was only fourteen when
she was married."

"I had no idea you were such a Methuselah!" I
rejoined, "have you learned to look forward with
equanimity to maidenhood during your declining
years?"

"That can only come from my declining men, I
assure you," she retorted, and then after a moment's
pause went on, "Men are so silly! They seem to
be always falling in love and offering themselves!
They are ready to swear everlasting devotion to
girls they have not met a dozen times! The fun-
niest part is that I think they really believe what
they are saying, at the time, and sometimes almost

persuade us to believe it too! They rant and rave until they have reduced us to a terrible state of agitation and remorse, and within a week after they have left us, some other girl says to us, ' O, my dear, I had such a scene yesterday with Mr. so-and-so! I feel very badly about it too, for I think he really cares for me; but what could I say?' The joke of the matter is, that the men most given to that sort of thing, are the very ones who could not afford to marry, if we should say yes!"

" Why, then, do they do it, if it can lead to nothing?" I asked.

" Why do they do it?" she replied, with a little laugh, as she poised her head slightly on one side, and looked up at me, " Who can tell? Really I am unable to enlighten you! However, perhaps, they like the excitement of scenes! Thrilling love scenes without the audience! Then, too, I do not think they would object to being engaged, even if they could not marry!"

"I can imagine little pleasure in that." I answered, prosaically.

" Ah! what charming innocence!" said she, with a quizzical smile, " How utterly devoid of imagination you Northerners are! You must, as you said, be the personification of discretion! And yet, do you know, I thought discretion was the result only of experience."

" No!" I replied, " you do me more than justice, I assure you, I fear discretion with me, has been merely lack of temptation. But, honestly, I cannot imagine offering one's self without being thoroughly in earnest."

"Oh! they all are that," she said, "but I do trust that nothing will happen this winter to disturb the beauty of your philosophy. I shall warn all my friends not to lead you into temptation. It would be a terrible pity to spoil such an excellent young man!"

"Such certainly does not appear to be your intention," I answered laughing.

"You would not have me, would you?" she said, looking up again into my face. But at this moment we drew up at the garden gate, where Jim stood waiting for us, and nothing more was said.

Jim drove the horse to the stable, and, as I followed Madge through the garden, she stopped to pick a rosebud and then turning to me, said—"I see you have kept the flower I gave you this morning, so you shall be rewarded with a fresh one." So saying she took the faded rose from my coat and put it in her hair.

Then in a hesitating tone she added, while she fastened the fresh bud in my buttonhole, "But perhaps you do not care for it?"

"How can I do otherwise?" I answered.

"Very well, then," she replied, "as long as I consider you sufficiently polite and attentive, I shall keep you well supplied; but remember, I am very exacting!" and with that she ran lightly up the steps and into the house.

That evening, on the piazza, after dinner, Mrs.
Jackson said, "I am worried about this trouble of
yours with Armstrong, Jim."

"Why so, my sweet sister? I think Harry
and I taught him a lesson to-day he will not soon
forget."

"Well, I am afraid of him, Jim! He is such a
desperate character. He is not a man to forget
what he considers an injury and would hesitate at
nothing to avenge it. I am confident he will attempt something in retaliation! Do take good care
of yourself, Jim. You know, as well as I do, how
dangerous he is."

"Don't let your anxiety get the better of your
good sense, my dear girl," said Jim, "He knows
after what I told him, that it will be as much as his
life is worth to venture on this side of the river. He
is, no doubt, an insolent, daring, fellow enough, but
still, he has some appreciation of the value of his
black hide!"

"Has he ever done anything before?" I asked.

"O, yes," said Mrs. Jackson, "for the last ten
years there has been no piece of rascality committed
in the county, in which he has not taken part. He
used to belong to the Lees and was supposed to
have shot their overseer, against whom he bore a
grudge. But it was never proved, and he escaped
the hanging he, no doubt, richly deserved. After
that, he was· sold to some one in Alabama, but
eight or ten years ago, he wandered back to his old
haunts. If your rifle had been accidentally dis-

charged to-day, it would have freed the County of a great pest ! ”

“ By the way, Madge,” said Jim, changing the subject, “ your friend, the Major, is coming up to-morrow to dine and pass the night. Now don't flirt with the poor fellow ! I warn you ! We should prefer not to have him shooting wild on Friday, as we are going to the “ ten acre drive,” where the stands are at best rather uncomfortably near each other !

“ What do you mean by flirting, Jim ? ” asked Madge, looking up at her brother with innocent composure, as he stood beside her chair.

“ You little goose ! ” he answered laughing, “ask any of the half-dozen men you have seen in the last six months.”

“ Really, if you wish me to mind you, I think you might tell me what you mean. Now, when, for in-stance, you say awfully sweet little things to Mary, do you call that flirting ? ”

“ Do not tempt me to box your ears and send you to bed, Miss Impertinence,” said Jim, laying a hand on each of her shoulders, and, at the same time, bending down his smiling face to hide his blushes.

“ Well, I think I understand you, Jimmy,” she rejoined, “ and I promise not to say any sweet little things to the Major ; but you must be equally good to Mary, or I shall not ask her to dinner to-morrow.”

“ Why, when are they expected ? ” he asked quickly.

"They arrived to-night. So Scipio told us at the gate."

As the twilight deepened into night, Jim retired to attend to some business in his study, and shortly after, the ladies went into the house, leaving me alone with my reflections and cigar.

I had much to think of, for to-morrow I should, in all probability, see Miss Lee again ; and the many hints let fall since my arrival at the Eustis's showed me plainly how delicate my position would become, if I allowed my admiration for her to grow into a deeper sentiment.

If I had been actually in love the problem would have been altogether different, and, to my mind, capable of but one solution ; but, as I told myself, I, very fortunately, had not yet arrived at that point, and was, therefore, free to forward the interests of my host. And, in view of these plain facts, why could I not dismiss the matter ? Why should I feel a vague depression at the thought of my friend's good luck ? Well, perhaps it is always rather hard to part with any romantic possibility of life, even if it is first recognized when we must give it up.

I assuredly had not been in love, and yet there had been a certain sentiment—a sympathy—a something indefinable in our intercourse, that made the recollection of our voyage very pleasant to me ; and now, for the first time, I realized with how much interest I had looked forward to the renewal of our acquaintance.

It was fortunate—most fortunate—that I had discovered the state of the case in time. Not of course that I should have become Eustis's successful rival, but I might, at least, have made my own life wretched. And when, for the hundredth time, I had come to this sage conclusion, I retired for the night to dream of a girlish face, blushing at the rude kiss of the southeaster.

CHAPTER X.

THE OAKS.

THE next day, before breakfast, while Madge and I were chatting together on the front piazza, we saw Jim come riding up the avenue at a canter on his thoroughbred, " Dangerous," and soon after he joined us.

" Why, Jim," said Madge, when he had kissed her, " where have you been at such an early hour? "

" I went over to ' Palmetto Grove ' to arrange with the Captain for the hunt to-morrow."

" O, you went to see the Captain, did you? " she asked, in a half-bantering tone.

" Why, child, who else should I have been likely to see at this time in the morning? " And then, turning to me, he continued, " We shall probably have Major Barnwell, Colonel Shorter and Mr. Holland with us to-morrow, and that, with the Captain, will make six in all; so we shall cover the ' ten-acre drive ' well. It will be somebody's fault, I expect, if we don't bring home some good venison."

" Yes, but Jim," persisted Madge, " are you quite sure you saw nobody but the Captain? "

" No, I saw Peter. He held my horse. By the way, speaking of Peter, Harry——"

"I was not speaking of Peter, Jim, nor of Harry, either," she said, laughing. "Who else did you see?"

"Mrs. Lee, for a moment, and she asked me ___"

"And Mary?" interrupted Madge, determined not to be driven from her point.

"And Mary, confound it!" he assented, laughing, "yes, yes, yes, a thousand times yes! and looking as bright and fresh as a rose in the morning! Now please let me alone, you plague! you good for nothing tease!" he continued, patting her gently on the cheek, as she looked saucily up into his face.

"Fresh as a rose in the morning!" she repeated. "O, that reminds me, I have not given Harry his rose to-day!" and with that she ran gayly down the piazza steps, while Eustis and I went to the breakfast room.

A moment later she returned with a bright flush upon her face.

"Why, Jim!" she exclaimed, "there is not a good rose left upon my bush, and I saw at least twenty there last night! Who can have taken them?"

"Probably, Jim thought the bush needed pruning," said Mrs. Jackson, demurely. "I saw him wasting a good deal of his valuable time in the garden, before he set off this morning! Perhaps he took the clippings to Mrs. Lee, she is so fond of flowers, you know!"

The guilty color betrayed Jim's ill-concealed

little secret. But he said nothing, and received Madge's expostulations with a half-conscious smile, which seemed to say that he had no reason and, indeed, no longer the desire to defend himself from her attacks.

Did I envy him his canter to " Palmetto Grove ? " Well, yes, perhaps I did, a trifle, for the day was fair, and the woods cool and fresh in the early morning !

After breakfast, Jim and I rambled about The Oaks, but, as the day promised to be a warm one, the ladies did not join us.

We visited the stables, with their half a dozen well stalled horses, and perhaps as many mules.

We inspected the kennel, with its pack of short-legged, long-eared, sleek, sullen-looking hounds. Dogs that could be trained to follow the trail either of deer or man. Their enclosure was surrounded by a high picket-fence, with rails sunk a foot or more into the ground, to prevent them from burrowing out, and in the centre stood a low, roughly built shed, by the side of a sluggish brook that made its way through the yard.

Near by was the old log cabin of the huntsman, its chimney built of laths and clay against the gable end. An oak-tree cast its shadow on the mossy roof, and at the door sat Pompey, adjusting a leathern thong to his hunting horn. He arose at our approach and touched his hat. He was a tall, thin, white-headed old man, with bright clear eyes, and erect, vigorous carriage. He had acted as huntsman at the Oaks for two generations, and was familiar with every swamp and brier patch in the County.

"We are going to try the 'Ten-acre Drive' to-morrow, Pompey, and shall start at six in the morning. There will, probably, be six of us, Captain Lee, Major Barnwell, Colonel Shorter, Mr. Holland, Mr. Strong, and myself. I shall take the stand on the Schoolhouse Road, and shall place Mr. Strong by the three trees in the woods on my right, where I shot that doe last spring. Has 'Spotted Tail' come back yet?"

"Yes, Massa Jim, ums come in las' night—all use up and fag out. I'se hea' um barkin' in de woods yesday. Guess ums arter de rabbits. Ums no good, Massa Jim. Better shoot de old bitch!"

"Well, leave her in the kennel to-morrow. Be on hand sharp at six, Pompey. Hear?"

"Yes, Massa Jim."

"By the way, here's a plug of tobacco, Pompey. It will keep that old pipe of yours full for a day or two."

Leaving the old man and the hounds, we strolled on down the woodland path for a quarter of a mile or more to the bank of the river which separated, with its dark current, The Oaks proper from the rice plantation.

From the bluff, on which, after emerging from the woods, we stood, some twenty feet above the river, we looked down upon the rice-fields, and the marshes stretching away for many miles beyond, to where a narrow strip of blue told us they ended in the sea.

Along the belt of open land upon the bluff, both to the right and left of us, was a row of cabins, some twenty or thirty in number, facing the river, and backing upon well-tilled kitchen gardens.

This was the plantation settlement, and as there was but little work in progress at this season, most of the negroes, men, women, and children, were sitting and lying about in the sunshine before their cabins, doing absolutely nothing; although a few, more energetic than the rest, were fishing in a lazy way from flat-bottomed boats anchored in the stream below the bluff.

The first cabin to the right was larger than the others, and boasted the additional luxury of a covered piazza, entirely surrounded by a high railing, with access by a gate above the steps.

This, Jim informed me, was the nursery, and thither, when in busy times the men and women were alike called into the fields, all the little children of the settlement were carried in the morning, and left in charge of some old crone whose working days were over, to be again distributed among their parents when they returned in the twilight from their labors.

Poor youngsters! I did not envy them their quarters! And I pitied, even more, the unfortunate old woman whose lot it was to keep watch over this squalling, turbulent throng, through the long hot hours of a midsummer's day!

They were a rough, unkempt community, scantily and raggedly dressed. The women wore colored calico dresses, with skirts falling just below the knee, and gaudy turbans, mostly red and yellow, which gave a certain picturesqueness to their appearance; and some of the men, in lieu of coats and shirts, wore burlaps, with slits for head and arms, and with the brands of the grain or fertilizer for which they were originally intended, still legible upon them.

We hailed a boat, and, crossing the river, walked for a time over the long straight dikes. I examined the rude dams and sluice ways, and gathered some information as to the method of flooding and draining these vast fields, and of drawing up and nurturing the sprouting rice under the gentle influence of a gradually deepening irrigation, until it should have gained sufficient size and strength to withstand, unaided, the scorching summer heat. A method of culture requiring careful handling, but rewarding with its magnificent results all the attention it demands; and happy is the man who, spared by the dreaded autumnal flood, gathers the well-earned crop into his cribs and mill.

We returned home in time for lunch, having heartily enjoyed our morning ramble and very sharp-set for the mid-day meal.

After lunch as I was sitting on the piazza, smoking and glancing through the columns of a local newspaper, the blinds of the parlor window near me were thrown open and Madge, leaning out upon the window sill, interrupted my reading.

" What do you find so absorbing in that old paper, Harry?" she asked.

"I had just finished," I replied, "this glowing obituary upon Mr. Dibbles and a brilliant description of Miss Elmira Tompkins and her wedding, and was wondering whether all the men about here are as wonderful and the women as beautiful as these two!"

"Of course our men are great and our women beautiful," she exclaimed, "you must see that yourself!"

" I suppose, at any rate, I shall have to admit the latter," I answered.

She waited a moment before answering, and then said, hesitatingly,—

" I am going to ask a great favor of you, Harry! Do you feel very tired this afternoon?

" That depends somewhat upon the extent of your demands, Miss Madge! Now, if you wish an egg from the nest at the top of that old pine down there, I may be obliged to plead fatigue, for the sun, you know, was very hot on the rice-fields this morning. But if, on the other hand, you ask me to stroll with you down the avenue, or through the woods to the river, you will find me possessed——"

"You do talk as if you were possessed!" she cried, interrupting me. "No, I am not going to require anything so adventurous or delightful as you suggest! But it seems Jim forgot to ask the Lees to dinner to-night, and now he has been sent for to go down to the plantation, and sister and I are both busy this afternoon. Would you mind going over there with a message for me?" she asked, as if half doubting my reply.

I felt my face flush, but restrained the alacrity with which I was about to answer, and said, quietly,— " No, certainly not, if you wish it."

She evidently mistook my expression and added, as if to lighten an unwelcome task, " You know, you need not stay. But I have no doubt you will find them very pleasant. They are always kind and hospitable. You don't really mind going, do you?"

" O, not in the least, I assure you. It is just a pleasant walk."

" You can ride if you prefer."

" No, thank you, I would rather walk this afternoon."

" Very well, then, I will bring you a note in a moment. I am ever so much obliged," she said, with a smile as she closed the blind. Presently, she returned and I started on my way. When I reached the garden gate I turned for a moment to look back. Madge was still standing. upon the piazza leaning against the railing, and, as she waved her hand, she said, " When you come home, Harry, I will try to reward you for your good nature."

I walked down the avenue and along the public road until I came to a footpath diverging into the woods on my right, which, I had been told, would lead me by a short cut to Palmetto Grove.

It was a pretty winding path with the underbrush growing thick and green on either side, and,
as I strolled slowly on, my thoughts were so full of
the coming meeting and of Jim's attachment for my
fair travelling companion, that I was not altogether
pleasantly surprised, on emerging suddenly from the
woods, to find myself at the end of my walk.

An acre or more of rose garden lay before me
with well-trimmed box borders around beds of every
shape and size, and across it stood a long, low, white
house with its broad piazza closed in with vines.
Behind the house rose the dark background of
forest pines, while to the left and half shut out
by the shrubs bordering that side of the garden,
was the universal white picket-fence of the back-
yard.

The afternoon sun lay bright on house and garden.
Not a soul was in sight, and scarce a sound disturbed the peaceful stillness of the scene, as I stood
for a moment in the shadow of the woods to enjoy
its quiet beauty.   Suddenly the silence was broken
by the notes of a piano coming from the open windows of the house, followed by the music of a voice
whose sweet full tones I could not mistake.   I knew
the song.   It was "Waiting," and as I listened to
the pensive expression of its opening bars, for a moment I felt that it might be sung for me.   It was
only for a moment, and then smiling at the absurd-
ity of the thought I left the woods and went quickly
up the garden path.

The last cadence had died away upon the air before I reached the house. I ascended the steps, and walked along the piazza to an open window at the end, making at the same time, sufficient noise to give warning of my approach. On reaching it, I looked in and saw Miss Lee sitting at the piano opposite and just across the room. As if to ascertain who the intruder might be she had turned half round and faced the window. She uttered a faint exclamation of surprise, and came forward to meet me with smiling face and outstretched hand.

" Why, Mr. Strong! I am very glad to see you," she said. " It seems a long time since we took our sea voyage together, does it not ? "

" Yes," I replied, " it is impossible for me to realize that I have been here such a little while, the Eustises have managed to make me feel so thoroughly at home ! "

" I knew you would like the girls ! Is not Madge as pretty as I told you ? " she asked.

" I think her handsome, rather than pretty," I answered, " and altogether one of the most attractive girls I ever met. And such a flow of spirits ! "

" Yes, she is always bright and pleasant," she said, motioning me to a chair near the open window. " I am sorry my father and mother are out driving this afternoon, they will be so disappointed not to have seen you ! "

" By the way, that reminds me of Miss Madge's note," I said, handing it to her. " They hope you will all come over to dinner this evening. I believe Jim forgot to deliver the message."

"Yes? he is rather forgetful, but you must forgive him this time, for he was too much interested in telling of your adventure at the polls yesterday to think of anything else!"

"Well, I am very ready to forgive anything that gave me the opportunity of coming here! But tell me," I added, to change the subject, "why is your place called 'Palmetto grove?'"

"If you are not too tired for a little stroll, I will show you" she said, and in answer to my prompt reply she left me to get her hat.

It was a pretty parlor in which I sat—low-studded and cozy; furnished in an old-fashioned way, and free from the bric-a-brac, old-curiosity-shop, appearance of the modern drawing-room. Old portraits, more or less good, hung upon the walls, and among them I recognized one by Copley of some ancestral grandmother, taken in the prime of womanhood. The square, low-cut black silk dress displayed to full advantage the marble neck and swan-like throat; while one wrist resting on the corner of a table, near which she sat, gave ample opportunity for those gentle curves of arm and drooping hand that the artist loved so well. On the mantel-shelf stood a miniature by Malbone, in a velvet frame, of a young man with long black wavy hair and incipient beard. The complexion was clear and ruddy, and the bright piercing eyes seemed to look with the expression of life, frankly and fearlessly into your own. It was painted with all the delicacy and strength of the master's hand,

and was, no doubt, a portrait of the Captain's father, taken during the great and gentle artist's sojourn in the South.

At one end of the room was an open fireplace, with brass andirons and fender, on either side of which stood large Chinese vases of white and blue.

Most of the furniture was of mahogany inlaid with brass. Some old-fashioned, straight-backed chairs were placed here and there against the wall, but to better accord with the more luxurious fashion of the present generation several heavily upholstered easy-chairs were scattered about the room.

The entire arrangement of the parlor bespoke a refined and homelike taste, while the books and papers on the centre-table showed plainly that this was the general " living-room " of the family.

On a little table, near the garden window, was a vase of roses like those with which Miss Madge had made me familiar, and I did not doubt that they were the spoils of Jim's morning depredation.

Miss Lee soon returned and we went out together into the grove of pines, on the opposite side of the house from the rose garden, and on emerging from it found ourselves standing near the edge of a bluff some thirty or forty feet above the river and its marshy banks, and with an extended view to north and east and south.

It was a landscape with which I was rapidly becoming familiar. The only type of scenery in this level land which could boast the attraction of distance, and, perhaps, on this account, it had already

found much favor in my sight, who had been
accustomed to a hilly country with its comprehensive
views.

The broad river wound in and out among the
marshes and in the middle of the stream, a quarter of
a mile or more away, was a little island covered with
a dense growth of trees and shrubs reaching to the
very water's edge in tropical luxuriance. The western
sun fell full upon it, and it rose high above the vast
expanse of marshes around it, like an oasis in the
desert. Many birds were skimming through the air
above it in circling and uncertain flight, and as I
looked a large white heron rose from amongst the
verdure on its banks, and winged its way across
the marshes until lost to sight in the soft hazy distance.

There was a rustic bench beneath the shadow of
the pines and we sat down together to enjoy the
view. A gentle breeze came in from the sea, laden
with the peculiar odor of the salt marsh. How
long we sat there I do not know, nor do I remember
what was said, probably nothing of importance in
itself. But we drifted half idly on from thought to
thought in pleasant sympathy, forgetful of the hour,
until at last we were warned by the lengthening
shadows and arose to return to the house.

As we walked back through the pine grove, it was
flooded with a golden light, that seemed to fill
all the air above and around us, and—a sensation
rarely experienced elsewhere—we appeared to be
not simply looking at the sunset, but absolutely

standing in the midst of its bewildering brightness!

"How beautiful this is!" I said as we left the woods and approached the house, "I never saw such a deluge of golden light! Do you remember what a fine sunset we had at sea, the first day I met you?"

"O yes," she answered "and how you said you should not remember it!"

"No, not that exactly," I replied, "I think I said I should not remember it simply for itself. But I do remember it well!"

"Then, I suppose, you must have had a particularly good supper that evening!"

"Yes, that was probably it!" I returned laughing.

"Have you heard from your friend, Mr. Brown, since he went to Florida?" inquired Mary.

"No." I answered, "but I hardly expect to hear from him. We have never corresponded. I hope the change of climate will do the poor fellow good and, no doubt, this trip will at least widen his mental horizon."

"Why, do you think him wanting in intelligence?" she asked.

"No, not at all! But this is his first experience of the outside world, and it will probably remove some of his provincial prejudices."

"I think papa took rather a fancy to him," she said. "He considered him original, and altogether a character! He has asked him to stop with us when he leaves Florida."

"Has he? That was very kind of him!"

"O, not at all," she answered. "He likes to meet new people, and especially young people." By this time we had reached the piazza steps, and, as I held out my hand to bid her good-by, I said,—

"By the way, you have forgotten to show me the Palmetto Grove. I shall reserve it for my next call."

"Very well," said she, "I will not be so remiss when you come again! Tell Madge she may expect us at dinner. Good-by, for the present!"

I shook her hand and left her standing there in the deepening light. The vines so full and green trailing up the lattice at her side and waving their sprays above her head, seemed a befitting framework for the sweet face and graceful form, thrown out in strong relief by the dark shadow of the piazza. If I had been an artist I should have passed many an hour in striving to reproduce the picture, and, no doubt, in the vain endeavor should have sacrified the vividness of the impression that now remains upon my mind.

CHAPTER IX.

THE DINNER.

THE twilight settled down rapidly into night, and when I reached home it was almost dark. The lights were burning in the parlor, and Madge was sitting by the centre-table reading. I delivered my message through the open window, and sat down on the piazza for a few moments to rest.

Presently, I heard Mrs. Jackson enter the parlor, and say,—

"Did you have a pleasant walk with Harry, Madge?"

"No, we did not go," she answered, very quietly.

"Why, Madge, I thought when I saw you putting on your hat, you said you were going out together."

"Well, we did not," she replied, with some little impatience.

There was a short pause, and then I heard Mrs. Jackson say, inquiringly,—

"Surely, you have not been quarrelling, Madge?"

"What perfect nonsense, sister. Of course not. Harry went over to the Lees for me, and did not return in time, that was all."

I arose and went to the open window.

"Madge," I said, "why did you not tell me you expected me back to walk with you?"

"Really, it was not of sufficient consequence," she answered.

I saw that she was not in an altogether amiable mood, and, thinking it best to say nothing more, I went to my room to get ready for dinner. I remembered Madge's promise to reward me for my errand, and supposed she was provoked at being thwarted in her kindly intention by my delay. It seemed, however, rather unjust to make me the victim of her displeasure, when she had given me no intimation of her plans.

"Well," I thought to myself, as I finished my toilet. "Although I do not pretend to understand the caprices of woman, certain I am that you, for one, Miss Madge, shall not take up arms against me on such slight provocation as this."

As I descended from my room, a light buff overcoat and a spick-and-span sole leather portmanteau in the hall, told me of the arrival of Mr. Amsterdam Holland, of New York. Mr. Holland had, like myself, come South for the winter in search of pleasure. He was of an excellent family, and reputed to be rich. He had brought letters to Jim, and had, in consequence, been asked to spend a week at "The Oaks." As, however, he has little to do with my story, it will be enough to state that he was a youth of medium height, light hair and sandy whiskers, and distinguished principally by the perfection of his dress, which impressed me deeply, even in the momentary glimpse I had of it, before Jim carried him off to make his preparations for dinner.

Soon after I had entered the parlor, Major Barnwell and Colonel Shorter arrived, who, after their introduction to me, seated themselves on either side of Madge at the further end of the room, thus leaving me at liberty to speak to Mrs. Jackson, and learn from her something of their history.

"That Major Barnwell, Harry——" she began.

"Which Major Barnwell?" I asked.

"There is only one, you stupid fellow, the stout, thickset one, with a pleasant face."

"Ah! yes, I see. It is a pleasant face, and particularly pleasant in its expression of devotion to Madge."

"Well, between you and me, Harry, he is very attentive to her. He would offer himself in a minute if she gave him the slightest encouragement, and she might do far worse."

"Why? Is he rich?"

"I might have known you would ask that. All you Northerners are so mercenary. No, not particularly—but riches are not everything.

"True, but they can procure everything."

"Well, perhaps they can at the North. I am quite ready to believe you. But, thank goodness, we have not been educated up to that, yet, in this part of the country, the young men and women of the South—"

"Now, excuse me, sister Kate, for interrupting you," I said laughing, " but you really must not deprive me of the pleasure of personal discovery, by a summary of their virtues; besides, I am interested to hear more of the gallant Major."

"Well, there is not much to tell you about him— he is not rich, he is not particularly bright, nor particularly handsome, nor particularly anything; but, nevertheless, he is an excellent man. He owns a rice plantation some three or four miles from here, at least his family used to own it, but he was obliged to mortgage it very heavily to run it after the war. He had a hard time at first to make the ends meet, but was careful and energetic, and is doing much better now, they say. Colonel Shorter is staying with him, and for that reason is here to-night, for to tell you the truth, I do not like the Colonel. I think him a dangerous man. He has been in ever so many scrapes and shooting affairs; not all of them very reputable."

"He is rather handsome," I said, looking at this sprig of Southern chivalry with growing interest.

"O yes, he is good looking enough. He considers himself a great lady-killer, and, I regret to say, he has had more success in that direction than he deserves. Many women think him very fascinating and romantic."

"He does not appear to exert himself to be especially attractive just at present," I said.

He was leaning back lazily in a low chair near Madge, taking no part in and apparently indifferent to the conversation between the Major and herself.

"O no," replied Mrs. Jackson. "He is what one

might call a *tete à tete* man. It is then only that he displays his wonderful powers. He never wastes his light upon general conversation. I hardly know why I have taken such a dislike to the man. Have you noticed how cold his eyes are?"

" No, I have not. What does he do?"

" He is a merchant, or factor, or something of the kind, in the city. He sells rice for all the planters, you know. I believe he lent the money to the Major to enable him to begin planting. Why! there are the Lees. I must go out to meet them," and so saying she arose hastily and hurried from the room, followed by Madge.

I was very glad to meet the Captain again, with his cheerful, whole-souled way. He seemed to diffuse his sunny nature through the room, until everybody caught and reflected back a portion of its genial rays. I could not but feel flattered by his apparent interest in me, and his affectionate manner which arose, no doubt, from the recollection of his early intimacy with my father.

Mary wore that evening a white muslin gown, cut open and pointed in front, showing to advantage her snowy throat and neck. I had never seen her look so lovely. She had on no jewelry nor ornaments, with the exception of a single rosebud in her hair, which I recognized as one of Madge's favorites.

Mrs. Lee was, as usual, in black, and, as usual, silent and dignified.

Mr. Holland, who made his appearance presently

with Jim, was in full dress, and, no doubt, pleased to think himself the only suitably dressed gentleman in the room. After a few minutes passed in general introductions and handshaking, dinner was served, and we filed into the dining-room, led by Captain Lee and Mrs. Jackson. Jim went in with Mrs. Lee, Mr. Holland with Madge, and I had the good fortune to be allotted to Miss. Lee, while Major Barnwell and Colonel Shorter were left to take care of themselves, or of one another, as they might prefer.

The table was well lighted by silver candelabra, and in the centre, stood a handsome *épergne* of flowers. Usually, the minutiæ of the great event of the day make but little impression upon me. I rise from dinner pleased or otherwise by its *tout ensemble*, but if called upon to give a reason for the feeling, find myself utterly unable to do so. The present occasion, was, however, an exceptional one, and, contrary to my custom, I do remember it well; the delicious white stew of terrapin, with which the dinner began ; (had I not in the morning, watched them basking in the sun, on a barrel head that lay beside the pool in the back-yard?) and the royal wild turkey, roasted to a turn before the kitchen fire, and running with juice at the first touch of the carving-fork ; the melting slice of home-cured ham that imparted such a relish to the roast; —what well-bred sideboard in the South is ignorant of its spiced fat and pantaletted bone?—the small game birds; the ivory palmetto cabbage, signal-

ling the death of a forest tree ; the profusion of vegetables with every course ; the tempting and insidious
dessert, made from some great grandmother's re-
cipe, an heirloom in the family; the smooth, fragrant Madeira, of three voyages and a hundred
years, that by some special dispensation had escaped
the eager eyes and thirsty lips of the invader;—
such a dinner as is seldom seen nowadays, except
in Southern country houses.

The conversation soon became general, turning
upon the latest local news, the expected gayeties of
the coming winter, the domestic affairs of people
with names unfamiliar to me, the prospects of the
coming crops, and, finally, upon the elections, and
thence, naturally, to our adventure at the polls.
Many questions were asked about it, and to my annoyance most of them were addressed to me; nor
was my embarrassment lessened when I heard Jim
exclaim, in an animated voice,—

"Yesterday was the second time that Strong
saved my life. If it had not been for him I should
never have pulled through the winter I was im-
prisoned at Johnson's Island."

Almost for the first time in my life I felt thoroughly provoked with him! I tried to catch his
eye, but could not; and every inquiry that his remark drew forth was answered by him in full, thus
drawing upon me the attention of the entire company.

As a rule I am not troubled with diffidence, but,
at this moment, I had not a word to say, and sat

there in silence, and apparently with the modest blush of conscious merit on my face.

My position was indeed absurd; for I felt that it must be evident to all, that, on the occasion referred to, I had merely sent him a few trifles to soften the hardships of imprisonment, for which he was over-grateful, from the fact, no doubt, that he had found it so pleasant to be remembered at all at such a time. However, before I had sufficiently recovered my self-possession to speak, the subject was changed, and the opportunity lost.

Although I cared comparatively little what others might think, I wished, if possible, to set myself right with Miss Lee. I would not have her do me the in-justice to suppose I gave undue weight to such a trivial act of friendship.

So when at length a general discussion arose as to the relative merits of fox and deer hunting, I turned to her and said,—

"I do wish Jim had held his tongue about that Johnson's Island affair."

"Why?" she asked.

"Because it is absurd to make so much of such a trifle!"

"Do you think it a trifle to have saved his life?"

"No. But I did not. If I helped him at all, which I doubt, I am very glad of it. But what merit is there in any act without at least a touch of self-sacrifice, and there was none in that; it cost me nothing!"

"I do not suppose, when he spoke of it to-night,

that Mr. Eustis was thinking of the pecuniary obligation!" she answered dryly.

"I believe you wilfully misunderstand me!" I exclaimed with indignation. "I am sorry you should think me capable of such a consideration!"

"If I was unjust I beg your pardon," she answered quickly, looking up at me. "But how should I know? I do not understand you Northerners, and always expect to find something about them that I do not like. I wish I were not so suspicious. I cannot help it. I am very sorry."

I felt at once disarmed and reproved by her earnestness and simplicity, and, anxious to make amends for my over hastiness, I replied in a low tone,—

"You see how much I dislike to be misjudged by you, Miss Lee. I hardly know why I care so much for your esteem, but such is the fact, and I beg you not to be so ready to think ill of me. Like, or dislike me if you must, for myself, and not because I am a Northerner. Do not begin by suspecting me —but trust me until I prove myself unworthy of it —even then do not condemn me without a hearing. Will you not promise me this?"

While I was speaking the ladies had risen from the table, and as Mary arose she turned to me with a slight flush and said,—

"I will try—, yes, I will promise!"

At the same moment Madge approached us.

"Why, you look as guilty as two conspirators!" she exclaimed. "Don't trust Mr. Strong, May, he never keeps his promises or his engagements. I have found him altogether unreliable!" and with a laugh and a discarding sweep of the hand, she linked her arm in Miss Lee's, and they passed together out of the room.

Before they were out of hearing I heard Madge say,—

"I am very glad to see you and Mr. Strong get on so well together. I was afraid——"

After the ladies had left us, we sat for half an hour over our wine, making arrangements for the coming day's hunt.

"What horses will you and Harry ride to-morrow, Jim?" asked Captain Lee.

"I shall ride ' Dangerous ' and Harry ' Gray Bess.' The mare is not handsome, as you know, but she is a very comfortable hunting nag. Then I thought Mr. Holland might ride ' Beauty,' she is working very well this fall."

"Beauty gone carse ur shoe to-night, Massa Jim," said David, a mulatto, who acted either as Jim's body servant, coachman, or waiter, in which last capacity he was at present filling Col. Shorter's glass with Madeira.

"Is that a fact? Well I'm sorry to hear it," said Jim, then after a moment's reflection, he added, "I don't see, then, but that Mr. Holland must make his choice between the pony and ' Vixen,' and ' Vixen ' has not been ridden much lately. I am afraid she might be up to some of her old tricks."

"Then, let me ride her, by all means," said Mr.

Holland, cheerfully. "I like a good lively horse!
I always say to my riding-master in New York,
'Riddle, give me one of your right down runaways.'
I hate a horse that just goes walking along the street
as if he took no interest in anything. Give me a
horse with some life about him!"

"Very well, then, David, Mr. Holland will ride
'Vixen,' but put the curb on her. Do you remember that day, Captain Lee, when she pitched me over
her head into the brook, while you stood by laughing, as if it were a good joke?"

"Ah, ah!" shouted the Captain, as he recalled
the scene, "It was enough to make a saint laugh!
When you dragged yourself out on to the bank,
what with mud and water, you were a sorry sight,
Jim! And there stood 'Vixen,' staring at you
with a reproachful air, as much as to say she was
mortified to think her master could not keep
his seat better than that! You lost a great deal,
Jim, by not seeing it as I did."

"I hope you will give me a chance some day,
Captain," returned Jim, laughing.

It was settled that the Captain should join us at
The Oaks, and that we should start at six in the
morning.

Barnwell and Colonel Shorter were to ride their
own horses, which were already standing in Eustis's
stables.

When we joined the ladies in the drawing-room,
Madge and Mary were sitting on a sofa near the

open window, and Major Barnwell and I, who were talking together as we entered, crossed the room to join them.

After chatting for a few moments, the Major asked Madge to show him some fancy-work that she was doing, and as they left us to examine it near the light, I took the seat that Madge had left by Mary's side and settled myself for a talk. But my hope was not to be fulfilled, for a moment later Mrs. Jackson asked Mary to sing, and without hesitation, she arose and crossed the room to the piano.

Much as I regretted the interruption, I could not fail to admire the grace with which she complied.

"Do you not object to sing before so many people?" I asked, as I opened the piano.

"Yes," she answered, with decision.

"I should never have guessed it from your manner," I said, and then added, as she turned over the music for a song she knew, "Please don't sing any of the songs you sung at sea."

"Why? Did you not like them?" she asked, stopping and looking up at me with an expression of surprise.

"Yes, every one of them," I said, "and so well that I do not wish to hear them again now. I would rather remember them as I heard them first."

She looked down at the music again while I was speaking, but did not answer me.

I would willingly have recalled the words a moment after they were spoken, for I felt that I had overstepped the bounds within which, I had persuaded myself, it was my duty to keep. I was provoked at having done so, and, at the same time, provoked to think I was not free to speak my mind. Thus it happened, that when Mary asked me to turn the pages of her music while she sang, I answered thoughtlessly and almost rudely,—

"No, if you will excuse me, I will listen to you from the piazza."

I did not wait for her reply, but turned away, and walked slowly out of the room, pausing just long enough at the door to see Eustis join her at the piano. I did not catch his words, but I saw the bright, frank smile with which she greeted him, as she began the prelude to her song.

For one who considered himself a philosopher I felt very thoroughly disturbed. I sat down alone on the piazza and lighted a cigarette. I called myself "fool" and "idiot," and by other names of equal severity; but even this failed to afford the customary relief; partly, no doubt, owing to a lack of sincerity in my self-condemnation, and partly to the combined influence of the sad, sweet-voiced song within the house, and the blackness of the night without into which I was looking.

At length the sound of the singing ceased, and in its place arose the chatter of many voices.

Presently, Madge's tall figure appeared in the lighted doorway, and after standing a moment in silence, she asked, turning towards me,—

"Is it you smoking there, Harry?"

"It has a disagreeably strong likeness to me, Miss Madge. Won't you come and amuse me for awhile?" I replied, getting up and moving a chair for her near my own. "You know you promised to reward me for my gallant services this afternoon."

"Well;" she answered, with a tone of resignation, as she sat down beside me. "But I don't think you deserve it at all after breaking your engagement with me."

"I had no idea you intended to go to walk."

"You should have known," she said with severity.

"How, pray?" I asked.

"By—by intuition."

"Well," I answered, "I fear my intuitive faculties are very imperfectly developed. Please don't make 'intuitive engagements' for me in the future. It really is hardly fair! Suppose a young woman should put a ring on her own finger, and then hold a man guilty of breach of contract unless he offered himself. What a predicament he would be in!"

"You need not have the least fear of that, I assure you."

"O, I beg your pardon. I should not be uncivil enough to make the application personal, even in thought. I was only speaking of girls in general."

"And so was I," she exclaimed, with a hearty laugh; and then we made it up, if our little misunderstanding deserved the importance the words "make up" imply.

We chatted on for awhile to the accompaniment of several duets by Miss Lee and Jim who sung very pleasantly together. Jim had a good baritone voice and used it well; nor was singing his only musical accomplishment; for with a natural aptitude, as pleasant as it is rare, he could play upon various instruments, and if not with great skill, yet with sufficient taste to give pleasure to all but the most critical. He played altogether by ear, but with so much vigorous sentiment and spirit, that his occasional liberties with the music could be forgiven.

By the time the duets were finished, and Madge and I went into the house, the loquacity of my companion had restored my spirits. On entering the parlor, we found the party on the point of breaking up, owing to the early start expected for the morrow's hunt.

I saw Mrs Lee to her carriage, which was waiting at the garden gate, and after she and the Captain had taken their seats, as Mary did not come, I went at their request to look for her.

I met her walking slowly down the garden path with Jim. The shrubbery concealed me from them, and they were so deeply absorbed in conversation that they did not notice me until I spoke. I heard Jim say, "To-morrow night," and her answer spoken in a tone full of entreaty.—"Ah, Jim! please don't, I beg of you!"

"Your mother asked me to look for you, Miss Lee," I said, as I approached them; and they both started at the sound of my probably unwelcome voice.

"Oh, I am so sorry to have kept her waiting! Good night, Mr. Strong!" said she, and she hurried past me toward the gate.

Jim followed her and I returned to the piazza thinking of her pleading tone, and wondering what her words had meant.

Shortly after the departure of our guests, the men went down to the smoking-room to take a last pipe and nightcap. I, however, did not join them, wishing to secure an additional hour's sleep against the fatigue of the coming day.

I took a few turns up and down the piazza, and then entered the house on my way to bed. I stopped for a moment at the drawing-room door to bid the ladies good night. Madge was sitting in a recess at the further end of the room talking with Colonel Shorter, who stood leaning against the win. dow near her. The Colonel was evidently in his ele- ment and to judge from Madge's animated face, was. whispering to not unwilling ears. They appeared to be so much engrossed, I thought it best not to disturb them, and as Mrs Jackson was not there, I passed on without entering the room and retired for the night

CHAPTER X.

DEER-HUNTING.

THE morning of the hunt broke bright and clear. I was up and dressed before the gray light in the east had given place to the streaks of red and gold that followed it.

I am fond of early rising, and often have I crept noiselessly from the house in the obscurity of the dawning, to watch in the growing light, from some near height, the mists in the valleys and the rosy tints on the hilltops.

How vigorously the grand old monarch rises from his couch, with beams of light and life and hope for all mankind !

As we watch him, the pulse quickens, and the ambitions rise ! We feel a restless desire for action ; a longing to begin at once upon our allotted tasks.

Full of new-born strength and energy we hasten home to our breakfast, newspaper, and cigar, and then —well, then we relapse into our ordinary, easy going selves, and get through our daily troubles as best we can.

Must we attribute this pitiable result to inherent

weakness, an inborn lack of power for continuous
effort? or do the fumes of the tobacco rob us of our
manly aspirations?

Whatever it is that cuts down these shoots of
ambition in their early growth, it is, at least, pleasant
to have felt them sprout, if only for an hour!

With some such fancies in my mind, I descended
from my room and passed through the garden, in-
tending to steal a short morning walk before the
others had made their appearance.

My hand was already on the gate latch, when a
window was thrown open and Eustis, in his shirt
sleeves, called out to me that it was nearly breakfast time. So I returned to the house, and went to
the smoking-room to put my rifle in order and fill
my belt with cartridges. Shortly after, the men
came dropping in, and by half-past five breakfast
was announced.

Our meal of rolls, eggs, and coffee was a hurried
one, for all our little party were under the pressure
of excitement, and anxious to be off and away.

I said all, but should have excepted Colonel
Shorter, who seemed entirely unruffled, and continued to eat his breakfast with perfect equanimity,
even when the sound of the horns and the baying
of the hounds in front of the house, had caused the
rest of us to leave the table and hurry to the scene
of action.

It is always provoking to see apathy in others
when we are excited ourselves, and especially when
our excitement is of a healthy character, and one in
which those about us should naturally sympathize;

and certainly Colonel Shorter's nonchalance, on the present occasion, prejudiced me against him.

There are, no doubt, times when calm self-control, amid scenes of extreme agitation, marks the great mind; but, on the contrary, it is a sign of a mean intellect to be conspicuously selfish and unsympathetic in the little excitements of daily life; and such a man might be the first to lose his self-possession in the event of a great crisis. Yet, strange as it is, men will pride themselves upon this lack of impressibility, and will, with those about them, mistake it for coolness and depth of character.

What a lively, bustling scene was now taking place! Old Pompey, the huntsman, was there, mounted upon a small, angular-looking mule, and surrounded by a pack of a dozen or more howling, whining hounds, which, by dint of horn and voice and lash he managed with difficulty to keep together.

Three or four negro boys were walking back and forth with the horses we were about to mount.

The horses themselves seemed to share in the general excitement, and their capers and antics gave the boys in charge all they could do to keep them from going a-hunting by themselves.

I noticed that "Vixen" was particularly lively, and taxed to the utmost the powers of the groom at her head. She was a handsome thoroughbred; and while I admired her graceful movements, her bright eyes and distended nostrils, I thought to myself that a day in the woods might be passed more comfortably on a less ambitious animal. I

turned to see whether Holland appeared to be
pleased with the prospect before him, and saw that
none of the excited movements of the horse escaped
his notice. At that moment Eustis approached
him and said,—

"I think, Mr. Holland, I will first try 'Vixen'
myself this morning."

I had gone to the horse that I was to ride and
was adjusting the stirrups when my attention was
arrested by Barnwell's voice, crying,—

"Take care, Jim, slack your rein, or she'll be over
with you!"

I looked up over the pommel of my saddle and
saw that Jim had mounted "Vixen," and was doing
battle with her in dead earnest. She was plunging
and rearing so viciously that I expected her to fling
him over her head, or fall backwards with and upon
him. But he stuck to her like a man, and when she
found her efforts to dislodge him in this way futile,
she began to buck, and, jumping with all four feet
from the ground together, she arched her back, and
sent her rider up into the air a foot or more from
the saddle. Nothing but good luck settled him
upon her again, but his feet were out of the stirrups,
and before she could buck again he had wound them
under her, clinging like grim death. He looked cool
and determined, but I think the rest of us felt
anxious for his safety.

By this time Colonel Shorter had joined us and was
leaning indolently back against the fence near by,
with a supercilious smile upon his face.

"Vixen" had done her best in vain, but, not yet disheartened, she gathered herself together for one final effort, and with a rear and a plunge away she shot down the avenue like an arrow from its string! As they rapidly diminished in the distance, we saw Jim sitting as if welded to her. "I trust she will not throw him at the gate," whispered Barnwell at my elbow. No, out of the gate they swept and down the road, and before we finally lost sight of them in the forest, we could see Jim laying on the lash with every jump! "He's all right now," said Barnwell, "He'll be back in ten minutes or so, He's a fine rider and afraid of nothing."

"There's not much to fear in that horse," interposed Shorter. "Had she been mine I would have thrown her at once and then have beaten her into submission. All this is very pretty to look at, but I don't think it worth our while to waste any more time over it. We might as well start at once."

As no one opposed the Colonel's proposition we all mounted; Holland riding "Dangerous," and I carrying Jim's rifle across my saddle; and to the sound of much discordant music (for each horseman seemed to think it necessary to test the horn that was slung across his back) our little cavalcade proceeded down the avenue.

As we rode slowly along we heard the notes of other horns, in answer to our own, and at the gate met Eustis with Captain Lee who had joined him on the road.

A short delay ensued, while Jim exchanged horses

with Holland and took his gun from me, and at the same time arranged the different stands we each should take at the " Drive."

How lovely was the morning as we strayed off, now in single and again in double file, through the woods. The very atmosphere to breathe and live in ; so cool and fresh and fragrant. The light haze was fast dissolving before the slanting sunbeams that had already found their way to the feet of the pines, and the merry horns waked echo after echo in the distant and more distant cloisters of the forest.

With what distinctness the leaves rustled as the hounds went nosing along through the underbrush, and how sharply the dry twigs snapped beneath the horses' feet. And see, through the woods, in the shallow pool to the right, that tall white heron. How majestically erect he stands, poised on one foot, as motionless as a marble statue ! Wondering, no doubt, what noisy company dares thus invade his sacred solitude at this early hour. Let us not waste a bullet on the beautiful bird—but see! as if suspicious of the thought, he loses suddenly that haughty dignity of bearing, and with lowered and outstretched neck, with awkward skips and strident voice, he takes his flight, the sunlight playing with his snowy wings as he soars upwards through the pines !

On we went through the woods, until at last we came out upon a broad, straight road, stretching in either direction as far as the eye could reach. This road, I was told, bordered one side of the "Drive," and here Captain Lee and Mr. Holland dismounted to take their stands.

The huntsman, with the hounds, continued up the road to enter the woods half a mile to windward, while I followed Jim down a bridle-path that ran into the woods at right angles to the road. Some forty rods from the place where we had left the Captain, we halted at the foot of three tall pines. Jim bade me dismount, and showed me in what direction I must look for the deer, and, then, after one or two parting injunctions, he kept on down the almost imperceptible bridle-path, to a point some distance to my right.

Barnwell and Shorter were beyond Jim, and protected, so I was told, the third side of the quadrilateral.

When Jim had disappeared in the woods, I led my horse back twenty or thirty yards from my stand, and hitched him to a sapling near a copse of dwarf palmetto, that effectually concealed him. Then I returned to my post, and took a survey of my surroundings.

On my left were the open woods, through which I had come from the main road. In front of me, with, perhaps, thirty yards of "open" intervening, was an apparently impenetrable thicket running off indefinitely in either direction. This was the thicket that the hounds and huntsman were about to beat ; around it had our party formed, and within it lay the hope of the day's sport.

To my right, toward the spot where I supposed
Eustis to be standing, the woods were comparatively open, but with clusters of underbrush here and
there to intercept the view.

Behind me the trunks of the pines rose clear and
free from undergrowth, with the exception of the
palmetto thicket, where my horse was tied.

I stood for awhile, leaning against one of the
three pines, listening to the silence of the forest.
I could not hear a sound, save an occasional
movement of my horse.

But, hark! Yes! I hear the huntsman's horn,
blown at intervals, and growing fainter and fainter
at each repetition, until I lose it altogether.

Again silence reigns about me, but still I listen
on intently. I stand up and listen, until I tire of
standing. I sit down and listen, until the rough
trunk of the pine at my back drives me again to
my feet. Standing or sitting, I continue most persistently to listen, but nothing meets the ear but
the creaking of the branches above me, the falling
of the leaves from a withered tree near by, and the
infrequent neighing of my horse.

But one cannot listen intently to nothing forever.
The counting of falling leaves becomes monotonous,
and the number of times a horse can neigh in the
bushes, ceases to be amusing.

So I lean my gun against a tree and light a cigarette. I begin to ask myself how long I have been
standing here, and mentally reply, " Well, at a guess,
I should say forty minutes." I look at my watch,

and find to my astonishment that it is half-past ten. And, as we started at six and were on the ground before seven, I find I must have been standing at my present post for at least three hours!

What has become of the huntsman? Where are the hounds? Have my companions gone home and forgotten me, or are they following the chase in some distant part of the forest? Well, I certainly cannot stay here doing nothing and hearing nothing all the day long, and yet, as I dislike extremely to give it up and go home alone, I decide to remain where I am until eleven o'clock.

I have scarcely formed the determination when I hear distinctly the crackling sound of breaking twigs in the thicket before me, as of some animal forcing his way through it.

I seize my rifle, and stand ready at my post.

The next moment, the loud blast of a horn resounds within a hundred yards of me, and then the deep voice of a single hound, followed in an instant by the music of the whole pack as they open wildly on a fresh trail! Away they go under full cry, waking the echoes with their mad war song!

I see absolutely nothing, but that magic music sends the blood coursing through my veins, and I feel the strong throb of every pulse in my body! O, for one shot at the deer that leads the pack! But away they go—away they go! Now nearer, and now farther off, as he doubles and redoubles on his track, but never again so near as when they first broke in upon the dead silence of the forest.

Hark ! That was a rifle shot. It must be Jim or Shorter, for only we three have rifles. But hark again ! Another rifle shot, and still another. They must be doing brave work in the woods beyond me !

As I turned in the direction of Jim's stand, whence the reports had come, I caught sight, for an instant, of a figure disappearing behind one of the clusters of underbrush that lay in that direction, and not a hundred yards away.

I expected to see it emerge from the opposite side of the thicket, but no, whoever it was, he had evidently come to a standstill behind it. I whistled repeatedly but received no answer. I could not, surely, have been mistaken, and to satisfy my curiosity I walked rapidly to the spot. I passed round the thicket. Nobody was there, and nobody was in sight beyond. I called and whistled, but still there was no response. Had a man passed either way from the place I must have seen him, unless, indeed, he had retreated in a direct line from the spot where I had been standing, thus keeping the thicket between him and me ; but this appeared hardly possible, for at fifty yards from it in that direction, the land fell away into a dense swamp. I went down to its edge and examined it. The underbrush looked impenetrable, and I could see the water glistening through the leaves. I was greatly perplexed, but felt myself finally forced to the conclusion that I must have been mistaken after all, and that my eyes had deceived me. So, having taken my little walk for nothing, I returned slowly to my stand.

In the mean time the sound of the hounds and horns grew more indistinct, and at last died away altogether, but, inasmuch as after the first shots I had heard others at a greater distance, I had hopes that some of the party, at least, had been more fortunate in their hunting than I.

Thinking now that, so far as I was concerned, the hunt was virtually over, I unhitched my nag from the sapling, and throwing the rein over my arm, sauntered up the path to the road where we had left Captain Lee and Mr. Holland. There I found them sitting together on a bank in the shade (for the day had grown warm) smoking their pipes.

"Well, Harry, what luck?" called out the Captain as I approached. I explained that my only luck had consisted in hearing the hounds open near me, and added,—

"But that in itself was worth waiting an hour or two to hear."

"Yes, my boy," replied the Captain, "it is as thrilling as the bugles in a cavalry charge. But I am right down sorry you did not get a shot! We heard the rifles banging away there and supposed you were in the thick of it. But, between you and me, I rather suspect these excellent young huntsmen of sometimes shelving new comers like you, and old fogies like myself. They tickle our ears, you know, with the music, and our palates with the venison they have shot. But they tell us we must have made a noise, or been smoking at the wrong time, or that the wind changed. They have a thousand

good reasons to account for the one inevitable result
—that the deer run right away from us and on to
them! Well, a morning in the woods is pleasant, at
any rate," he added, as he rose from his mossy seat
and shook the ashes from his pipe. "But I think
we've had about enough of it for one day, and so,
gentlemen, if you feel disposed to leave the field to
our more cunning competitors, we may as well go
home to lunch."

Before leaving, the Captain gave two or three
long calls upon his hunting horn, but their echo was
the only answer, and we concluded that the rest of
the party had probably deserted their stations and
joined in following the dogs.

When, half an hour later, we entered the gate of
Palmetto Grove, we saw a lady walking slowly up
the avenue ahead of us.

"Why, there is Mary!" cried the Captain, and
forthwith blew a loud blast upon his horn. She
turned at once and waited for us, waving her para-
sol as we approached.

"Well, father, what luck have you had?" she
asked, at the same time greeting us, each in turn,
with a pleasant smile.

"We have had the good luck, my dear," replied
the Captain, "to get home in time for lunch, and
with no innocent blood upon our heads. I am sorry
we could not give these gentlemen a personal introduction to our game, but I tell them that next
time the best stands are allotted them, they must be
too polite to accept them. If you will show them

the way to the house, Mary, I will hurry on and order lunch."

When the Captain left us we both dismounted, and walked by Miss Lee's side. She looked very lovely in her well-fitting walking dress and broad-brimmed hat, that shaded her eyes and wavy hair. But then she always looks well, I said to myself with almost a feeling of impatience at the thought!

I had not forgotten my rude behavior of the night before, and knowing it could not be easily explained my position embarrassed me and, in consequence, I felt that my manner was constrained and cold. Mary, however, did not appear to notice it and treated us both with the same sunny serenity. But, from some inexplicable contrariness of disposition, this very sweetness itself rather piqued and annoyed me.

At the door of the house, a negro was in waiting to take our horses to the stable, and we went in to lunch. Owing to some slight indisposition, Mrs. Lee did not come down and Mary presided in her stead.

After an excellent luncheon, we retired to the piazza that overlooked the rose garden at the back of the house, and presently the Captain took Mr. Holland away to show him the stables and the view from the pine grove, and Mary and I were left together.

For awhile we spoke on subjects very foreign to my thoughts, but, at last, what was uppermost in my mind would find utterance, and I said,—

"I beg your pardon for leaving you so abruptly last night," and then, as she did not reply, I added inquiringly, "but, perhaps you did not notice it!"

"Why, yes, I think I noticed it," she answered slowly

"Did you think it rude?" I asked.

"It certainly was not very flattering, but I attributed it to Northern manners."

"You must, then, think them very bad?"

"I have not wholly made up my mind, but they do appear to be very uncertain, to say the least," she answered.

"Would you have us always the same! With emotions so completely under control as never to indicate them by word or act?"

"If they must take the form of rudeness, I cannot see the advantage of expressing them!"

What more could I say? I could not mend the matter! Why had I so stupidly referred to it? I had only strengthened her impression of my incivility by acknowledging that I was aware of it, and, at the same time, unable or unwilling to explain it.

How gladly would I have told her that she had caught a glimpse, not of my feelings, but of the strong curb with which they were controlled! The temptation was great, but after a moment's hesitation, I simply said,—

"Yes, no doubt you are right. I only trust you will never again be called upon to pardon such an exhibition of my boorishness!"

At this moment the Captain returned with Mr.

Holland and, declining the cordial invitation of our host to stay to dinner, we ordered our horses and started for home.

About four o'clock we reached The Oaks and found, grouped at the garden gate, Mrs. Jackson, Madge, and Major Barnwell, together with the huntsman and hounds. The latter had just returned from the chase and had brought home two good-sized does as the result of their day's sport. They were examining their prizes and explaining to the ladies, who had come out to meet them, the directions taken by the fatal shots.

" Well, Harry, where is your share of the spoils? " asked Mrs. Jackson turning to me.

" The fact is, Mr. Holland and I were so utterly famished, that we ate our two bucks in the forest, where they fell! " I answered.

"Did Jim kill anything to-day?"

" I don't know. Indeed I have not seen him since we first took our stands. But I heard his rifle just after the hounds opened. What luck did Jim have, Major Barnwell? "

" I don't know," said the Major, " We supposed him to be with you. We saw nothing of him after we left him at his stand. Has not Master Jim come home? " he asked, turning to Jim's body-servant, David, one of a group of negroes who had now gathered round the deer.

" No, sir, I hasn't seen um."

" See if his horse is in the stable."

" No, Massa Tom, I jes' done come from dar."

"Isn't he with Colonel Shorter?" asked Madge.

"No," replied the Major, "Shorter and I followed the hounds together—and, by the way, when I left him at the gate just now, he asked me to make his apologies for not coming up to the house to say good-by. He was obliged to go to town to-night and did not have a moment to spare."

Madge looked up with an expression of surprise while Barnwell delivered his message, but the only comment made upon it by either of the ladies was an almost inaudible, "O, I'm so sorry!" from Mrs. Jackson; a painful effort of good breeding on her part.

"Probably he went over to the Lees', " suggested Madge.

"No, Mr. Holland and I lunched at the Lees' and have just come from there," I said.

"I wonder where he can have gone then!" she exclaimed.

"No doubt he has ridden down to the Corner for the mail and then to the plantation settlement," Mrs. Jackson answered, and added, "Well gentlemen, as you must be hungry after your long day in the woods, we will have dinner at five. It is half past four now. Jim will undoubtedly be back by that time," and with that she and Madge left us and went into the house.

Mr. Holland retired to his room, and Major Barnwell and I, thinking we had a few minutes to spare, went to the smoking-room to take a short pipe together and clean our guns.

After chatting awhile on matters of little moment, the Major said, "I don't know what got into Shorter to-day! He must have gotten out of bed with the wrong foot foremost. I did not like to speak of it before the ladies, but he and Jim had a fuss this morning. Did you not notice his ill temper before we started?" I answered affirmatively, and he continued. "Well, nothing seemed to please him! First he wanted us to go to a different drive, then he was dissatisfied with the place where the hounds were put in, and finally found fault with the stand allotted him. He was altogether in an ugly mood. We stopped at Jim's stand and when he came up Shorter took him to task. Jim bore it as good naturedly as possible, but this only seemed to make Shorter more provoking than ever, till at last Jim lost his temper and gave him a piece of his mind in very plain language; if I had not been there to quiet them down there might have been serious trouble. I was sorry for it—but I must say it was entirely Shorter's fault. That is the reason he did not return to the house. It will probably all blow over but he is very ugly when he once gets the bit between his teeth!"

At this moment David entered the room, and said,—

"January's jes' done come from de corner, Massa Tom; say he see nuffin' of Massa Jim! and I'se been to de settlement and Peter tell me he ain't gone dar all day!"

The Major looked perplexed and puffed away at

his pipe for a few moments without speaking. At length he said,—

"David, get out the horses for you and me and Mr. Strong at once, and lead them down to the thicket at the end of the Avenue; keep quiet about it, for you might disturb the ladies," and, as David hurried off on his errand, he added,—

"I think, upon the whole, we had better hunt Jim up! I heard him fire just after the hounds struck the trail and I remember thinking it odd, that when the deer got by us, and Shorter and I decided to follow, he did not join us, for we called him several times, and he isn't the man to lag at such a moment! At first I supposed that he must have taken some short cut, to head the deer, for he knows the woods almost as well as they do; but as he did not turn up, after all, I came to the conclusion that he had gone back to you and Mr. Holland. We had better ride first directly to the stand and see if we cannot get track of him there."

In the mean time we had left the house and hurried to the spot where David was to meet us with horses. He was there a moment later, and without a word we vaulted into our saddles and swept down the road at a quick gallop.

It was not far to the hunting ground and in a few minutes we were entering the woods at the point where we had left Captain Lee in the morning. We passed the three tall pines where I had kept watch so many hours and proceeded more slowly down the scarcely visible bridle-path.

A hundred yards or so further on, the Major, who was in front, drew up his horse, and said,—

"He must have taken his stand somewhere about here," and at the same moment, we heard the neigh of a horse and the rustling of the leaves, as he pulled and twitched at the saplings to which he was tied. We turned our horses at once in the direction of the sound, and found "Dangerous" hitched in a thicket near by.

He seemed very restless. His saddle had slipped from his back and was hanging under him, and he had gnawed half through the slender trunk, round which the bridle rein was knotted. We dismounted in silence, and, after hitching our horses to the trees, followed Major Barnwell still further into the woods.

The Major, who was a little in advance, had not gone a dozen yards, when, as he was passing a low clump of scrub palmetto, he suddenly stopped and exclaimed, in a low, suppressed voice,—

"My God! here he is—and shot!"

I sprang forward to where he stood, and bent down with him over the prostrate form at our feet. He was lying on his right side, with his right arm stretched at full length above his head. His face had dropped forward on the ground. His bare left arm told the story. A rifle ball had passed through it just above the elbow, and the red stains upon his arms and hands and clothing, showed how freely the blood had flowed. He was without coat or hat. He had torn the shirt sleeve from the wounded arm, and just above the bullet hole had wound and tied his handkerchief as best he could, and its ragged corner marked, how, with his teeth, he had striven to draw tight the knot.

We saw his gun, coat, and hat, together with the remains of his shirt sleeve, some dozen yards from where he lay, and between them and him the ground bore evidence of his having dragged himself along in a desperate attempt to reach his horse before his strength failed him.

We took little note of all these details, however, until later on, for, at first, our only thought was to discover, if possible, some sign of life. From the appearance of the wound, we judged that the blood must have stopped flowing several hours before we found him.

We raised his head and laid him gently on his back, and as I held his wrist, I felt an almost imperceptible beating of the pulse. Oh! what a thrill of joy it gave me! For a moment, I scarcely dared to breathe lest that gentle throbbing might cease!

" He is still alive! " I whispered, looking into Barnwell's livid face. " Have you any whisky with you ? "

He drew a flask from his pocket, and handed it me without speaking, and I, placing the boy's head in my lap, poured a few drops of the spirit between his tightly clenched teeth.

" Go, get a wagon, David," I said, turning to the negro, who had been standing by with clasped hands, the picture of misery. And as he hurried off to his horse, I added, "Wait a minute. Fill the bottom of the wagon with straw, and mind to send some one you can depend upon to the city for a doctor, without a moment's delay, and, if possible, don't raise any alarm up at the house."

"I'se get de wagon from Isaac's store, Mister Harry, and send um down heah. Den I'se ride right on to de town, and I'se fetch de doctor."

"That's good; now be quick; don't waste a second. How soon will the wagon be here?"

"Quarter an hour, sir."

"Well, make the best time you can. Remember, don't spare the horses."

Almost before I had done speaking, he had galloped out of the wood.

It seemed hours that we waited with our unconscious friend. We spoke little, but listened intently for the sound of coming wheels. Barnwell, however, did say to me in an undertone, "He must have shot himself." And I had answered, "No, I think not; you see the ball entered on the outside of the arm." But neither felt inclined to continue the conversation, though, no doubt, both were busy with conjectures.

At length the welcome sound of the approaching cart was heard, as the dry leaves crackled beneath the wheels, and presently, to our relief, old January appeared with the mule team.

He drove close up to where Jim lay, and we gently raised him from the ground, and laid him upon the straw in the open wagon.

We gathered up his gun and coat and hat, and placed them beside him.

Barnwell unhitched the restless "Dangerous," and led him by the bridle, and having again mounted our horses, our sad little procession, with the wagon in advance, filed slowly out of the woods.

How I dreaded that home-coming, and the breaking of the news! But before we reached the gate of The Oaks, I had made up my mind that the unpleasant task should be mine. So I spoke a word to Barnwell, and cantered on alone down the dark avenue.

I will not describe the scene that followed in the brightly lighted drawing-room, where Mrs. Jackson and Madge were waiting for their tardy guests.

They did not give way to useless lamentations, but, as soon as they had recovered from the first shock, set themselves to work, like the thoughtful, loving sisters that they were, and hastened to get everything in readiness for Jim's reception.

How their practical good sense and forethought warmed my heart towards them! It was far more affecting to me than if, as I had expected, they had given way to their feelings.

Thus when the wagon arrived and, with the assistance of Mr. Holland and January, we carried Jim to his room and laid him upon his bed, every possible preparation had been made for his comfort. I lingered yet a little while to help them in rebandaging the wounded arm, and then left him to their tender care. By the time the doctor came

it was ten o'clock, and meanwhile Jim had regained his consciousness and taken a little nourish-
ment. As the doctor ordered him to be kept
perfectly quiet, I did not see him again that night.

Holland, Barnwell and I sat till a late hour in the
smoking-room, discussing the pros and cons of the
affair, but arrived at no very satisfactory conclusion.
According to the best information we could obtain
from the negroes, Armstrong, towards whom our
suspicions tended, had not been seen in the
vicinity since election day and was supposed to have
left that part of the country altogether. If the
suspicion crossed my mind that Shorter might
be in some way implicated, it was set at rest by the
fact that according to Major Barnwell's statement
they had been together for the greater part of the
day.

Hence it was evident that we must wait until
Jim had sufficiently recovered to throw some light
upon the matter himself.

CHAPTER XI.

HOME LIFE AND THE NEW REGIME.

JIM passed a comfortable night and the doctor told us, at breakfast, he was doing so well that his own services would be no longer needed. Rest, nourishing food, and good nursing he must have, and would have, and with these, in all probability, he would be himself again in three weeks' time. But he must avoid excitement or exertion of any kind, and obey implicitly the instructions that had been left with his sisters.

The ball had passed entirely through the arm, but fortunately had not touched the bone.

The doctor who was a brusque but good-natured and withal a loquacious man, monopolized the conversation at breakfast, as we were glad to have him. It was wonderful what a sunny effect his dogmatic manner had upon us, and he left us in an altogether more cheerful frame of mind. Upon his getting into his gig, Holland, Barnwell and I vied with each other in plying him with cigars, and as he drove off down the avenue Barnwell turned to me and said,—

"I reckon there ain't many better doctors than that, anywhere. He knows just what he wants to say, and doesn't waste much time saying it either ! "

I assented, feeling at the moment that he must indeed be a remarkably clever physician or surgeon or both.

It is strange how readily we confound good or evil tidings with the bearer of them, however innocent in the matter he may be. If they provoke the frown, we frown directly upon him; if they awaken smiles, he is the centre of them. So it is with our physician : when he banishes our hopes, we distrust him and his skill ; when he allays our fears, words fail to express our admiration for him and our confidence in his ability !

Soon after the doctor's departure, Barnwell told us that he, too, must return home at once, and ordered his horse to be saddled and brought to the gate. This was done, but the animal stood, hitched to the picket, for nearly an hour, while the good Major still lingered, walking up and down the piazza, or sitting upon the railing tapping his long boots with the end of his whip.

Guessing at the cause of his delay, at length I took pity upon him and went in search of Madge. She had not come down that morning, but, as good luck would have it, I met her in the upper hall carrying a tray of breakfast things from Jim's room.

" Good morning, Madge ! How does Jim seem to be ? " I asked.

" He is getting on splendidly, Harry. He has eaten some breakfast and has just fallen asleep. But you don't know how thin and pale he looks ! I should never have supposed such an accident could have altered his appearance so suddenly and completely," she answered, rather mournfully.

"Well, Madge," I returned, cheerfully, "I have the utmost confidence in your ministrations, and expect to see Jim down on the piazza in a couple of days at farthest. You must lend him a little of the coloring you use, to brighten up his cheeks. You cannot make me believe you sat up with him all last night!"

"I shall not try," she answered.

"You must, at least, allow you took just a few winks of beauty sleep!"

"You are very saucy, sir, this morning!" she said, smiling brightly at me, as she turned away to carry the tray downstairs.

"O, stop a moment, Madge!" I called after her. "I forgot to tell you that the Major ordered his horse an hour ago, but evidently cannot tear himself away, until he has said a word to you."

"What does he wish to say?" she asked in a tone of impatience.

"Really, he has not taken me into his confidence; but probably—good-by!"

"Well, I have no time for such nonsense this morning," she answered, petulantly, "and you can tell him so."

"O, that would be too cruel after all this waiting! Why, he would be in such ill humor, that when he reached home, he would order all his darkies out and flog them in a row!"

"Well, I will see," she replied, doubtfully, "but I do wish he would show some sense!"

"I think he shows a great deal!" I exclaimed laughing, and leaning over the banisters to watch her as she went downstairs.

I returned to the piazza and found the Major still pacing the quarter-deck, watch in hand, and a moment later Madge made her appearance.

When he saw her, his troubled face lighted up at once.

"Good morning," he said, advancing towards her, and then added, hesitatingly, "I am going home now and wish to say good-by."

"Good-by!" she answered, looking at him, without a smile.

He still stood there for a moment in silence, and then asked, with some embarrassment of manner,—

"Is there anything I can do for you? I may be going to town in a day or two; perhaps I can get you something."

"No, I thank you," she answered with perfect unconcern. "I can send for anything I need."

"Well, then, good-by," he said, coming to where she stood.

"Good-by," she answered icily, as he took her hand, and then added more cordially, as if conscious that she had been a trifle too discourteous, "I hope you will come to see Jim when he is able to sit up."

"Oh, yes, thank you," he replied, his face again brightening. "I shall come often."

Poor fellow! I pitied him; his whole manner showed so plainly that he was in love. Ah, my good Major, you cannot hope to win it in return until you have learnt how to control yourself—no matter how deserving love may be, the ill-advised expression of it is never acceptable.

I was provoked, too, at Madge's treatment of the Major, for I liked what I had seen of him, and the events of the day previous had afforded me no little insight into his character. He was a manly, straightforward fellow, not over bright, perhaps, but full of good feeling, and I was sorry to see the trouble in his face as he mounted his horse to start for home.

Mr. Holland only remained at The Oaks for a day after the accident. He probably found our country life rather dull, and, perhaps, feared that his presence might be a burden to the ladies of the house while so much of their time was required in the sick room.

At first Jim regained his strength slowly, and it was not until about the middle of December that he was well enough to leave his room and join us downstairs. But from that time his recovery was rapid, and a week later he was almost himself again.

In the mean time, the Lees were unremitting in their attentions, and hardly a day passed that did not bring from them some act of kindness. A mould of jelly or some fruit, brought by Mary to tempt the palate of the invalid, or a brace of birds (shot or bought, probably the latter), by the good Captain, who also took it upon himself to attend to the affairs of Jim's plantation, coming every morning for his orders, and doing it all in such a simple, matter of course way, that it was impossible to believe he thought for an instant he was conferring a favor.

Nor was he less thoughtful of me, and under his tutelage, during Jim's convalescence, I acquired a very general knowledge of the methods of rice and cotton culture, the social polity of plantation settlements, at present and in times past, and the difficulties that planters had been obliged to overcome at the introduction of the new regime.

" It was very hard at first upon the negroes," the captain said to me one day, " for their main ideas of freedom, were freedom of motion and freedom from work, and it took a heavy dose of privation and suffering to cure them ; to bring them back to scenes and occupations in which alone they are fitted and able to keep the wolf from the door ; and to make them understand that by work alone could freedom from work be attained. It was a hard lesson to learn, but they have at least partially done so, and are fast settling down into a quiet and useful peasantry. It is not unnatural, however, that until the negroes fully appreciate the fact that the planters interests and their own are identical, they should occasionally,.under the influence of bad men, break out into exhibitions of lawlessness and folly such as you witnessed the other day at the polls. It is a mere question of time, however, and I am certain that all will come right in the near future.

"There are, no doubt, some exceptions, but I venture to say the vast majority of my fellow planters will bear me out in pronouncing the new system an immense relief. No, sir, we would not return—if we could—to the old order of things.

"There is no use denying that slavery gave opportunities for cruelty, it is patent on the face of it ; and no doubt at times they were taken advantage of, but on the other hand it opened the door to liberality, kindness, and a deep personal affection such as seldom exists in any other relationship between master and man.

"Why, our own slaves, for instance, were devotedly attached to Mrs. Lee and she to them. Many's the night I've known her to pass in their cabins administering comfort by the death-bed of some old crone, or helping some mother to watch with her sick child! And she was by no means the only planter's wife who made herself a slave to her own slaves ! "

Alas! that the thought of self-interest should inevitably attach itself to stories such as these in the minds of those who have been born and bred without the pale of slavery. How difficult for them to attribute such acts of kindness to purely disinterested motives! Nothing but close intimacy with characters differing so much in thought and education from their own, will set their suspicions at rest, and enable them to mete out impartial justice.

From time to time Eustis' friends came out from the city to see how he was doing and to pass a day or two at The Oaks ; and on several of these occasions we went hunting under the lead of Barnwell or Captain Lee, and had some very successful days in the woods.

Barnwell frequently rode over from his plantation on one pretext or another, and rarely came without some little tribute, a bunch of flowers or a box of candy, to be offered at the shrine of his inamorata.

Sometimes Madge would receive his attentions with good grace and would almost warm in her manner towards him ; but then again she would hardly notice him and would preserve in his presence a quiet indifference that took all the light out of the good fellow's face. It was painful even to me, a mere looker on, to see how closely he watched her every look and movement, endeavoring to divine her thoughts and wishes, and how in his eagerness to do what might prove acceptable, he overshot the mark and covered himself with embarrassment and mortification.

As already said, I had taken a liking to the man and his frank, blunt manners, and, from the close companionship into which we had been thrown by Jim's accident, had rather expected our intimacy to grow stronger ; but such was not the case, for I soon observed, without suspecting the cause, that although courteous and polite, he treated me with a marked reserve that seemed foreign to his character.

Who shot Jim still remained a mystery, and as

Mrs. Jackson said that he was very unwilling to talk about it, the subject was avoided in the sickroom during the first few days of his convalescence.

Subsequently, however, while sitting with him one evening, I told him of my success that day in killing the first Churchill County deer that had given me a shot, and seeing how much he was interested, I exclaimed,—

" How I wish you could have been with us! I thought of you so often while we were in the woods! I cannot tell you how sorry I have been about this unfortunate affair. In fact——"

" O, never mind, old fellow!" he broke in, evidently to stop me. "Accidents will happen, you know. Besides it makes no difference now, for you see I'm getting on splendidly, and shall be as well as ever in the course of a week or two."

There was something so peculiar in Jim's manner that I suspected at once that he knew more than he was disposed to tell, and I continued earnestly,—

" I really think, Jim, you ought to tell us all you know or suspect about this affair."

" But I don't care to talk about it," he answered, emphatically.

"I can see no possible good in concealment," I replied. " If it was simply an accident you can and should explain it, and if not, you should tell us what you know, to prevent us from suspecting perhaps those who are innocent."

He was still very stubborn but finally acknowledged, to my utter astonishment, that he attributed

his misfortune to my own carelessness or misdirected
zeal! He believed me to be ignorant of the mis-
chief I had done, and intended to let me remain
so!

How heartily I laughed at my quixotic friend! It
did not take me long to undeceive him and to show
him how unworthy I was of such consideration!
But when we had talked the matter all over we were
no nearer the truth than ever, and could hit upon
no satisfactory solution of the mystery. Inquiries
set on foot by Captain Lee and others corroborated
the former statements of the negroes, that the man
Armstrong had quitted his old haunts and gone no
one knew whither. Of course, the place had been
carefully examined where, on the day of the hunt, I
thought that I saw a man disappear into the swamp,
but no traces were to be found; and as our suspicions pointed in no other direction, we were obliged
for the present to let the matter rest.

Meanwhile, I was becoming day by day more intimate with Mrs. Jackson and Madge.

The former treated me with all the kindness and
familiarity of an elder sister. She was a most charming hostess and always unobtrusively mindful of my
happiness and comfort. With rare tact and the
true spirit of hospitality, she left me entirely my
own master, yet with the consciousness that I was
never neglected nor forgotten.

She had been pretty as a girl and still retained a
fair portion of her good looks and figure; but her
complexion had lost its freshness at an age, when,

in a colder climate, the roses would have lingered still in her cheeks. Early in life she had married a gentleman of her own State, who, dying shortly after, left her a rich and still young widow.

As she had always been, more or less, a woman of the world and a favorite in society, her friends had expected her to marry again, but although the days of her widowhood had long since past and there were said to have been many suitors for her pretty hand, she remained single and devoted her life to the care of Madge.

As for Madge, she and I generally got on very well together. She was a high-strung girl, with a temper rather variable at times, but withal full of kindly impulses and feelings. Her very changefulness lent her a certain charm, especially as it seemed to lie altogether on the surface of her girlish and coquettish nature.

One rainy morning, which she and I were trying to while away over a desultory game of billiards, I asked,—

"Why has sister Kate never married again Madge?"

"O, don't interrupt me, sir, just as I am going to hole your ball! There!" she exclaimed as she made a fluke, pocketing her own ball instead and giving me the game, "it is all your fault, but I shall take my revenge by making you play another with me."

"If that is the worst punishment you can inflict. I shall keep on beating you all the morning, if I can!" I answered, arranging the balls. "But you have not answered me."

"How should I know why my sister does not marry? Probably because she is a sensible woman! Besides, what would Jim and I do without her?"

"Get married too!"

"Perhaps Jim might. In fact, I suppose he and Mary will arrange matters before long, if she can only tell her own mind! But think what a forlorn position that would leave me in!"

"Possibly some one might take pity on you,—the Major, for instance," I suggested.

"Please don't, if you love me!" she said, with a comically beseeching expression.

"Of course I love you!" I answered with mock solemnity. "But, all the same, I am certain you will marry the Major!"

"Never! Not if he were the last man on earth," she replied emphatically, and then added lightly,— "There now isn't he just the man for sister? She admires him so much, you know!"

She was standing with her back to the door and before she had done speaking, who should appear but the very gentleman whose hand we had been disposing of so freely! He wore a faded gray velveteen coat cut short and fitting close to his solid figure. His corduroy trousers and spurred top-boots, that reached above the knee, bore unmistakable evidence of the miry condition of the roads. In his hand he carried his black sombrero and short-lashed whip. His face was broad, ruddy and clean-shaven, and as he stood there in the doorway, he did not look unlike an English country squire.

" Good morning, Major," I said. At the sound of my words, Madge turned suddenly from the table and faced him. The color mounted to her cheeks and with marked embarrassment she exclaimed, as he took her hand.

" Why, Major Barnwell ! I had no idea you were here. When did you come ? Have you seen Jim ? "

The Major could not have failed to observe her heightened color and confused manner, but apparently mistook the cause.

" I came only a few minutes ago," he answered, with a bright cheerful smile that made his face for the moment almost handsome. " I had a little time to spare and thought I would ride over and see how Jim was. I have just come from his room and am glad to find him so much stronger and better ! " then stopping short, he took a little bunch of flowers out of his hat and added, hesitatingly,—

" There are a few violets, Miss Madge, not very pretty—the first I have had from my garden this winter—but they are very fragrant. I thought you might like them."

" Thank you ! " she said, as she held them to her face. " They are lovely and so sweet ! "

" I am so glad you like them ! " he replied looking very happy. " I shall have much better ones before long. And now I must—I must say good morning ! "

" Why, surely you will stop to lunch ! "

"No, thank you. I wish I could, but I must get back home at once. Good-by,—good-by Mr. Strong," and he was gone.

She looked very bewitching as she stood there facing him, with one hand on her cue and the other pressing the flowers to her lips, and I doubt if the good major recovered his senses till his horse floundered in the first bog on his way home.

After he had gone, she turned to me and said in a serious tone,—

"I hope he did not hear what I said of him, Harry."

"If he had he would not believe it now." I answered. "I am very glad I am not in that poor fellow's shoes!"

"Why, what do you mean? I thought I was particularly polite and nice to him."

"Yes, too much so, if you really meant what you said to me ten minutes ago."

"I certainly did mean every word of it!"

"Well, then, I pity the poor fellow. However, it's no business of mine!"

"You are perfectly right in that!" she answered, looking at me with sparkling eyes. "If I had been rude to him you would have said the same thing. You are very disagreeable this morning,—I shall not stay here any longer to be found fault with," and without taking any further notice of me, she laid her cue upon the table and sailed out of the room.

I indulged in whistling to myself and knocking

the balls about in a purposeless way for awhile, and
then retired to my room to write.

I sent a long letter to Alice that day, and in reply
to some sisterly inquiries contained in her last, I
wrote : " Madge is certainly an interesting and attractive girl, but I assure you, my dear sister, that
there is not the least danger of her becoming too
fond of me. Of course, we have seen much of one
another since Jim's accident, and I have become
sincerely attached to her, but regret to say she does
not seem to return my regard and at times, I think,
almost dislikes me. It is fortunate, however, for
your peace of mind that it is so, for if she had seen
fit to weave her enchantments around me, as she has
about some of her unfortunate countrymen, I would
not answer for the consequences.

" Do you remember my writing you of the Lee
family who came out in the steamer with me? They
live near us here in the country and Jim is engaged
to Miss Lee, or is about to be engaged to her,—that
is, there is an understanding between them. It is
an excellent match. You know what I think of
Jim, and she is very lovely both in face and character. I wish you could see her! "

And here I rather abruptly closed my letter.

Ah, how I wished I could keep that fair young
face out of my mind! But it was impossible! I
thought of her constantly, although well aware of
the folly of this self-indulgence.

CHAPTER XII.

MR. BROWN'S VIEWS OF FLORIDA.

ON a beautiful bright Monday, about a week before Christmas, Eustis, Madge and I were
sitting on the front piazza, reading and talking together at intervals. Although in the middle of
.December the day was warm and sunny, with just
a slight chill in the air, to remind us that it was
not summer.

Jim had recovered his wonted appearance of ro-
bust health, although his strength had not yet wholly
returned, and he still was obliged to make conces-
sions to his weakness that were chafing to a man of
his energetic nature.

He had been to the plantation that morning,
and after walking about the rice-fields, had come
home completely tired out. He was reclining in a
low easy-chair with swinging canvas back, and was
amusing us by the half comical way in which he
stigmatized himself and his worthless condition,
when our attention was called to two figures in the
distance, coming up the avenue. From where we
sat we looked directly down the long vista under
the Spanish moss, to the gate a quarter of a mile
away, and as the visitors drew nearer, now in deep

shade and again for a moment in a shimmer of sunlight, it was easy to recognize the lady as Miss Lee,
although the identity of the gentleman continued
to puzzle us until they reached the garden gate,
when to my surprise I recognized my friend and
fellow-townsman, Brown.

" Why, Brown," I exclaimed (after the necessary
introductions had taken place), " I had no idea you
would be able to tear yourself away from the palm
and orange groves so soon ! "

" Well, Harry, it doesn't take more than a month
or six weeks to do up Florida pretty thoroughly.
There's not much to be seen down there, except St.
Augustine and the St. John's River, and ten miles of
that are just as good or better than a hundred ! Why,
man, there isn't a hill or a pretty place anywhere
along it ; nothing but palms, pines and cypresses on
either side for miles and miles ; the most dismal and
monotonous scenery I ever saw. Things are bad
enough on board the boats, but when you land it is
worse still. Green Cove, Magnolia, and all that
sounds very pretty," he continued, contemptuously,
" but what does it amount to ?—a few rows of shanties, that the Irish would refuse to live in in our part
of the country, and full, too, of consumptives and
fleas. The fleas are the more fortunate of the two for
the consumptives get nothing to eat, and it is no wonder so few of them manage to drag themselves back
to civilization at the end of the winter. And then,
as for musquitoes and sandflies, I certainly never
saw anything like it ! No, it is all very well to

have been there, for I think a man ought to see all
he can of the world, but one visit is enough for
me ! ”

When Brown began, I observed a puzzled look
on Madge's face, but before he ended it had given
place to an expression of amusement.

“ I hope you found St. Augustine more attractive
than the St. John's, Mr. Brown,” she said.

“ Well, yes,” he replied, “ it was rather nice when
I once managed to get there, but it took half a day's
journey through the woods in an old horse-car
drawn by mules. Why, if the horse-cars up in our
village didn't make better time than that, the people
would be up in arms in a twinkling.”

“ That the people were up in arms so long in
Florida, probably accounts for their having such
poor travelling facilities,” suggested Madge.

“ Really, they are such a lazy-looking set,” he
answered, “ I can hardly believe they ever were in
arms since they were babies ! ” at which we all
laughed except Fred, who continued quite earnestly,
“ and I can't imagine what they had to fight for ! ”

“ Their homes,” said Madge, sententiously.

“ It doesn't seem to me they were worth it.”
rejoined Brown. “ If I hadn't a better home than
that, I should be glad to lose it. St. Augustine,
however, was rather an interesting place on account
of its history. I read up a good deal about it while
I was there, and expected to find out something
from the natives themselves, but though I questioned
them about the state of their society and their

schools and politics, etc., they were too ignorant or too lazy to answer me. I could make no headway with them at all ! ”

Thinking it as well to change the subject, I said, “ Well, Brown, I am glad to see you looking so much better than when I left you. You must have gained ten or fifteen pounds, even if they did starve you ! ”

“ Why, yes, I am better, thank you,” he replied. “ And I have certainly gained in weight, but I’m in a perfect quandary as to where the flesh came from.”

Jim was much amused at Brown’s garrulity and his quaint way of looking at things, and the young ladies apparently did not know exactly what to make of him. As they told me afterwards, they could not understand whether he was speaking in jest or seriously, and on this point I was unable to enlighten them ; for Brown was one of those men who always appear to speak in dead earnest, and never to appreciate the humor of their own speech.

The visitors stayed to lunch with us, and afterwards Madge and Jim and I went with them as far as the gate on their way home. As we walked back Madge said to me,—

“ What an extraordinary little man Mr. Brown is ! What a comical contrast he and Mary made. It reminded me (excuse my saying it of such an intimate friend of yours, Harry), but it did remind me of ‘ Beauty and the Beast.’ ”

“ You do him great injustice I assure you,” I answered, “ there is very little of the beast about Brown. He is eccentric, but his mind has altogether the upper hand."

"Well," she continued, gayly, "of course I did not mean that he really was. But did you ever knew anybody so inquisitive? And such funny questions as he asks, and such queer things as he says! One scarcely knows how to treat him. Among other things he inquired about the schools I had been to; what was taught in them; what books I had studied and read. Then he advised me to continue my education, pointing out what I had better take up next and so on; and ended up by remarking, in the coolest manner possible, that it was a great pity there were no good schools at the South; I should certainly have been angry with him, if he had not talked all the time in such an innocent way."

" I hope you tried to impress upon him, by your own edifying conversation, that he was entirely mistaken," I said.

" Not a bit of it," she answered laughing, "on the contrary, I tried to appear just as ignorant as possible, and asked him all the most stupid questions I could think of! I told him we girls were too busy hunting and shooting to have much time for study; that I could hit the buckle of my belt at fifty yards with a rifle; and that Jim often called upon me to break his horses for him. You should have seen him open his eyes! It was too funny for anything. I believe he was taking notes of it all, and I only hope Mary will not undeceive him."

Mrs. Jackson had been passing the day in the

city, and so missed the opportunity of meeting our
visitors.

During Jim's illness, I had, on several occasions,
gone home to lunch or dine with Captain Lee. At
first, I refused his invitations under various pre-
texts, but at length yielded to the temptation, and
though in so doing I recognized my folly, I gradually became a frequent visitor at his house.

But as Jim grew better, we usually went over to
Palmetto Grove together, and from that time my
pleasant chats with Mary came to an end. For
Jim, with easy grace and the familiarity resulting
from long intimacy, would monopolize her attention
either by practising duets with her at the piano, or
by coaxing her out of the house for a stroll in the
garden. If out of politeness she remonstrated
against leaving me, as once or twice she did, he
would only say,—

"O, never mind Harry! he and your father are
busy discussing the affairs of past generations."

I would hear the words, and without looking up
feel that they had gone; and then my thoughts
would wander with them from the house and the
Captain's inexhaustible anecdotes !

Jim's *affaire de cœur* seemed to be progress-
ing as favorably as even he could wish, and evidently met with the entire approbation of Mary's
parents. Sometimes even Mrs. Lee would unbend
at his light-hearted jests ; and she always appeared
to feel the affectionate solicitude of a mother in
his plans and doings.

What was my own state of mind at this time? Changing every hour! At one moment full of sympathy for my friend; at another crowded with emotions that daily were taking stronger and stronger hold upon me. Sometimes, forgetting Eustis altogether, I allowed my thoughts to wander on and on through mazes of fascinating possibilities, to be, perhaps, suddenly and roughly awakened again to the realities that faced me!

Ah! better never to discover the essence of our life's happiness, than at the same time learn we are debarred from it forever!

CHAPTER XIII.

AT SCHOOL.

CHURCHILL County boasted of a negro school, which was supported by the contributions of the planters who lived in the vicinity. It had been started shortly after the close of the war by Captain Lee in the face of considerable opposition ; but owing to his earnest and continued efforts, it had been placed at last upon a firm footing in the community.

The former teacher had absconded with a small sum of money given him for the purchase of school books; and after much trouble an intelligent mulatto woman had been secured to fill his place.

For a year or more she had worked faithfully and economically in the discharge of her duties; and now, anxious to display the results to her patrons, she announced that on a certain evening before Christmas an exhibition would be held, and she begged them " to honor and encourage it with their presence."

It was consequently arranged that our household should dine on that day at Palmetto Grove, and that after dinner we all should drive together to the schoolhouse.

When the day came, however, Mrs. Jackson was slightly indisposed and decided to remain at home. So Jim and Madge and I drove over to the Grove without her.

The Captain and Jim were both in the best of spirits that evening and kept the table in a constant state of merriment. Even Brown was less serious than usual and, for the time, yielded awkwardly to the prevalent frivolity.

The exhibition was to begin at eight, and shortly after seven the carriages were ordered to the door. Just as we were about to leave the house, Jim came to me and said that, as Mrs. Lee was not going, the Captain had offered him the spare seat, and he wished I would drive Madge over to the school.

" Certainly," I replied, adding to Madge who was standing near, " if you will trust yourself with me."

" I'm afraid I must, whether I wish to or not," she answered.

By the time we were ready to start, the Captain's carriage had disappeared in advance and we were left to follow at our leisure.

It was a beautiful night, with the moon almost at the full. In the plot before the house it seemed as bright as day; and as we drove slowly along, the white light came streaming down through the pines and casting their dark images sharp and well defined across the road. Through the open forest on either side the moonbeams glistened and shimmered, playing strange pranks with the stately trunks and moss-draped branches of the trees. What a night for fairies to revel in the recesses of the forest and ride the fallow-deer in swift races through the checkered glades! There was a fascination in peering into those mysterious depths, half hidden, half revealed by the soft lights and shadows: and at every little opening, where the tall pines stood back to let the moonlight fall, one half expected to catch a glimpse of elfin sports or hear their cry of warning and alarm as they took fright and vanished at our coming!

Neither of us had spoken for some time, until at last I said, almost with a sigh,—

"What a depressing influence the beauties of Nature have upon us! Why should they make us sad, instead of filling us with joy to think what a lovely world we have to live in?"

"They do not sadden me," she answered gently. "I feel very happy and contented." Then, after a moment's pause she added, turning towards me, "Does anything in particular worry you to-night, Harry?"

"Yes, many things," I answered moodily, "Both in the past and future."

"Of your past, of course, I know nothing," she said; "but why should you worry about the future? You seem to me to have everything a man can desire."

"And yet what I desire most of all is beyond my reach!" I replied, hardly thinking what I said.

"What do you mean?" she asked earnestly.

"My peace of mind," I answered, cutting the dry

leaves from the underbrush with my whip as we passed.

" Why, Harry ! " she exclaimed cheerfully. " How very gloomily you talk this evening ! Tell me what has happened to destroy your peace of mind ? If you would only make me your confidante, perhaps I might help you ! ", and then as I remained silent, she added presently, " Surely, you are not in love ? "

She was leaning slightly forward, and as she raised her face to look up into mine the moonlight fell full upon it. Almost unconsciously I dwelt for a moment on its loveliness, and as I withdrew my eyes, I answered,—

" That I cannot tell, myself."

" Well, Harry," she said very quietly and turning from me. " If you yourself do not know what the matter is, of course I cannot help you."

I was so entirely absorbed in my own thoughts, that I did not at the time lay any weight upon our words, but long afterwards they came back to me with a new meaning.

For awhile both of us were silent; and when Madge spoke again it was in her usual tone.

" I heard you say you were going to Florida in January, with Jim," she said, " you know, we move to town next week for the winter, and I hoped you would come with us to see something of our city society."

" I should think you might have had enough of mine already," I replied.

"I shall not answer you!" she rejoined smiling. "But the next month will be our gayest season and it would be a pity for you to lose it!"

We had just drawn up in front of the school-house, and as I got out of the wagon, I said,—

"If it would really make any difference to you, I will not go. I can run down to Florida later, if I care to, just as well as now."

"Ah, thank you, Harry. I know you will not regret it!" she answered, pressing my hand lightly as I helped her down.

"Well," cried the Captain, who stood waiting for us, "we thought you must have lost your way. Why, we have been here for fifteen minutes or more. Come on, they are only waiting your arrival to begin the ceremonies."

"The night was so lovely, we drove very slowly, to get the full benefit of it!" I answered, as we followed him into the building.

The schoolhouse was a log cabin with its gable end facing the road. When we first entered, it seemed darker than the night without, so dim was the light of the three kerosene lanterns (its only means of illumination) hung against the wall at the further end of the long, low room.

We followed the captain between the rows of wooden benches, filled with negroes, to those in front, which, being near the little platform under the three lanterns, had been reserved for the white guests. Besides our own party, we found there a dozen or more ladies and gentlemen from the neighboring plantations, among whom I recognized Major Barnwell. Somebody made room for us, and the few minutes of solemn silence that ensued, for all was as still as a graveyard, gave me a chance to study the quaint scene.

At one end of the platform sat the colored school-mistress, a spare, sharp-featured little woman, whose keen black eyes wandered restlessly over the faces of the people before her.

In the centre of the same platform, on a throne of state, sat a well-favored young yellow girl, dressed in a white tarleton gown drawn in at the waist with a broad yellow sash, and all bedecked and bedewed with spangles. On her head she wore a broad tiara of tinsel pasteboard, and in her right hand she held, with one end resting on the floor, a long staff, wound spirally with variegated tissue papers and crowned at the top with a huge rosette of green and yellow.

She sat there motionless as a statue, with head erect and eyes fixed straight before her.

The exact place which she filled in the educational system I was unable to discover.

I hardly think her exalted position could have been a tribute to her scholarship, for her utterances later on did not seem to warrant the supposition. Possibly she was selected as the favorite of the school, or the belle of the colored community. I incline, however, to the opinion that she was simply placed there as a vision on which to feast the eyes during the interludes, a metaphorical drop-curtain.

Indeed, she was a fine specimen of yellow woman-hood with the composure and dignity of a queen at Court.

Behind me the room was almost hidden in dark-ness, but out of the shadows, here and there peered the shining faces and white teeth of the negroes.

Suddenly the silence was broken by the voice of the schoolmistress exclaiming in a clear, command-ing tone,—

" Shadrach Houston, My breeches ! "

The order was altogether startling and I half expected, for a moment, to see our preceptress don the masculine attire and favor us with a genuine breakdown ! But, instead, a negro youth arose from one of the back benches ; shambled down the aisle ; made a quick bow and scrape with his foot to the audience on either side ; and then, turning his back upon them, he faced the goddess on the platform, and began, in a clear, mellow sing-song, the story with which Dr. Holmes has made us familiar, of an inex-perienced youth upon whom one of our ordinary New England equinoctials made such a profound impression. His voice grew stronger as his woes increased, and the closing lines were delivered with considerable dramatic energy, but he never for a moment lost his strong musical accentuation of the metre. When he had finished he turned quickly round, paused for a moment, made another jerk of the head and scrape of the foot and shuffled rapidly away into the obscurity, amid the loud clapping of our hands.

After this, young people of both sexes and of all sizes, treated us to various recitations, gay or pathetic, as the case might be. In fact the innocence and simplicity with which they were uttered gave a touch of pathos to them all. A dialogue between the queen and another girl of about her own age especially struck me. The latter held out the temptations to a marriage for wealth, luxury, and social position, which the queen rejected in words expressive of the loftiest sentiments, in favor of a union for true love's sake in a lower sphere. A trite old story and commonplace enough to ears familiar with it from infancy; the moral of many a nursery tale ; the favorite gag of the circus clown ; the threadbare topic of the family circle; the last gasp of ballroom conversation; yet clothed with a new and touching charm when discussed in earnest tones by these ignorant negroes for whom the situation could only exist in imagination.

Toward the close, Miss Josephine Polite was called to the front. She was a tiny little four year old, with face as black and shiny as a lump of cannel coal. She wore a low-necked, short-sleeved gown of yellow tarleton, and the broad green ribbon round her head bound down her short crisp wool. She was a comical-looking little figure with her gaudy dress, bright eyes and quiet self-possession.

She curtsied to the schoolmistress, she curtsied to the queen, she curtsied to the company, and then, with eyes fixed straight before her down the aisle, and without an expression on her face, she

threw back her head, opened wide her mouth and
sang out at the top of her lungs, in a shrill, piping
voice, but tuneful withal, the following verses,—

"O I have a beau, mamma, mamma,
O I have a beau, but don't you tell pa,
For he wouldn't like it, you know, mamma !

"He kissed me last night, mamma, mamma,
He kissed me last night, but don't you tell pa,
For he wouldn't like it, you know, mamma !

"He gave me a ring, mamma, mamma,
He gave me a ring, but don't you tell pa,
For he wouldn't like it, you know, mamma !

"To-morrow he'll marry me, dear mamma,
To-morrow we'll marry, so you can tell pa,
For then he won't mind it, you know, mamma !"

This was the climax of the evening and the little
vocalist was greeted with long continued applause.

At the close of the exercises, the captain called
up the performers in turn and gave to each a silver
dollar and after complimenting the teacher in ap-
propriate words on the progress and proficiency of
her scholars, he announced that the exhibition was
over.

As we filed out of the building, Major Barnwell
made his way to Madge's side and I heard him ask
her, in a low voice, if he might not drive her home.
"No, I thank you, Major," she said, "I am going
with Mr. Strong. Am I not, Harry ?"

"I depend upon it," I answered, and he left us,
without another word.

At the first sign of the breaking up of the entertainment the negroes had hurried out, and when we reached the door, we found they had lighted a large bonfire in the woods near by and were preparing for some of their songs and games. So after we were seated in our carriages, we all remained awhile to watch them.

In the uncertain mingling of the moon and fire-light it was difficult to make out the points of the games that they played, but with joined hands they circled round and round, and their rich voices rung out loud and clear in time to their solemn-measured tread.

What an uncanny ring they are! Now lost in deep shade, and now again with the firelight blazing full upon their black faces and sparkling eyes!

Listen to the flute-like notes of the soloists, as in turn they sing apparently impromptu rhymes! With what full harmony the chorus follows with the oft repeated, dirgelike refrain! Hark to that deep bass breaking in upon them all in syncopated time, so unexpected, yet so invariably true!

I sat there watching them, silent and fascinated, until Madge suddenly recalled me to myself by saying,—

"Don't you think we had better start? The others left some time ago."

I had been too much absorbed in the unusual spectacle to notice the departure of the rest of the party, but at Madge's words I slowly gathered up the reins and started on our way home.

Madge was in one of her gayest moods, laughing and running on about the recitals we had heard, the odd dresses of the negro girls, and the expression of Mr. Brown's face when the teacher asked Shadrach for her breeches; and I drove along in the moonlight listening to her merry talk, and oblivious to the thoughts that for the past few days had worried and depressed me.

The air had grown colder as the night advanced, and drawing out from under the seat a shawl that I had persuaded her to take when we left home, and putting it round her shoulders, I said, " There, Madge, you see it has come into use after all ! "

" Yes, " she answered, " I must admit that you were very pleasantly thoughtful, to-night."

" Why, am I not always thoughtful ? "

" Yes, always thoughtful; too thoughtful at times, but not always pleasantly so."

" What do you mean, Madge ? I do not understand you," I stupidly asked.

" Well, forgive my saying so, but perhaps you are, you know, just the least bit apt to find fault about trifles. Don't you think so ? " she said, glancing up at me demurely, " it seems to me you are very hard to please."

" No, I do not think so," I replied, " at all events I am quite sure I have been pleased to-night, for when we left home I was thoroughly blue and low-spirited, and now—well—now I should be very happy to drive on till the moon sets ! No, I never find fault with people unless I like them ; but when

I imagine my friends are not doing themselves justice, I find it very hard not to speak."

"O I am so glad to know, then, that at least you like me!" she responded laughing.

"I shall not answer you," I said, smiling in return.

"No, I don't believe you ever paid a compliment in your life, Harry! you are the most matter-of-fact, prosaic man I ever knew!"

"What is the use of paying compliments to women? It only makes them more conceited and exacting. I do not care to tickle their vanity by repeating what a dozen men have, no doubt, said to them before. O no, handsome women do not need to be told of their own attractions, they are sufficiently 'early discoverers' themselves. If I were to tell you, for instance, that you were pretty and fascinating, it would only incite you to brighten up your armor a trifle, or waste a moment more before your mirror! If I should say you were always charming, it would not be the truth; but if I said you always had the power to charm—well, I should be encroaching upon the Major's rights and prerogatives!"

"Nonsense, Harry, you know the Major has no rights! However, I shan't accuse you again of never saying pretty things. Poor man, I only wish it came a little easier to you! You should take a course of lessons in the art!" she said, laughing at me mischievously.

She was quite right, and, though I joined in her

laugh, I felt a little abashed that she should have detected so easily the effort of my unusual attempt at gallantry.

When we reached home we found Jim awaiting us in the garden. He was walking up and down the path, in the broad moonlight, smoking, and seemed very happy, with a quiet self-contained happiness, that spoke of some pleasant thought lying near the heart.

CHAPTER XIV.

CONFIDENCES.

CHRISTMAS came on a Friday, and on Thursday the household was busy with preparations for the approaching holiday.

Nevertheless, Madge found time, at Mrs. Jackson's suggestion, to take a canter with me through the woods in the morning. She was an excellent horsewoman, and never looked prettier than in her riding-habit and with the flush of exercise upon her cheeks.

We rode that day to one of the headlands on the coast, and on our way home made a long circuit through the forest, that we might stop at the corner for the mail.

Soon after we had left the post office, and as we were cantering on again (or " loping," as Madge would have called it), we overtook, at a bend in the road, a horseman ambling leisurely along on a quiet looking nag. It proved to be Colonel Shorter on his way to Major Barnwell's, and as his road lay past The Oaks, he joined us. I had not seen the Colonel since the day of the hunt, nor had Madge. On the present occasion he appeared to be in a good humor and made himself more agreeable than when I had last met him. Still, from his asking nothing about Jim, I concluded that he had not yet forgotten their little difficulty.

"You have not been to see us for a long time, Colonel Shorter," Madge said as we were parting from him at the gate.

"No," he answered, "I have been too busy lately to leave the city, but I am looking forward to your coming to town after Christmas, for such is your intention, I trust?"

"Yes, we shall be at sister Kate's next week, and I shall depend upon your coming to see us."

"You may be sure I shall not deny myself that pleasure," he replied, and making a low bow, he put spurs to his horse and galloped down the road.

"I don't like that man, Madge," I said as we turned into the avenue.

"Why not?" she asked.

"I cannot give an exact reason. I feel as Kate does about him. It is, perhaps, more a matter of feeling than anything else, but, to my ear, he does not ring true. I dislike both his manners and his face."

"There I cannot agree with you. I think him decidedly handsome, and as for his manners, they are charming. He can say the very prettiest things in just the nicest way possible! Why, Harry, he is the man of all others you should take lessons from! He is exactly your opposite. If he did not care in the least for a woman, he could make her believe he did, while you—well, you—"

She stopped and looked saucily up at me.

"Go on, ungrateful woman!" I exclaimed, laughing, and as she turned away without speaking I continued, "You see I was brought up in a different school. I fear I am too old now to learn over again. However, as you are so quick to see my failings, I hope you will be equally ready to forgive them."

Jim had passed the early part of the morning at Palmetto Grove, and after lunch, while he and I were sitting together before the log fire in the smoking-room, he broached the subject that filled his thoughts. I had previously noticed his restless and preoccupied manner, so that when at last he spoke, I was not altogether unprepared for his disclosures.

"Harry," said he, getting up from his chair and poking the fire in a purposeless way, "of course you have heard the girls tease me about Mary Lee, and though I have never spoken to you on the subject, I daresay you may have suspected that I was in love with her."

"Well, yes, Jim," I answered with a smile. "It would not have required a very powerful pair of lenses to make that discovery!"

"Well, I have asked Captain Lee's consent this morning, and he has given it," he said, turning from the fire and facing me.

"I congratulate you with all my heart," I exclaimed, jumping up from my seat and shaking him warmly by the hand.

"Thank you, Harry," he said, returning the pressure, with an embarrassed smile, " but I don't know yet whether I am to be congraulated or not."

"Don't know! Why, what do you mean?" I asked.

" Well, I haven't spoken to Mary," he replied, blushing like a girl ; and as he stood there, almost the perfection of manhood, I felt that he need have little doubt of winning, wherever his heart was fixed.

After pausing for a moment he went on quietly.

" I believe I loved her when she was a little girl, and I taught her to ride her first pony, and my affection has grown stronger and stronger as she has changed from a child into a woman (how could it have been otherwise—she is so good and lovely), until now I feel there is nothing else in life worth living for. And yet," he continued, seating himself again and stretching out his feet towards the fire, " and yet, now that the time has come at last, I dread to speak, for I have been very happy, and my first words may ruin it all."

" She can give but one answer, Jim," I said with confidence, " for, surely, she must know your feelings towards her."

" Yes, I think so, and yet I cannot tell, for I have never told her that I cared for her."

" But she could not be ignorant of what is so plain to every one about her. If she had not liked you she would have shown it in a thousand ways ; I do not believe she is the woman to lead a man on and then desert him at the crisis."

"O no, she would never do that, I am certain—
quite certain," he repeated as if to reassure himself,
"But we have always been so intimate—such good
friends—that she may never have expected more to
come of it, and have accepted my attentions as a
matter of course. Besides, after all, a woman cannot tell a man she does not care for him, until he
gives her a chance; in fact, she often does not even
know it herself."

"Come, come, Jim, this is altogether unlike you!
You do yourself injustice. Cheer up, man. I wish
I had half the chance of ever being as happy as you
will be in the course of a day or two. What did
the Captain say?"

"He was very kind and said both Mrs. Lee and
he had always wished this to come about, but even
if they should have the good fortune to welcome
me as a son-in-law, it could hardly increase their
affection for me! He could not answer for Mary,
but, of course—he added with a smile—he thought
I ought to be able to do that. O, the old people
are all right, as far as good wishes go!" He said,
brightening up and speaking more cheerfully again.

After this we talked the matter over and over,
for an hour or more, until at last he regained his
usual hopeful frame of mind.

He was to see Mary on Monday and until then
would not go to the Grove.

He told his sisters how matters stood and they
were both as full of sympathy and excitement as
they were certain of Mary's answer.

In the afternoon Jim and I took a long ramble. We went first to the plantation settlement and then for a mile or two followed the winding course of the river towards the sea, now along the pine-capped bluffs and now across the level springy surface of the marsh. The air was cool and clear and the dark hummocks of the Sea Islands, on the horizon, rose in bold outlines against the sky.

Of course there was still but one topic of conversation, Jim's plans and speculations for the future. The doubts that had harassed him in the morning gave way to the natural buoyancy of his disposition. He ran on as gayly as a schoolboy, and with such utter confidence in my sympathy that I could not, at that moment, have betrayed it, even by a passing thought. All selfish considerations were scattered to the winds and I entered heart and soul into his projects. In fact, before we reached home, his good spirits had infected me to such an extent, that I felt as if to my own lot some great blessing was about to fall.

On my way to my room that night I found, in the upper hall, a miscellaneous assortment of wearing apparel of every shape and size, piled upon the tables and chairs and floor. There were dresses and under-garments, coats and trousers, boots and shoes, large and small, bright colored neckerchiefs and bandanna turbans, in endless profusion, and in the midst of the confusion Madge and sister Kate, busy as bees, assorting and labelling the different articles. I paused a· moment to watch them at

their work and said, " Well, Kate, do you intend to
clothe the whole County to-morrow?"

" Not quite that, Harry," she replied, getting up
from her knees, " but we do like to have just some
little things for the negroes at the settlement. So
much was made of the day in old times, that we
cannot now let it pass by altogether unnoticed. I
should hate to have one of them come to the house
to-morrow and go away empty-handed! Each must
have something, if it is only a plug of tobacco. But
you must leave us, Harry, or we shall not get to
bed to-night. By the way, it is growing cold, is it
not?" and upon my answering in the affirmative,
she continued "I told David to light a fire in your
room and to leave plenty of wood there. I think
we are about to have a cold snap and you don't
know yet how severe one of our cold snaps can
be!"

" Many thanks, my thoughtful hostess. I may
safely defy the elements while in your hospitable
keeping," and turning to Madge, who had not allowed her work to be interrupted by my presence I
said,—

" Good night, fair Madge; will there be a mistletoe bough in the house to-morrow?"

And without awaiting her reply, I took my candle
from a pile of blankets where I had put it and betook myself to bed.

No—not to bed—but to a seat before the fire
that blazed and crackled upon my hearth where,
undisturbed, I could think of all that Eustis had

told me and of the life so soon to become a part of his.

Had I already forgotten the one short romance of my own life ? In Jim's presence I had believed so; but alone, in the silence of the night, thoughts arose that I could not fight off single-handed, and the first hours of the Christmas morning found me still in my chair before the dying embers.

CHAPTER XV.

CHRISTMAS—" THE POINT."

THEY may talk of the severity of our Northern winter climate; but for downright bodily discomfort give me the southern country-house during one of their periodical "cold-snaps!"

How the wind hisses and whistles through the cracks of the loose-jointed rattling windows! With what audacity it attacks the very sides of the house, and forcing its way through floors and wainscotting puffs up the carpets into great balloons!

The flames from the logs in the open fireplaces blaze and roar in their hopeless effort to impart warmth to the waves of frosty air that sweep through the rooms.

We revolve and revolve before the fire, in the vain attempt to warm ourselves all round at once, but no sooner have we thawed out the tingling frost on one side than circulation ceases on the other! It is a useless task. There is no such thing as comfort "within doors;" (there is satire in the words themselves for they are never shut;) but, for out of door exercise, no weather can be more perfect than this keen, frosty air with the thermometre at 20° Fahrenheit.

Such a morning was that of the Christmas on which I awoke to the crackling of a bright log fire that David had rebuilt for me; but when I arose I found that my pitcher and the pail of water for my bath were frozen solid, and had been placed by the fire to thaw. So, nothing loath, I returned to my bed for another nap.

When, at length, I came down from my room it was very late, and the house was astir with life and bustle. There was a swarm of negroes on the back piazza and in the yard, among whom Mrs. Jackson and Madge were busily engaged in distributing their Christmas gifts. Bows, scrapes, courtesies, and " merry Christmases " were to be seen and heard on all sides, and I stood there for the half hour before breakfast, which had been delayed for the occasion, watching the happy faces of the negroes and listening to their caustic wit.

After breakfast Jim ordered the wagon and drove me down to the plantation settlement. His pocket was filled with coppers, and as we passed slowly along the road between the cabins, he scattered them to right and left for the children to scramble for. They evidently had expected him and were out in full force for the occasion. It was very amusing to see the little imps with their grinning faces and wide-open eyes, rushing, pushing and tumbling heels over head in their eagerness to get possession of the shining coins! Of course the big boys had the advantage of the little ones in this rough sport. But Jim's quick eye took in the situation at a glance, and, thanks to his adroitness, a fair portion of the spoils fell to the lot of even the most diminutive and clumsy.

We drove, at a walk, through the settlement and back again, followed by the noisy crowd, and when we finally left them, they gave expression to their gratitude in a parting yell!

Barnwell was to pass the day and take his Christmas dinner with us, and so from the settlement we drove down through the woods to his house for him.

He lived three or four miles from The Oaks, and although we were well muffled up and the sun had taken much of the frostiness out of the air, we found it still very cold in the depths of the forest, and the pools and swamps covered with thick ice.

At the end of our drive we drew up at a rickety gate, that gave entrance to a field or clearing of twenty or more acres, surrounded by a Virginia fence. The land was uncultivated, with the exception of a half acre or so, which showed signs of having been used as a flower and kitchen-garden. A couple of native cows and a lean horse were taking a constitutional together around the enclosure, while here and there flocks of poultry scratched and pecked at the brown stubble and sandy soil.

In the centre of the field, under the shadow of a solitary live oak, stood a small, weatherbeaten, one story, pitched-roofed house, resting upon wooden posts.

Near it, in the rear, were a couple of still smaller

buildings, used for the kitchen and servant's quarters, and farther off, the stables and the cabins for the farm hands.

The side of the cleared land opposite the gate skirted an irregular bluff, and, as we drew near the house, a view of the salt marshes and the blue waters of the sound stretched away as far as the eye could reach.

When we alighted at the steps, some sullen looking hounds got up from where they lay basking in the sun, and with surly growls slunk off behind the house.

At the same moment, Barnwell came out and greeted us most cordially, and then after calling long and loud, but in vain, for "Jerry," jumped into the wagon himself, and drove to the stable, while we entered the house to warm ourselves at the fire.

Within, the house was as desolate and unattractive as without, its accommodations consisted of two sleeping-rooms, and the one in which we were standing, which was evidently used by its bachelor owner for all other purposes. A few old prints in tarnished gilt frames adorned the unpainted and unpapered walls, and over them, as well as over all the doors of the room, were fastened antlers of every size and shape.

The floor was covered with musty straw matting, and in one corner stood a rifle and a double barrelled shot gun, while beside them lay, in a disordered heap, powder horns, shot flasks, tin canisters and other hunting paraphernalia.

A three shelf bookcase hanging upon the wall; a mahogany sideboard, with wine glasses and, a half-empty decanter upon it; a round table; half-a-dozen delapidated cane-bottomed chairs; a black horsehair rocking-chair, and brass andirons in the fireplace,—completed the furniture of the room.

Its appearance was by no means cheerful and might itself, in the absence of stronger inducements, have furnished a sufficient excuse for its master's frequent visits to The Oaks.

The family homestead had been burnt during the war—and this house, so Jim told me, had been occupied formerly by the overseer. "The Point," was Major Barnwell's home thoughout the year, for situated, as it was, on the "Salts," or salt marshes near the sea, it was considered perfectly healthy, even through the torrid summer months.

Forlorn as the place seemed to me, I found that the good Major regarded it with considerable pride and spoke enthusiastically of the sea breezes, the view, the oyster beds, and the unequalled fishing in the creek below the bluff.

"Not a stylish place you know," he said to me, "but rather cosy and comfortable, everything, in fact, that a bachelor needs. Take care Mr. Strong, that chair has only three legs, try the rocker! It is always cool on the piazza even in the hottest weather. There's no use going North in summer, when a man has such a place as this to come to. I don't know anything pleasanter in life, than to lie there in my hammock on a summer's evening, and

look off over the marshes to the sound, with a cool
breeze blowing, and a net over me to keep off the
mosquitoes and sand-flies."

Not being to the manor born, I could not fully
appreciate his ardor, especially in view of the un-
tidiness and shiftlessness about me. It seemed
strange to see such utter indifference to all things
that render the interior of a house comfortable and
attractive, in a man who was not cut off from them by
absolute poverty. As I became better acquainted
with the people among whom I was stopping, I
found the Major's case by no means an exceptional
one, but that, not infrequently, men kept their thor-
ough-breds at the expense of hall carpets and well-
furnished drawing-rooms; and I accounted for it,
on the supposition, that the out of door lives of the
people lessened, to some extent, their interest in
matters of domestic comfort.

The Major was full of hospitality, and insisted
upon our trying his favorite brands of whiskey and
tobacco, while we waited for him to make a hurried
toilet. He soon appeared again, and the wagon
was brought to the door in answer to his loud calls
from the piazza, whither the hounds had returned
to their corners in the sun.

"Jerry," said Barnwell to the coachman, a half-
grown colored youth, dressed in a superabundant
old coat of his master. "Come over for me, with the
sorrel mare at ten o'clock, and mind you shut the
gate after you—hear?"

"Yes sir!"

"Maria!" he called to a slatternly-looking yellow girl who put her head out of the kitchen door, as we drove past, "don't forget to feed the hounds at one." She only answered with a sullen nod, and stood there looking after us till we were out of sight.

As the Major reseated himself, after getting out to open and shut the pasture gate, he said,—

"I am sorry you didn't have a pleasanter day to see my place, Mr. Strong; it isn't looking its best just now. You must come and spend a few days with me in the spring, when my roses are in bloom. It looks very pretty here then."

I thanked him, and congratulated myself that probably duty would not compel me to accept his invitation.

We reached home in time for lunch, and found the ladies awaiting us in the drawing-room and resting after their labors of the morning. We all passed a pleasant afternoon and evening together, although forced, perhaps, by the requirements of the day, into slightly overstrained hilarity.

The Major created some amusement, from the fact, that he had secreted about him a box of candy for Madge, upon which he unfortunately had seated himself during the drive to The Oaks, much to his own chagrin and Jim's delight, who let the cat out of the bag at the dinner table, and brought down upon the bashful Major a storm of merriment from Madge and Kate!

He strove most gallantly, however, to take his

revenge under the mistletoe that Jim had hung in the centre of the hall; but was thwarted and only succeeded in getting his ears very soundly boxed! His attempt, however, was so thoughtless and awkward that he richly merited his punishment.

Now perhaps I speak from the conscious superiority of a successful tactician and perhaps from my recollection of the whispered suggestions of the fay in the mistletoe; but if, let me ask, when all were about to retire for the night, he had handed her her lighted candle, and asked her also at the same time to hold his own for a moment, could she have refused? Well—yes—perhaps she could.

Would she have refused? Ask the fairy conspirator in the mistletoe bough! Alas! I cannot tell you!

CHAPTER XVI.

THE OLD NURSE.

WITH one of those sudden changes so common in the South, on the following Sunday evening the weather moderated, and at midnight a heavy thunder-shower passed over us, startling me from my sleep, with a strange feeling of confusion and surprise. The blinds rattled, the rain beat furiously against the window panes, the lightning flashed into the room making it as bright as day—and above all the thunder rolled and crashed, shaking the house to its foundations. Was it indeed mid-winter, or had I been only dreaming that this was the night after Christmas !

For a time I was utterly bewildered ; but little by little I began to realize the situation, and listened with mingled curiosity and pleasure to the wild tempest, counting the seconds between the flashes and the discharges of musketry, and hoping that each successive peal might be louder than the one before. But the storm was as short as it was severe and passed away as rapidly as it had arisen. Yet, though the wind and rain ceased and the thunder grew fainter and fainter in the distance, the first wild outburst had so thoroughly aroused me, that I could not sleep again, and, as on Christmas

Eve, my mind called up the experiences of my short
Southern life and passed them again and again in
review before it—with one fair image ever floating
in and out among them.

How exquisitely sensitive we become to the influence of our thoughts in the darkness and silence of
the night! How resistlessly and completely do our
joys or sorrows take possession of us—while the
mind self-centred panders to the most extravagant
emotions of the heart! I don't know how long I
lay awake, but think the light was already glimmering in the east, when, for the second time, I fell
asleep.

The morning came in warm, sunny and spring-like,
and soon after breakfast Jim's thoroughbred was
brought saddled to the garden gate. A few minutes
later Jim himself joined me on the piazza, where I
was walking up and down with my cigar.

He wore a dark blue, doubled-breasted coat, cut
short and square, corduroy trousers fitting close to
the shapely legs, long cavalry boots with shining
spurs clinking at either heel, and a military hat of
soft black felt; and over his arm hung a hunting
whip.

He stopped to speak to me for a moment while
he drew on his leather gauntlets. His handsome
face was somewhat flushed and his eyes bright with
suppressed excitement. He was, indeed, a goodly
specimen of ·manhood—with his intelligent face,
faultless physique, and erect, graceful carriage.

" Well, Jim," said I, looking upon him with an

affectionate admiration, "may the small god with the bow and arrows guide you safely to-day!"

"Ah, but when the blind lead the blind, you know!" he answered smiling, and looking up from the glove that he was buttoning.

"Yes, but in point of fact," I answered, "I give you credit for seeing much better than you pretend. It is my private opinion that you need no guidance whatsoever, and are fully capable of finding your way by yourself. However," I continued, laying my hand on his shoulder, "my blessing goes with you, my son, notwithstanding your hypocrisy, and my best wishes for the happiness you so little deserve."

He laughed and shook my hand, and then descended the steps into the garden, where he paused before the rose bushes to pick a bud for his buttonhole.

"Which would you take, white or pink?" he asked, turning towards me with an air of uncertainty as grave as if the decision were a matter of moment.

"Red, by all means," I answered promptly, "this is no day to show the white feather." He followed my sage advice with apparent hesitation, and having mounted "Vixen," kissed his hand to me and cantered slowly down the avenue. It is strange, said I, musingly, how the mind, when overburdened will seek relief in trifles, upon which, if untrammelled, it would not bestow a second thought!

That morning I took a walk with Madge down to

the settlement, to visit an old negro woman who had been her nurse when she was a child. She had been confined to the house for several years with an incurable disease, and Madge often went to read to her, or to carry her some little delicacy from The Oaks.

I waited for my companion at the gate of the little garden, in front of the cabin, and when she again appeared the old nurse came with her to the door, supporting her bent and heavy frame upon two stout canes.

"Good morning, mauma," I said, "you should leave your front door open to catch a breath of this spring-like air."

"Huddy, massa," she replied, "it's too late now for de air to do good or ill to dis ole woman; but it's no doubt good for dem dat likes it." And then speaking to Madge in a half "aside," but keeping her eyes fixed on me, she muttered, "Is dis the gemmun dey was tellin me 'bout? de gemmnu what Massa Jim gone to school wid? He ain't got Massa Jim's smile, has he, miss? But he ain't so bad looking neither—for a Yankee! Well, honey, mebbe you might ha' done wuss arter all!" Madge blushed, and hastily kissing the old woman good-by, rejoined me at the gate. When we were out of hearing of the old mauma, who still stood watching us from her cabin door,—

"Well, Madge," said I, laughing, "your nurse seems to draw speedy conclusions, doesn't she? How do you like being settled for life without an opportunity of expressing yourself on the subject?"

"Isn't she queer, Harry?" she replied without answering directly. "The negroes about here consider her a sort of witch, and would no more dare to rob her hen-roost than a graveyard at night. She has been devoted to me as long as I can remember. She was mother's nurse, too. I am very fond of the poor old thing, with all her peculiarities."

When we reached home it was lunch time, but as Jim had not returned we waited for him, sitting on the piazza in the sun, where Mrs. Jackson joined us. Lunch was put off for an hour, but still he did not come, and just as we had concluded that he would probably pass the afternoon at the Grove, we saw him turn in at the gate and gallop rapidly up the avenue. A moment later he drew up at the garden fence and dismounted.

The steam was rising from Vixen's back, and her chest and legs and flanks were spattered with foam and mud. The jaded beast hung down her head, and gave every indication of a long, wild run through the heavy roads. Jim threw the rein over a picket, and walked slowly up the garden path with eyes bent upon the ground. He, like his horse, was covered with mud from head to foot. He did not see us sitting on the piazza until he reached the top of the flight of steps, when, with apparent effort, he straightened himself up, and with a forced smile on his haggard face, and a painful attempt at cheerfulness, he said,—

" Well, girls, it's all up ! "

" Why, Jim, what do you mean ? " they asked, in astonishment.

" Just what I say, my dears. It is over ! I was mistaken, that's all ! " he answered quietly.

" Well, then," exclaimed Madge with vehemence, jumping up from her chair, " all I can say is, she is a heartless flirt ! "

" It's false ! " he cried, turning angrily upon her with flashing eyes, the hot blood rising to his pallid cheeks. " You are unworthy to be mentioned in the same breath ! How dare you speak so of her ? "

" O Jim ! " she uttered in a low, beseeching tone, her eyes fixed intently upon him and her right hand extended as if to ward off a blow.

He turned slowly away and without another word strode heavily into the house.

She stood there for a moment as he had left her, staring into vacancy. Then she covered her face with both her hands and walked, sobbing, to the end of the piazza.

Kate was at her side in an instant, and putting her arms around her neck, she drew her head down upon her shoulder.

" There, my darling," she said tenderly, " do not cry. He did not know what he was saying. Pity him, Madge. The poor boy is beside himself ! "

I left them by themselves and went up to my room, where I threw myself into a chair, in front of the empty fireplace. But I had not sat there long, staring at the heap of white ashes and the half-burnt back-log, before there was a knock at the door and David entered with a tray of luncheon.

He put it on the table, kindled some sticks of wood upon the hearth and left me.

As it would have seemed ungracious to leave untasted what Kate had so thoughtfully provided, I went to the table and tried to eat, but it was impossible. I had no appetite and soon returned again to my seat by the fire, full of conjectures as to the result of this blow to Jim and its effects upon the little colony of friends whose interests had become so thoroughly my own.

I remained in my room till nearly twilight and then went out for a walk before dinner. As I passed the open door of the drawing-room, I saw Jim and Madge sitting together on a sofa in the embrasure of the window. She was nestled close to his side, and looking up into his face. His arm was round her waist, and bending down his head he gently touched her forehead with his lips. What an effect this little tableau had upon my spirits! It was like lifting a weight from off them. It was in keeping, too, with Jim's hot-headed affectionate disposition; and as I had felt keenly his injustice of the morning, so now my heart proportionately warmed towards him at this exhibition of tender repentance.

I admire this quick, impulsive character, too ready, perhaps, to take offence, but equally prompt to ask forgiveness—a nature that cannot find itself in the wrong without instantly striving to set itself right again!

Dinner, that evening, was a very quiet meal, although, I believe we all exerted ourselves to make it cheerful. Jim was not himself. He strove to appear the same as usual, but scored a signal failure.

Both he and Kate disappeared at an early hour and Madge and I were left for a while by ourselves in the drawing-room.

Madge was sitting opposite to me, near the centre-table, crocheting from a blue pyramid of worsted, that lay upon her lap. I had been glancing over the columns of a home paper, but put it down at length, and said,—

" Madge, I can hardly tell you how glad I was to see that you and Jim had made up again so quickly."

" It was the first time in my life he had ever spoken harshly to me; and I was so sorry you should have heard him," she answered. " I did not mean to provoke him. I would not have hurt his feelings for the world, he has always been so sweet and good to me! But I was so astonished and indignant, that I could not help saying what I did. Even if she could trifle with other men, as some say, Jim never deserved such treatment at her hands. She knows his character too well to think he can take it lightly, poor fellow! It makes me hot to think of it! " she exclaimed, " I cannot understand it, can you? "

" Indeed, I cannot," I replied.

" If I were he I should not give it up so easily," she went on, somewhat inconsistently. " I am sure she does not care for any one else, and she has known Jim all her life and always seemed to like him so much! I cannot believe her answer was final; but Jim feels differently about it and won't even listen to such a suggestion; and when he has once made up his mind there is no use trying to argue with him. At any rate, I am glad he is going to Florida. It may bring her to her senses, and the change will no doubt do him good and help him to get over it, for, after all, men's hearts are not easily broken."

" Are women's ? " I asked.

" I have read of instances, but I never knew one," she answered, sagely. " I cannot imagine a sensible woman allowing herself to care for a man until she is certain he is in love with her."

" And it is equally absurd," said I, " for a sensible man to fall in love and offer himself to a woman until she has given him very evident and ample encouragement! So, for sensible men and women, at least, we seem to have very effectually obstructed the paths to matrimony ! "

" The case is different with men. They should be free and independent as air. An occasional mistake cannot hurt them very much, " she replied, " but a conscientious woman must act with caution, you see ! If she likes a man—without being in love with him—of course she must give him just a little encouragement, or she would never really know him; and if she likes him better as he becomes more attentive, she can continue to encourage him little

by little and so on ; and, on the other hand, if at any
time she likes him less, she can stop, and any
sensible man will understand her ; don't you see ? "

" O yes, I see the sophistry of the coquette!"
I answered laughing. "Allure him to the edge and
then topple him over ! Alas ! poor Barnwell ! "

" Why will you always bring up Major Barnwell,
Harry?" she replied, the color mounting to her
cheeks ; "you know he is nothing to me ! You only
do it to annoy me ! "

" It is very becoming to you, to look annoyed !" I said, "but you would not be so if you
didn't feel some slight interest in him ! There,
don't go !" I added, as she arose as if about to
leave the room, "I will promise not to tease
you again. I know it is very impertinent. I am
astonished that you put up with me at all." She
hesitated a moment and then sat down again.

" Madge," I said, after, a short silence, " I really
think you are very sweet and forbearing with me.
I wrote my sister Alice about you, the other day."

" What did you say to her ? " she asked, looking up
from her work.

" Much in praise and nothing against you," I replied. " Still, I think I had better not repeat it, for
even the truth does not always bear repetition."

"Ah, yes, do tell me !" she said, with a pretty
affectation of interest, leaning slightly forward, her
hands clasped across the feathery pile of worsted in
her lap.

" Well," said I with a slight smile, " I wrote her

how fortunate it was for me, that you had not tried to include me in your list of victims ; and how kind and hospitable you always were, notwithstanding a dislike that you evidently found it hard, at times, to struggle against ! "

While I was speaking, she rose and went to a table at the side of the room, in which she kept her work, and when I stopped, she said quietly and with her back toward me.

" I must go now, Harry, good-night."

" Wait a moment ! " I called to her before she reached the door. " Tell me, did I not write the truth ? "

She faced me, with a bright crimson flush upon her face. " Yes, I do dislike you," she said emphatically, and then closed the door and left me to myself.

These were plain words, but I had only myself to thank for them ; and although I had suspected the truth before, I realized now what an unpleasant difference there was between a mere suspicion and the actual knowledge of the fact.

However, I determined henceforth to do all in my power to make amends for the past. I did not feel piqued, nor was my vanity wounded by what she had said, for I was conscious that my conduct had justified her dislike ; but, at the same time, I could not allow any unpleasantness to exist between such an important member of Jim's family and myself without at least an attempt on my part to dispel it.

22222222222222222222222222222222222222222222222222 stop.

CHAPTER XVII.

THE BALL.

DURING the following week our pleasant household at The Oaks was broken up. Mrs. Jackson and Madge moved to town, and Jim started on
his trip to Florida. The latter, however, before he
went, established me in rooms at the best hotel in
the city, put my name down at the Club, and did all
he could to make me comfortable until his return.

He was rather disappointed at my not accompany-
ing him; but left me with the understanding, that,
if I grew tired of city life, I should join him later
in the winter; although he hardly expected me to
do so, as he thought I would find Southern society,
under the guidance of Kate and Madge, preferable
to travelling alone with him under the present circumstances.

My rooms, although not well furnished and with
unmistakable signs of Southern shiftlessness about
them (for the negro servant in room-cleaning always
"circles the square"), were cheerful and sunny,
with a pretty outlook on one of the many city
parks.

The hotel was tolerably well kept and the table

good ; but what struck the New England mind as especially odd in such a warm climate was the absence of all bathing facilities within its walls.

My rooms were conveniently near the Club, where I usually spent an hour or so after breakfast in reading the papers, or talking with the affable set of rice-planters, who frequented it in the morning.

The Lees also had moved to town and I often met Fred Brown, who was still stopping with them, either at the Club or in the street, when he and I would go off together for a walk about the city or a drive through its environs.

One day as we were walking in the park I said to him, " Well, Fred, have you changed your mind about the Southerners yet ? "

" I can't thank you enough," he answered, " for having introduced me to the Lees. Otherwise I might have passed the winter here without really knowing the people. There is nothing like living in the same house for getting to understand people thoroughly. Yes, I have changed my views of them in some respects. I always thought them awfully down on Yankees, but I find they are just as kind and hospitable as possible. Still they are exceedingly prejudiced, and I have to be very careful what I say. For instance they don't much like comparisons with the North. I suppose they are sensitive because they're so far behind us, and know it's their own fault ! The Captain is always ready to discuss anything, but when he and I were talking about slavery the other night, Mrs. Lee gave me rather a setting down ! I didn't know she was listening and was sorry she took it so hard."

" Why, what did she say ? " I asked.

" Well," he replied, " I was comparing the progress of our two States, and I believe I said that no State had worked like ours against slavery, and that with a sort of poetical justice, no State had become so prosperous ; whereat Mrs. Lee flared up and said something about our State having given up slavery only when it was found to be unprofitable, and her grandfather's having bought his first slaves from one of these exemplars of high morality ; or words to that effect ! I was not quite satisfied, but as she seemed rather excited, I didn't exactly like to question her further about it and so let the matter drop. To be sure, Miss Lee took it pleasantly enough and was inclined to laugh it off ; but, still, I see that ladies can't look at these things in the perfectly reasonable and dispassionate way that men can. They seem to fly out when one least expects it. However," he concluded meditatively, " I really think they have a good many fine points about them, don't you ? "

" Well, yes," I replied. " When one comes to look at it seriously, I think perhaps they have ! "

I called upon the Lees shortly after their arrival, and to call once was to be asked often by the Captain either to dine or sup with them, and his invitations were seldom declined.

Then, too, through the influence of Mrs. Jackson and the Lees, I went very generally into society, and was treated everywhere with great consideration, the hostesses taking care that I should know the most attractive women in the rooms, and the hosts plying me with old and rare Madeiras.

Many houses to which I went were scantily furnished and shabby looking in the extreme, and excepting at Mrs. Lee's and Mrs. Jackson's very little of modern art and modern taste was to be seen. They were, indeed, but relics of a past generation. But where could one find more delicious dinners, or more tempting suppers, and served with such whole-souled, lavish hospitality! They were not French, they were not English, they were not even fashion-able, but they were broad-smiling, generous repasts that cheered the heart and made glad the inner man!

Mrs. Jackson had begged me to use her house as if it were my own, and it was understood that she and Madge were to command my services at all times.

They had brought their horses to town and Jim had placed Vixen at my disposal; so Madge and I took frequent rides together in the frosty mornings and glowing afternoons. Thus we saw much of each other, and in the course of a few weeks I succeeded, or thought I had succeeded, in establishing our relations on a thoroughly friendly footing. I gave up teasing her almost with a sigh, and did what I could by my brotherly attentions to disabuse her mind of its unfavorable impressions. Her manner toward me became easier, and her temper—if I may use the word—more even, and I knew by many signs that she was not unobservant of my good conduct. I was naturally pleased at the change, which in truth I had scarcely expected, for I knew that in trying to dispel dislike one was only too apt to strengthen it.

"Why, Harry," she said to me one evening when I gave her some flowers for a party to which we were going, "you have grown so polite of late that I should hardly know you!"

"You see," I replied, "I have not forgotten what you said to me that night at The Oaks. Will you not take it back?"

"No, sir!" she answered, as she stooped to gather up her train, "I cannot trust you yet. I am afraid you might return to your old ways!"

The party that evening was an assembly given by the Terpsichore Club, and Mrs. Jackson, who was one of the patronesses, went with us. The hall was extremely plain and bare, and the walls and ceilings absolutely innocent of the decorator's art. But the gas was bright, the floor was good, and the music, furnished by a German band, was, to say the least, loud enough to be heard without difficulty. But the essential elements of every pleasant ball were there, in groups of pretty young women and well-favored men, in light hearts and feet, and merry voices; and had the dresses been the costliest that Worth or Macdonald could devise, the general effect would not have been better than that of the clouds of simple tarleton and muslin that floated about the room.

When we entered the ballroom Madge was seized upon and whirled away to the music of a Strauss waltz. The hall was already crowded, but Mrs. Jackson and I managed to secure seats where we could watch the people undisturbed, and as far as possible from the music. I was to dance the German with Madge, but until then had no engagements. My companion told me about the people as they passed before us, with running, sometimes spicy, comments impressing upon me the salient points in their lives and characters.

"I do wish Colonel Shorter would let Madge alone!" she said as he passed with Madge upon his arm. "Ah! there, Harry, who is that with Mary Lee? O I need not ask, for although I have never seen him before, I am certain it is your friend Mr. Brown. Who could mistake his being a Yankee!"

"No one would wish to, Kate; you could not pay him a higher compliment."

"Nonsense! I can't agree with you, at least not in the way I mean. Just see!" she continued, still watching Brown as he promenaded with Miss Lee, "how he stares through his eyeglasses at everything and at everybody, as if he were studying a collection of curiosities! Meanwhile he seems to have quite forgotten Mary. He is evidently collecting items, jottings, for his family circle or some newspaper at home, and nothing will escape his exhaustive observation. He looks the very personification of inquisitiveness. I do believe that man must have been born with a question in his mouth!"

"What?" I asked.

"Am I a boy or a girl?" she answered laughing. "I should think he might almost ask the same to-day."

"If you knew him you would not speak so! However," I added, " I have no doubt it is only because he has never sought an introduction."

"Not at all," she replied decisively, "I have no wish to know him. I do not like to be catechized, and I feel sure he would question me about slavery and the war. He looks fully capable of it! And there are no subjects I so much dislike. I should probably lose my temper and send him home with a strong impression of the urbanity of Southern women. Well, I believe I do cordially detest these ·Yankees!"

"You surely forget yourself or me, Kate!" I exclaimed, feeling a little nettled by the sincerity with which she spoke.

"O, but I don't call you a Yankee, Harry!" she cried quickly.

" But I assure you I am one, heart and soul, Mrs. J., so beware how you arouse the sleeping lion!"

"Codfish, did you say?" she asked laughing, with a thrust at one of New England's industries, and then continued more soberly, "You need not try to be angry with me, for I shall not permit it; besides, you know perfectly well what I mean. Well-bred people are pretty much the same the world over, but there is a class that I call Yankees of whom I should take Mr. Brown to be a fair example. They come here ill-disposed towards us in the first place, and then condemn everything in which we and ours differ from them and theirs. It irritates me beyond measure to see them walking about our streets with their hats on the backs of their heads, leaning over our front railings, prying into our back yards and, occasionally, even taking roses and japonicas from our very gardens! They seem to have no modesty; nothing escapes their open-eyed curiosity, and I cannot tell you what a relief it is, when spring takes them away with their boxed alligators and Florida beans!"

"Why, Kate," said I, "I had no idea that you could be so venomous. How indignant you would become if I should abuse you Southerners in this way! But I shall set you an example in good manners by restraining myself and leaving Brown to vindicate his fellow-countrymen."

At this moment I rose to speak to Miss Lee and Brown who were passing, and then turning to Kate, I said, "Mrs. Jackson, allow me to introduce my friend, Mr. Brown."

As I left them with Miss Lee, Kate gave me a look as much as to say, "You shall pay for this, young man!"

I had not spoken to Mary before, that evening, and, in fact, since Jim's refusal, although I had seen her often, we had seldom been alone together. For some reason I found it difficult of late to talk with her. Either her suspicion of my knowledge of that affair, or my own consciousness of it,

was a constraint upon us. There was one subject constantly present to our minds, and always to be avoided in our conversation. Then,
moreover, owing to this unexpected turn of affairs, I had suddenly become free to act according to my impulses, and with the possibilities had
come also the responsibilities of freedom, which for
a time kept me in an uncertain, vacillating state of
mind, that found expression only in embarrassed
words or still more awkward silence.

When we stopped walking I looked over Mary's
card and found that there was but one more dance
before supper.

" May I have the last half of this next dance ? " I
asked.

" Thank you, no, I am engaged to Mr. Benjamin.
Why, is not his name down?" she asked, glancing quickly over her card. " Your eyes must have
failed you, Mr. Strong ! "

" Surely," I answered, looking quietly into her
face, "surely, you cannot think that I asked you because I saw you were engaged. No, I only hoped
that I might take you to supper. I wanted to talk
with you ! "

" Why ? " she asked, looking at me, almost anxiously ; and it flashed across me that she expected
me to speak of Jim; perhaps thought I had some
message for her.

" Why do you ask the question ? " I replied. " I
simply wish to speak to you, but have nothing in
particular to say."

"O really I cannot, Mr. Strong," she said, after a moment's hesitation. "Mr. Benjamin expects to take me to supper. Ah, here he is!" she added, as that gentleman came up and claimed his dance.

I stood for a while watching them as they wound in and out among the dancers, and then made my way back to Mrs. Jackson. She had been joined by Madge; and Mr. Brown, who was still in attendance, was calmly and complacently exposing himself to a volley of light artillery from that young lady.

Presently we went into the supper-room together, and, after Brown had left us, I congratulated Kate upon having kept her temper with the Yankee. "O yes!" she replied, "he was altogether pleasanter than I had expected; decidedly bright, I should say. He made himself extremely agreeable till Madge came and interrupted us. And you never heard such nonsense as she talked! She is perfectly irrepressible! Why, the poor man scarcely knew whether he was on his head or his heels!"

"O he is such fun, Harry!" Madge broke in, laughing gayly. "I have been trying to persuade him to go snipe-shooting with me. I told him I had a regular outfit for that kind of work—bloomer costume, and long boots! He said it seemed to him rather unfeminine for ladies to shoot, but I told him it was the only recreation we countrywomen allowed ourselves during the war. He said he had supposed that young ladies were too tender-hearted

to kill things merely for amusement; he had heard
them say so."

"He was thinking of what Miss Lee said on our
passage out!" I exclaimed, hastily recalling her
words.

"Oh!" said Madge, looking up at me, as if struck
with the earnestness of my manner; "judging from
her treatment of Jim she must have greatly changed,"
and then returning to her subject she continued,
"O, then Mr. Brown asked me, if, when I saw the
little birds fall fluttering and wounded at my feet,
my conscience did not reproach me? ' In the first
place, Mr. Brown,' I said, 'it is very seldom that my
shot is not immediately fatal, but when I am so
unfortunate as only to wing a bird, Jim has taught
me how to bite it in the neck so as to produce in-
stantaneous death. It is not pleasant at first, you
know, but one soon gets used to it, and then it puts
the poor little thing out of suffering so quickly!' His
eyes opened until they were the size of his glasses.
I think he regarded me as a sort of amateur canni_
bal. I wish you could have seen his face, Harry,
it was as good as a poor play!"

"It is my private opinion, Madge," said Mrs.
Jackson, "he is not half as foolish as you think
him. It would not surprise me one bit, if all that
innocence of manner were put on, simply to draw
you out."

"O nonsense, sister!" exclaimed Madge with some
warmth. "He is just as verdant as he can be!"
But evidently the suggestion did not please her, for

she dropped the subject and for a time became unusually silent.

After supper the German began. Kate decided not to stay for it, but to leave her sister in my charge. So I saw her to her carriage and promised to bring Madge safely home before daybreak.

I will not enter into the details of the German, which were the same here as everywhere. The same favors, trinkets, ribbons, flowers, and figures, the same success of the few and disappointments of the many, the same disconnected talks and long lapses in the conversation, the same suppressed yawns and lengthening faces as the hours drew on, the same torn and tattered skirts, and the same weariness of mind and body.

My partner was a general favorite and seldom off the floor. In fact, she and Mary and a Madame Alvari, a gay and pretty widow from Florida, divided the honors of the evening.

Colonel Shorter had no partner, and, to my annoyance, asked Madge to dance on every possible occasion, and was to be seen at all times hovering about her. He was unquestionably a handsome man, and his devotion was not thrown away upon my partner, who coquetted with him to his heart's content.

I had heard enough of Richard Shorter and his life from men at the Club, to despise him thoroughly; and it worried and provoked me beyond measure to see Madge receive and encourage attentions, which, in view of the existing difficulty be-

tween him and her brother, appeared to me almost
in the light of an insult.

She had just left me for the twentieth time to
dance with her admirer, when Miss Lee crossed the
room to me and offered me a ribbon.

"Will you take it?" said she, holding out her
hand.

"What?—your hand?" I asked smiling, as I arose
to meet her.

"No—only the ribbon," she answered. "Is not
that enough?"

"No," I said, as we began to dance, "for whatever
some give, only makes us desire more. They should
give everything or nothing!"

"You are very ungrateful, Mr. Strong, especially
when—" But she did not finish her sentence.

"You have danced so much you must be dreadfully tired," I said, after we had taken a short turn.
"Won't you come out upon the piazza?"

On one side of the ballroom the windows opened
to the floor upon a broad verandah that was closed
in with awnings from the night air and lighted dimly
by Chinese lanterns. As we entered it, the only
couple that were there arose and went into the
room, and we were left alone. We took several
turns up and down and then seated ourselves upon
a bench, near one of the open windows; the cool
air and half light were refreshing after the heat and
glare of the ballroom, while distance lent harmony
to the music of the band and the noise of the merry
voices within.

For a few moments we were silent, but at last I said,—

"I feel as if I had not seen you for ages."

"Why we met at the Izards' and Houstouns' last week, and you dined with us night before last, did you not?" she asked, with an expression of feigned surprise.

"True. But I mean it is an age since we have had a talk together. To meet you with others is simply an aggravation."

"You must be easily provoked," she answered. "I am afraid good temper is not your strong point. But tell me, has it not been your own fault? If I had not too good an opinion of myself to suppose it possible, I should have thought at times you had avoided me.

"You are right, always right. I cannot tell you how hard I have striven to keep away from you!" I exclaimed excitedly.

"I do not quite understand you, Mr. Strong, but certainly you are not very flattering," she said, tapping her hand lightly with her fan. "Have I then made myself so very disagreeable? One might almost suppose you were afraid of me!"

"I believe I am of you and of myself. I hardly know which I fear the most."

"Then you are cowardly as well as ill-tempered. What a charming picture you draw of yourself!"

"If it is cowardly to fear soft eyes, or the sweetness of a voice; if it is cowardly to fear disappointment and regret, I am indeed a coward!"

Mary was looking down upon the fan that she was slowly opening and shutting in her lap. The light from the lanterns fell full upon the dazzling whiteness of her neck. I had moved close to her and was bending forward to catch the expression of her face, when I was suddenly startled by the unwelcome sound of Madge's voice.

"Why, Harry," she exclaimed, "I have been looking for you everywhere. It is our turn to dance, and they are waiting for us."

I knew that she was standing at the open window near us, but, without turning, I bent still lower down and picked up Mary's handkerchief that had fallen on the floor at her feet. Then slowly rising I answered with forced composure.

"I beg your pardon for keeping you waiting, Madge. I will be with you in a moment."

Then turning to Mary who had also risen from her seat, I offered her my arm, and we re-entered the ballroom together.

Perhaps after all the interruption was well timed, for I had completely lost my self-control. I seemed to have forgotten everything but the surpassing loveliness of the woman beside me, when Madge recalled me to my senses. Yes—no doubt it was most fortunate; what grounds, indeed, had I for hope? None whatever, and yet,—if she had only waited one moment longer, that I might have caught the expression of those downcast eyes!

By this time the German was nearly over, and shortly afterwards the ball broke up.

While I was waiting hat in hand in the hallway for Madge, Mary came down the stairs with her partner. Her cloak was white, and a white nubia was wound lightly about her head and throat.

"Allow me to leave you here a moment, Miss Lee, while I call your carriage," said Mr. Benjamin.

I had been partially concealed by the shadow of the staircase, but when her companion left her, I crossed the hall to where she was standing.

As I approached, her eyes were bent upon the ground and I thought that her face wore an expression of distress.

When she raised her eyes and saw me a slight flush suffused her cheeks, and she said, with an exclamation of surprise,—

"What! have you not gone yet, Mr. Strong?"

"No, I am waiting for Madge," and after a moment's pause, I added, "I am afraid you are tired to-night."

"O no!" she answered looking up. "Why should you think so?"

"I thought, as I came up, that you looked so."

"O no," she said, turning away her face, "you imagined it. I do wish Mr. Benjamin would find my carriage! What can have become of him?"

"Shall you be at home to-morrow evening, Miss Lee?" I asked, without answering her.

"Papa and Mr. Brown dine at Mr. Hazeltine's to-morrow."

"That is not what I asked."

"Yes," she answered, hesitatingly, "I suppose I

shall; that is, mammá and I will probably be at home."

"Then I shall come to call," I said, "if you will let me."

"Of course you may, if you wish, that is— O, here is Mr. Benjamin at last! Good night, Mr. Strong!" and she was gone.

Her last words, which sounded most unflatter-ingly like an exclamation of relief, provoked me, and, as is usually the case when anything happens to annoy one, my ill-humor was soon to be still further aggravated; for a few minutes after her depar-ture, Madge came down into the hall with Colonel Shorter, and when I joined them, the Colonel asked me in a tone better suited to one of his servants,—

"Is Miss Eustis's carriage at the door?"

"Yes," I answered, curtly, and then, turning to Madge, I said,—

"Let me carry your things, Madge, so that you can hold up your skirts."

"You need not trouble yourself, Mr. Strong," broke in the Colonel, in the same overbearing style, "for I shall see Miss Eustis home."

"That is a pleasure, sir, that I have no intention of yielding to any one," I replied, turning full upon him. "Come, Madge," I added, placing her arm in mine, "I am afraid you will take cold, standing here with nothing on your head."

I heard Shorter say something to the effect that it was for Miss Eustis to decide, but without noticing him further, I led Madge out to her carriage, and taking my seat beside her, closed the door. He had followed us half way down the steps, and then without uttering a word of good night even to Madge, turned suddenly on his heel and strode back again into the hall.

"Well, Harry," said Madge, laughing rather nervously, as we drove away, "that was one way of doing it! You certainly took forcible possession, didn't you? How dreadfully angry the Colonel will be, won't he?"

"I neither know nor care, but he certainly is the most insolent coxcomb I ever met," I said.

"O, what fun, Harry! Why, I never saw you provoked before."

"Do you think it funny, Madge? I think it very disagreeable. But, perhaps you are right, for after all there is, no doubt, something ludicrous about it. Do you know, I consider myself rather good tempered as a rule, but I must confess I cannot stand that man's manners! Still, I must beg your pardon for acting so hastily."

"O," she cried, "I assure you I have nothing to forgive! I am only too glad you insisted. I told him I was going home with you, but he would not take 'no' for an answer, and he was so persistent that I could do nothing with him. I believe I am a little afraid of him sometimes."

The drive was a short one, and when we reached home Madge asked me to go with Kate and herself on the following evening to a reception at a Mrs. Latham's.

"Thank you," I said, "but I shall not be able to go with you to-morrow night."

According to the custom of the place, I had opened the front door for her with her latch key and was standing in the hall, ready to put out the light when she should have gone up stairs.

"O, why not?" she asked in a disappointed tone.

"I am sorry, but I really cannot. You know I am not used to such continual dissipation," I added, laughing, "and besides, I have another engagement."

"Give it up, then," she persisted. "I don't believe you have any engagement. It is nothing but an excuse. I think it very unkind, when I ask it as a special favor. Ah, do come, Harry! Won't you?"

"No, you must forgive me, for indeed I cannot go. Good night!"

"Good night!" she answered as she turned and went upstairs. "I shall never ask a favor of you again. Good night!"

I shut off the gas and closed the door. The carriage was still waiting, but I dismissed it, preferring to walk home in the cool morning air.

CHAPTER XVIII.

AN EVENING CALL.

THE next morning, while I was sitting by the
fire in the reading-room of the club, glancing
through the files of the morning papers, Fred
Brown dropped in upon me. I knew it would be
useless to try to continue my reading, so I laid my
paper down upon the table and lighted a fresh
cigar.

"Well, Fred," said I, "the sun is bright, the
skies are fair, what do you say to a stroll to the end
of the bluff?"

"Very well," he answered, "I'm with you. I
need a little exercise this morning. You can sit up
all night, I suppose, with impunity, but I'm not
used to that sort of thing, you know, and these late
hours don't agree with me."

It was a fine, clear winter noon, and we strolled
down the broad street that skirted the top of the
bluff along the river.

The masts of the vessels lying at the wharves
rose high above the blocks of stores between them
and the street, and from the mastheads flags of
many nationalities flapped lazily in the light breeze
from the east. Endless lines of cotton loaded drays
were rattling along over the uneven cobble stones,

or descending, at intervals, through the cuts in the bluff to the wharves below. Saddle horses were hitched here and there to the posts and railings in front of the offices, under the sparse shadows of gnarled and sickly-looking trees with which the street was lined. Clusters of business men were standing idly in the doorways, or sitting in the sun on the office steps, smoking, whittling, and discussing the price of the great staple, the past and future of the markets, or national politics. Lean goats wandered about the streets and gutters in search of food, or struggled with each other for the possession of some bit of oily rag or paper. Negroes were everywhere at work or asleep in the sun.

We left the stores and the noisy business portion of the street behind us, and continued on until we reached a broad plateau which commanded a view of the winding river, the salt marshes, and a ribbon of blue, ten miles away, where lay the great Atlantic; and here we sat down on the stubbly grass, near the edge of the bluff, in the pleasant noon-day sun.

Just below us, a little tug, with a foreign barque in tow, was struggling for mastery with the yellow current of the river, while further on, a black-hulled steamer was winding her way among the marshes to the sea; and in the dim distance we could just descry the masts and sails of vessels lying in the outer port.

"How should you like to be on your way home in that steamer, Fred?" I asked.

" Well, I suppose it's time for me to be going
back to work," he answered, " but I am so well here,
I hate to leave. Then, to tell the truth, I have
learned to like the people. Of course they are very
different from what I have been accustomed to.
Most of them are a shiftless set and absurdly conceited about nothing. Do you suppose they really
think that they are the only men in the world that
possess personal courage? However, with all their
faults I like them, although I am not yet ready to
allow that being good horsemen and good shots,
and wearing small boots, more than makes up for
the want of education, as some of them seem to
think. But what I especially like is the ladies.
They have surprised me most. Why, I always
imagined that Southern women did nothing but lie
around in hammocks and easy-chairs all day—reading novels, drinking lemonade and eating candy.
But I have found that some of them at least lead
useful lives and know what it is to work. Take
Miss Lee, for instance, hardly a day passes without
her going down to the negro quarter of the city to
visit the poor or do some act of charity; and every
Sunday she has the little children from the back
yard up in her room and reads to them, and to any
of the older ones that choose to come, and she
teaches them too. She never speaks of it herself, but
I questioned Nero the other day while he was brush-
ing my coat and found out all about her doings.
She's a thoroughly Christian young woman, you can
depend upon it, and she's a stunner to look at, isn't

she ? It's no wonder if her head's a little turned by
all the flattery these Southerners give her. From
what I have overheard them say to her, I guess they
understand flirting pretty well," he said, shaking
his head sagaciously. "However," he continued,
" I suppose it does not have much effect upon her,
because, you know, she's dead in love with your
friend Eustis."

" Indeed, what makes you think so ? " I asked,
beginning to take an interest in his chatter.

" Why, everybody is talking about it," he answered. " I often hear it said that he is engaged. .
Nero don't know about that, but he says they have
been in love ever since they were children. He told
me that, when Eustis bade her good-by, just before
he went to Florida, she was crying, and he saw him
kiss her. What do you think of that ? "

" Think, Brown," cried I, springing suddenly to
my feet. " You should be ashamed to listen to such
gossip from a servant! I am astonished at your
simplicity or ignorance ! "

" Well," he replied, quite crestfallen, " I don't see
why you should take it so seriously. What am I
to do ? how can I help it, I should like to know, if
Nero will talk about such things?"

-" Help it, man ! Why, kick the insolent rascal
out of the room."

" It's all very well," he answered, " to talk about
my kicking him out of the room, but I'd rather not
try to kick Nero."

" Well," I said, " I will not discuss it with you.

If your own instinct has not taught you what is due to your host and his family, I cannot hope to enlighten you. But come, it is time to go home."

I was disgusted with Brown's want of gentlemanly feeling; but what good could it do to discuss the principles and obligations of good breeding with one who did not seem aware even of their existence? However, when my first indignation had subsided, I could not but feel sorry for him, he seemed to have taken what I had said so much to heart. He was very quiet, and I saw that he was mortified at his conduct and the construction I had put upon it. After all, thought I to myself, if you are so sensitive as this, there may be some hope for you yet. And upon the whole I was not sorry that I had spoken as I did.

I knew that he had sterling merit, notwithstanding his solecisms in manners, but feared that at any moment the latter might endanger his friendship with the Lees. Captain Lee had taken a fancy to him, and had showed him much kindness, while he on his part was giving valuable assistance to the veteran in some articles that he was preparing for publication under the title of " Reminiscences of the Southern Navy," looking up facts and dates, which demanded a larger amount of research than the Captain would have undertaken by himself. Brown never thought of personal trouble, and entered upon the work of those he liked as if it were his own ; and yet, in a measure counterbalancing these good qualities that he possessed, there was this painful want of tact, of delicacy, of decency even, that occasionally amused, but more often mortified me, for—having introduced him to my Southern friends—I felt in a measure answerable for his behavior.

When I reached the hotel I found a note awaiting me from Jim.

He had now been in Florida for several weeks, and I was glad to see from the tone of his letter, that he was more cheerful than when he left us. Among other things, he wrote, " I am off to-morrow with a hunting party to the Everglades, where we look for good sport. I shall probably be out of reach of the mails for a week or two, and then shall, without doubt, come directly home, for I cannot afford to lose any more of your visit. As it is, it seems rather rough to have gone off and left you so long, but I felt I must make a change, and knew you would forgive me under the circumstances. Nothing like plenty of work in the open air for restoring one's equilibrium. Take good care of the girls, and please remember me to Miss Lee if you see her."

That evening, at eight o'clock, I was on my way to the Lees, as I had proposed. I went with no settled purpose, for I was still in doubt as to the course I should pursue, though more than willing to subject myself to the influence of Mary's presence.

In answer to my ring the veritable Nero appeared and ushered me across the tiled hall to the room in which the family usually gathered in the evening. It opened into a drawing-room of stately proportions by folding doors which, in cold weather, were usually drawn to, as on the present occasion. Its heavy curtains were dark-brown and crimson, and many of the chairs were covered with the same material, or in colors that harmonized with the quiet tone of the room. Over the polished floor, a Persian rug and soft deep mats were spread. The centre-table (on which was a vase of flowers), the escritoire and bookcase were of inlaid rosewood, like the upright piano that stood at the end of the room with some of Mary's music open upon it. The hickory logs were burning brightly on the broad hearth. On one side of the fire sat Mrs. Lee, reading by the light of an astral lamp placed on a small table near at hand; and opposite to her sat Mary, in a low chair, busily engaged upon a piece of fancy work, with the firelight flickering on her gown and upturned face.

With the recollection of our last interview fresh in my mind, I entered the room with some misgivings, but Mary's manner was so cordial, so different from that of the night before, that it soon placed me at my ease.

After paying my respects to Mrs. Lee, I sat down between them before the fire; for Mary had already reseated herself, and her slender fingers were again busy with the intricacies of her work; while the diamond of the solitary ring she wore glanced in and out among the meshes of soft worsted. The open sleeves fell slightly back, revealing, now and

then, the small wrist and round white arm. What
a subtle fascination there is in the expressions and
motions of a perfect hand! Woman's greatest beauty
as it is the last to fade! We may possibly even
forget the features of a face we have loved, but time
can never steal from us the memory of a hand that
we have watched, admired and caressed. As the
lengthening network fell softly into Mary's lap
that night, her fairy fingers seemed to be forging
chains to bind me heart and soul forever.

" Were you not asked to the Latham's to-night,
Mr. Strong?" said Mrs. Lee, placing a ribbon in
the book she had been reading and laying it down
upon the table beside her.

" Yes," I answered, " but I have been out so much
lately, I did not care to go."

" You ought to have gone," she said, " their parties are always pleasant, I am told, and Lent is so
near at hand that all the gayeties will soon be
over."

At this moment Nero opened the door and announced Mr. Benjamin. I for one was sorry enough
to see him ; but my fears were soon set at rest, for
he was going to the Latham's, and had only called on
his way to ask Mary to drive with him on the
following afternoon.

He was a gentlemanly fellow, and although a
Hebrew, as his name and features indicated, he was
a leader in society, and appeared to be an especial
favorite with the Lees. I had met him frequently
of late and liked him, for he had always treated me

with marked courtesy; but none the less was I happy to hear that on this occasion his visit was to be a short one.

"Why, Mr. Strong," he exclaimed, as he was taking his leave, "aren't you going to the Lathams' to-night? They spoke to me yesterday of you and said they depended upon seeing you. I understood Miss Eustis, too, to say that you were going with her?"

"I did intend to, but your late hours at the ball last night made me change my mind."

"I am sorry to hear it, sir; they will be much disappointed," he replied.

After he had gone our conversation drifted on from one thing to another, until at last it settled upon the old subject of the war, still ever uppermost in the mind of Mrs. Lee. She was more communicative that night than usual, and related many incidents and episodes of their own lives during those stirring times, that I had not heard before, although I had gathered from others much of their family history.

Mary said very little, but sat quietly working in her corner by the fire, only occasionally looking up to ask a question or to add a word in explanation of her mother's stories.

Captain Lee, before the war, had held a commission in the United States navy, where his genial and manly character had made him one of the most popular men in the service; while his heroism, when in command of the merchantship "Albatross" (to which he had been assigned while on furlough), brought him prominently to the notice of the government, and in fact to that of the whole country.

She was (as many may remember) wrecked on Cape Hatteras in the winter of 1851, with a full cargo of freight and passengers, but through the signal courage and presence of mind of her captain not a life was lost. It is unnecessary to give the details of an affair that was so fully discussed in the papers of the day. Suffice it to say, that he became in consequence a conspicuous officer with a brilliant future before him.

Thus when, in 1861, his native State seceded from the Union, which he had served for many years so faithfully, it was a terrible blow to him, and it was only after long and anxious deliberation that he yielded to what he considered his first duty, sent in his resignation to the government, and gave up his position to follow the uncertain fortunes of his State.

It was a great trial, to one of his keen sense of honor, to be thus called upon to decide between allegiance to the flag under which he had sailed, and his duty to his kindred and his State. The associations, honors, hopes of a lifetime were not to be cast aside without a terrible struggle. But the decision once made, he entered heart and soul into the cause he had espoused, and offered his services to the Confederate Government. He was at once given a high command in their navy, and served with fidelity and distinction to the end of the war.

The Captain's only son, a young man of twenty, followed his father's example and enlisted as a private in a Southern cavalry regiment, having, shortly before joining the army, become engaged to a young cousin, to whom he had been attached from boyhood. By decimation of the ranks, and his own bravery he arose, step by step, until he became at length colonel of his regiment.

On the eve of the battle of Okolonee Swamp, only three days after he had received his last commission, and nearly three years since he had left home, the news reached him of the death of his betrothed; and when, on the morrow, his regiment made that hopeless, but gallant dash, he led the charge, and although his men were repulsed and driven back, he kept right on to his death in the midst of the enemy.

A letter was found in his tent written the night before to his mother. Its contents were never disclosed, but, undoubtedly, its burden was despair.

The Eustises and Mary had told me his story, but I had never heard Mrs. Lee mention his name. In fact, she had cherished this grief in secret until her mind had become unnaturally morbid on the subject of the war, and of all connected with it.

During those dreary years, Mrs. Lee and her little daughter lived at Palmetto Grove, surrounded by their slaves.

At long intervals the Captain would make his appearance among them, and gladden their hearts with his affectionate and hopeful spirit. But his vessel was seldom in port and his visits necessarily short, so that often months at a time would pass without a white man crossing the threshold of their door. Their slaves, however, proved trustworthy and faithful to the end.

In the hot summer months, Mrs. Lee would take Mary to some little village in the interior of the State to return again to the Grove with the first black frost.

Occasionally, during the long winters, the monotony of their lives was enlivened by a visit to the city, where a state of constant excitement prevailed; for although far from the seat of war, the home camps, the frequent departure of fresh recruits to the front, and the return of the sick and wounded, made work for one and all, and filled the streets with bustle and commotion.

In strange contrast, society ran mad with gayety. While parades, public meetings, relief clubs, sewing societies, and hospital attendance filled every moment of the day—Germans, sociables, parties, balls and masquerades came off night after night in rapid succession. Occupation for every waking hour—little time for rest—no time for thought !

Often when the dance was at its height a rumor from some distant battlefield would find its way in among the gay assemblage to blanch the cheek, and change the laugh into a cry of anguish ! It was a mad life indeed. Unbridled gayety waltzing in the arms of death !

What wonder that the excitements and horrors of

such times as these should have left their indelible impressions?

And when at last all hope had fled ; when the troops came straggling back to their desolated homes, barefooted, ragged, sick and dying ; the cause which they had regarded with religious enthusiasm lost utterly and forever, was it strange that the hearts of the Southern women should have hardened? Was it strange that for the time they should have hated their successful enemies with a hatred too intense to be concealed ?

Many of the Northern officers—to their honor be it said—who were stationed among this distressed people treated them with the utmost gentleness— avoiding with tact the open wounds, and endeavoring to aid them both by word and deed. Would that all had been animated by the same spirit of forbearance, the same manly good nature, the same kindliness of heart ! But some men are born gentlemen and some born brutes, and the *role* of conqueror brings out each character in its strongest light.

Upon these and kindred subjects Mrs. Lee talked for an hour or more, recounting her own participation in the sufferings and emotions of those unhappy times, and bringing them nearer home to me, by her earnestness, than they had ever been brought before.

With me bygones soon became absolutely bygones, and it both excited and depressed me, to find the past with all its passions and prejudices so present and vivid to the mind of Mary's mother. With each succeeding reminiscence she seemed to be adding a stone to the barrier she was consciously or unconsciously raising between her daughter and me.

From my first acquaintance with the latter, I had tried to measure the influence of the past on her mind, but had never until now given it sufficient weight. Though I had known full well how wholly our early lives differed in their associations and surroundings, never before had the natural consequences of that difference so strongly impressed me. Now I felt the strength of the invisible enemy, that through all her short life had been working against me, and was unable to cope with it. Love alone could blot out the past, but to inspire it in the face of life-long prejudice seemed indeed a hopeless task.

When Mrs. Lee had brought her story to an end, she was called from the room by one of the servants, and Mary and I were left alone together. Then I said,—

" Do you remember, when I first knew you, how indignant you were one day, at my saying I could make you care for me if I chose ? Although I spoke in jest, I more than half believed it then. It seems strange now how little I realized the deep-rooted prejudices that must stand between every Southern woman and me. In fact I never thoroughly understood them before to-night." And after a pause which Mary did not interrupt, I added with some bitterness,—" The outward cordiality with which I have been received deceived me. It gave no warning of the strong undercurrent that must, in reality, be always setting against me. Now I see it all. It is natural enough, no doubt. I only wish I had discovered it sooner. Now it is too late."

"But we—but people here do like you, Mr. Strong," she said, and then looking up from her work, she added, "You must at least believe in our sincerity."

· "How can I, when your dislike has been so clearly shown in every word your mother has just spoken? If you were to tell me with your own lips you liked me, I should almost doubt it now."

I had risen in my excitement, and with one arm resting on the mantelpiece, stood looking down upon her.

She had stopped working. Her hands were clasped tightly in her lap, and her eyes fixed upon the fire.

"And yet, fool that I am!" I exclaimed, almost fiercely, "I would give ten years of my life to hear you say so."

Did the color deepen in her cheeks? Or was it only the light from the sudden blazing of the log upon the hearth?

How still it seemed when I stopped speaking!

At last she said with a slight tremor in her voice.

"It is not worth the sacrifice, Mr. Strong. But have I ever given you reason to doubt my friendship?"

"No, never in words, of course, nor in act. Like all your people you have too much courtesy for that," I answered bitterly, growing harber and harder as I went on. "It is that very thing that I condemn. You are always civil to us, even more so than to your own friends, for this you think a requirement of hospitality; but at the very same time you are steeling your hearts against any sentiment or sympathy in common with us."

" Have we not the sentiments common to all humanity, truth and honor, as you yourself once said to me ? " she asked, with a faint smile, attempting to turn the current of my thoughts. But I had become too earnest to unbend, and I answered in the same uncompromising tone.

" I should not be willing to deny it now, but I believe they can be warped and twisted by prejudice almost beyond recognition. And so although in truth bitter and relentless, you do not hesitate to make us believe you like us, or at least skilfully conceal your hatred. And what is the result ? The natural and inevitable one, and you may well be proud of it. It is no doubt the Southern women's revenge ! "

" I shall not dispute what you say. I do not consider it necessary for me to defend them."

" I shall not dispute what you say. I do not consider it necessary for me to defend them," she answered quietly, but with a hot flush upon her face, " but even granting, for the moment, that we dislike and deceive you, as you say, would you have us treat you with incivility? Would that have made your winter among us any the pleasanter ? "

" Yes, a thousand times ! Better than to have found out, as I have to-night, that what I have taken part in, and believed to be earnest and real, was nothing but a sham, a hollow farce! That I have been the only puppet on the stage, even my fellow-actors, spectators! I despise deceit, whether I am its dupe or not, but I must confess there is something unique in a combination of sham hospitality and patriotic coquetry!"

I had spoken with more and more bitterness and excitement, and when I stopped Mary looked up at me with a face as white as the worsted in her lap.

"There is but one way of accounting for your ill-nature," she began.

"No, thank Heaven!" I exclaimed, somewhat inconsistently, catching at her meaning; "I have not been made a fool of by any woman! But, until to-night, I thought there was one, at least, as far above hypocrisy as——"

Before I could finish, she rose from her seat, her tangled work dropping from her lap upon the floor, and with tears in her eyes, and her voice trembling with emotion, she said,—

"If you have come here to insult me, sir, I will not submit to it. You are cruel! You are unjust! No, do not speak; I will not listen to you!" and she turned hurriedly away to leave the room. I sprang to her side, and seized her hand in both of mine.

"O forgive me, forgive me, my darling!" I cried, raising it to my lips and kissing it passionately, "I love you with all my heart and soul! I did not know what I was saying. I was beside myself! I was crazy with disappointment! I did not wish to hurt your feelings! I know I am a brute, but never thought you would care for what I said. Speak to me, Mary, speak to me, and tell me you forgive me ! "

I laid my hand gently upon her shoulder, and drew her to me. Her eyes were turned from me, and she had covered her face with her handkerchief to stifle the sobs that shook her frame like the regular pulsations of the heart.

Suddenly, I heard the rustling of a dress, and turned in the direction of the sound.

Mrs. Lee was standing in the doorway, looking fixedly at us.

CHAPTER XIX.

A RIDE.

MRS. LEE was drawn up at her full height. Her arms were crossed, and her expression was one of astonishment and indignation.

As I released Mary, she glided past her mother out of the room, and Mrs. Lee advanced to the opposite side of the centre-table near which I was standing.

"It is hardly necessary to ask you for an explanation of the scene I have just witnessed," she said, haughtily.

"No," I answered, impetuously, before she could say more. "Only one explanation is possible, Mrs. Lee, and that is, that I love your daughter with my whole heart. I have loved her ever since we first met, but never told her so until to-night. I hardly dared hope——"

"That is sufficient, sir," she said, interrupting me in an icy tone. "I believe I have already said no explanation is necessary. But before you go I must command you never again to speak on this subject to my daughter. It is extremely distasteful to me, and I have sufficient confidence in her good

judgment to feel sure that when she has had time
for reflection, it cannot be otherwise than painful
to her."

"I am sorry that I cannot obey you, Mrs. Lee," I
answered, in my turn amazed and indignant at
her tone. "On the contrary, I tell you frankly,
I will not stop trying to win your daughter, until I
know from her own lips that it is hopeless!"

"I am surprised," she replied, scornfully, "that
after what I have just said, you have not sufficient
pride to save yourself from a very humiliating position. I supposed it would be sufficient for me to
tell you that I should never sanction your attentions to my daughter; but, if you insist upon the
additional mortification of being refused by her own
lips, you can have it, sir. Still, I hope, after thinking
it over, you will see the uselessness and folly of such
a course."

"You are mistaken if you think I can be disposed
of in this summary way," I answered, excitedly.
"My mind is already made up. Much. as I regret
your opposition, it will not alter my course. I
would not give up hope—not if she herself said
'No'—unless fully satisfied it was the expression
of her own feelings, and not the result of pressure
or misrepresentation. Not even her own mother
has the right to control her freedom of action. I
should indeed be unworthy of her, if I obeyed
you."

Her air of calm superiority overcame all thoughts
of prudence, and I could not restrain. myself,

although I knew that every word I uttered made her more and more my enemy.

"You apparently forget, sir, the arrogance of your assumption," she replied, without any perceptible change in the expression of her cold face. "I do not admit what you have said, but I may say, that we have intentions for our daughter that are agreeable to us, and, I believe, acceptable to her. Even granting for a moment that she did return your affection, to speak, as frankly to you as you have to me, I would rather see her in her grave than married to a Northerner! However, inasmuch as I cannot shut her up, or prevent you from seeing her if you persist,—as you so courteously suggest,—I trust you will see fit to accede to one last request I have to make, which is, to give my daughter sufficient time for deliberation, and not to attempt to address her for at least a month to come."

"It is too much to ask," I exclaimed, "when every influence——"

"We will not renew the discussion," she interrupted. "Surely a month is not an unreasonable time. Will you give me your promise?"

After a moment's reflection I reluctantly consented. I hardly saw how I could refuse her request, and felt that under the circumstances some concession on my part was absolutely necessary.

"Thank you," she said, when I had given my promise, "and now, Mr. Strong, as there is nothing further to be said, I will bid you good evening."

I bowed and was about to leave the room, but at the door I stopped and looked back. She was standing motionless by the table where I had left her; but when she heard my voice she turned her head to listen.

"If in my excitement I have spoken rudely, I beg your pardon, Mrs. Lee," I said. "If you knew how dearly I love your daughter, you would understand how painful your words have been."

"I know nothing against you personally," she said, checking me with a slight gesture of her hand, "and shall no doubt forget your incivility; but I think I have made my own feelings sufficiently clear to render no further explanation on the subject necessary. Good evening, sir," and with a haughty inclination of her head she dismissed me.

Before returning to my room I took a long walk in the starlight through the quiet streets and parks. I tried to review my position in every aspect, and although distressed at the result of my interview with Mrs. Lee, I found consolation in the glimpse that I had caught of Mary's feelings, and the thought that my own line of action was now clearly defined. But a month seemed a long time to remain in this suspense, and if even then Mary should prove willing to marry me against her mother's wishes, the scenes that might follow and the unnatural relations in which we might be placed, were not pleasant to contemplate. However, it seemed hardly natural to suppose that if she should accept me, her mother would continue an opposition founded simply upon prejudice; but if the worst should come to the worst, I might take Mary to the North or abroad, until separation should soften her mother's heart.

I entertained no fears of the Captain. His kind and generous nature would regard alone his daughter's happiness. He was not the man to thwart her where her heart was fixed. Besides, I knew he liked me, and that, even if disappointed at her choice, he would cheerfully make the best of the inevitable.

On the following morning I wrote a full account of my affairs to Alice, who had always been my confidante, but as yet knew nothing of my attachment to Mary, and, in fact, very little of the Lee family.

Then, too, I had to write to Jim and tell him frankly of my position. He would hear of it sooner or later, and better that it should reach him through me than others. What effect the disclosure might have upon our mutual relations I could not tell, but I felt that it must be made, however hard the task, and after two or three unsatisfactory beginnings, I wrote him, briefly and affectionately, all that had come to pass.

In the afternoon I was to ride with Madge, and the appointed hour found me at Mrs. Jackson's door, mounted on Vixen.

The hostler was walking Madge's horse up and down before the house, and Madge herself was already standing in the portico, whip and gauntlets in hand.

She waved them at me as I stopped, and then ran lightly down the steps and through the little garden where the violets were in bloom, pausing a moment to pick a little bunch of them as she passed.

"You are late," said she, as she joined me on the sidewalk; for I had dismounted.

"No, I think not," I answered, looking at my watch, which vouched for my punctuality.

"Then I am early," she said gayly, "but it is such a lovely evening, I could not wait patiently in the house. I hated to lose a moment of it. Come, will you help me?" she asked, placing her slender foot in my hand. "Gently! Beauty! Be careful, Harry; Now! there!" and with a light spring, she seated herself in the saddle. A moment later I was at her side, and we cantered slowly through the sandy streets in the shade of the evergreens, that had not yet cast off their last year's dingy leaves. On we passed beyond the outlying settlements and into the thickly wooded country.

It was, indeed, a lovely evening, just cool enough for gentle exercise. There was scarcely a cloud in the deep blue sky, and the sun, within an hour of the horizon, threw long shadows over the road and sheets of light through the woods on either side. The spring foliage was not yet out, but the swollen buds betokened life within, and the grand carnival of nature, now so near at hand.

We rode for a long time through the cool woodland roads, seldom speaking, sufficiently content to breathe the life-giving air.

By and by we came out upon a little settlement that followed the windings of a bluff along a narrow inlet, that made its way up through the salt marshes from the sea. It seemed to be principally a fishing village; and huge banks of oyster shells reaching from the water's edge to the top of the bluff—a monument to good taste—gave evidence of one of the chief pursuits of the hamlet. But here and there little cottages with shrubs and flower beds in front, and market-gardens in the rear, and an occasional restaurant with its broad piazzas and long line of sheds showed that it was also, more or less, a place of resort for people from the city.

The houses stood some distance back, and the road passed between them and the edge of the bluff. The moss-grown oaks that lined the way cast their shadows far out over the marsh, that lay golden red in the sunlight beyond. The stream flowed smoothly and silently along at our feet without a ripple on its inky surface, and, making a deep cove near by, it mirrored leaf by leaf the dark, overhanging foliage. It was a hushed and peaceful scene. We paused under a live-oak to watch some negroes, in their narrow "dugouts," drawing in their nets, and although they were far distant, we could hear the words of the man directing their work; so clear was the air, so silent was all about us.

At length, remembering Mrs. Jackson's dinner hour, we turned our horses' heads towards home. Shortly after leaving the bluff, and as we wound our way through the wood, whom should we meet at a bend of the road but Mr. Benjamin driving Mary Lee.

We came upon one another so suddenly that we were obliged to pull up our horses to make way, though we did not actually stop.

The delay, however, gave me time to mark the embarrassment in Mary's face at our unexpected meeting; nor did it, I had reason to believe, escape the notice of my companion.

We cantered on for a while after this without speaking, but presently, when we had brought our horses down to a walk, Madge turned to me and said,—

" So you passed last evening at the Lees, Harry ? " and as I did not instantly reply she added,—

" Why do you not answer me ? You need not try to deceive me, for Mr. Benjamin told me he met you there."

" Really, Madge," I answered, " I had no intention of deceiving you.   Why should I ? "

" O of course I know no reason why you should ; but I think it was very unkind not to have gone to the Lathams with me, when you had no better reason than that."

" I am very sorry," I answered, " but I could not break my engagement."

" It can hardly be called an engagement simply to say you will call.   You know you might have gone any other night just as well.   I did not think you would refuse me the first favor I ever asked, and for such a trifle."

I was completely nonplussed at being thus unexpectedly called to account, and hardly knew what to say, especially as Madge's tone and manner indicated that she was very much in earnest.

"Believe me, Madge," I answered warmly, "I would do anything in my power to oblige you, and in any way. I am exceedingly sorry to have offended you. It is the last thing in the world I should wish to do."

"I hardly believe you," she answered slowly, and then, speaking with some hesitation and with her eyes fixed straight before her, she went on,—"You know, Harry, that we have seen very little of the Lees since Jim's refusal—and Mary certainly did treat him most abominably—and to speak candidly, considering your intimacy with him, I have been rather surprised at your going so often to their house. Do you think it seems quite true to him?"

Her question surprised me, for I knew Jim had particularly requested his sisters not to allow his mishap to break up the friendship that had always existed between the families. Besides, leaving my personal feelings out of the question, I should have thought it impertinent on my part to have shown even by my manner that I was aware of what had happened.

"Why, yes, Madge," I replied slowly, "I think Jim would not have had me do otherwise. The Lees, as you know, have been exceedingly kind to me, and it would have looked very rude to have suddenly avoided them. Surely you would not have me make a display of my knowledge of their family secrets? Jim would have been the last to wish it."

"Perhaps you are not aware," she continued without answering me, "that people say you are yourself very devoted to Mary."

"No! you astonish me!" I exclaimed, the tell-tale blood rushing to my face.

"Then it is not true?" she demanded.

"Why, Madge," I answered, becoming more and more confused, "you know yourself how much, or rather how little, I have seen Miss Lee since we came to town."

"You have not answered my question," she said, in the same quiet tone. "You do not deny it, then?"

"Deny what?" I asked, plunging deeper and deeper into the slough of embarrassment.

"Deny that you are very attentive to her."

What could I do? What could I say? A certain feeling of loyalty restrained me from a flat denial. With any one I had known and liked less well than Madge, I should not have hesitated. In fact, no one who had known me less intimately would have asked me such a question. But why should I not make her my confidante and confess to her the whole affair? The thought flashed through my mind, and under the impulse of the moment I was about to speak, when she stopped me with a gesture of her hand. For the first time she had turned towards me, her face was very pale, her lips firmly set, and her eyes glittered almost fiercely as she riveted them on mine.

"You need not speak," she cried, in a low, constrained voice, "you cannot tell me more than I already know, and a lie will not deceive me. Idiot! Fool that you are! She will never have you! Thank God, she will never have you!"

I was struck dumb by the vehemence of her passion. For a moment more she looked piercingly into my face, then, turning away with a loud, scornful laugh that echoed through the woods, she lashed her horse's flank with her short riding-whip and dashed down the road at a mad gallop! There was nothing for me, but to follow. What a wild race we ran through the deserted roads in the shadowy twilight! On and on, mile after mile, without a break in the pace! I did not dare to overtake her, but kept "Vixen" well in the rear. A thousand thoughts were surging in my mind. Words and looks, that had made little or no impression upon me at the time, and had since been utterly forgotten, came trooping up into the light one after another. "Idiot, fool that you are!" rung in my ears, marking time to "Vixen's" steady springs. Yes, idiot, fool that you are! You can do nothing now. You can say nothing now. It is too late! Explanation means insult. Regret means insult. The friendship you have striven so blindly to win is in ashes. Love you do not—love you cannot ask!

At last we reached the nearest of the hamlets that drew their cordon round the city. Should we continue our headlong flight through the streets of the town? No; Madge slowly curbed her smoking horse into a walk, and I again joined her. But neither of us spoke, and it was, no doubt, a great relief to both when we, at last, reached home. I at once dismounted to help her down, but before I could reach her side she sprang lightly from her saddle and hurried into the house without a word. It had grown quite dark, so that I could not see her face, but I thought that she was crying.

" Well, Massa Strong," said David, who had been waiting for us, and who now stood stroking the horses, " I guess youse been runnin a race. Miss Madge's a great han' for runnin. It takes a heap o' pluck to keep along wid ur sometime."

" Yes, we had rather a lively time of it for a while. You'd better see that the horses are well rubbed down."

" Ain't you gwine to ride down to de hotel, Massa Harry ? "

" No, I'll walk, thank you. Have ' Vixen ' at the door at four to-morrow. Good-night."

CHAPTER XX.

COLONEL RICHARD SHORTER.

IT is not my purpose to speak at length of the many
questions that filled my mind at this time; although the practical dilemma in which I was placed
by the events of the last few days cannot be passed
over without a word.

If I were to continue my visits to the two families
with whom I had hitherto been most intimate, it
must be with the unpleasant consciousness that, to
at least one member of each, my presence would be
unwelcome, if not actually painful.

Yet, on the other hand, I could not give up
going as usual to Mrs. Jackson's, for any change on
my part would be remarked at once by her, and,
no doubt, frankly questioned; while explanation
would be impossible.

I, therefore, concluded with regard to the Eustises
to behave as if nothing whatever had happened;
and as to the Lees, that it would be best to base my
own line of action upon the conduct of the Captain
towards me.

This last question was soon definitely settled,
for shortly afterwards I saw Captain Lee at the
Club. He met me with unchanged cordiality, and

insisted upon my going home to dine with him. His manner satisfied me that he either knew nothing of what had taken place, or was determined to ignore it altogether, most probably the former, for his frank nature seemed incapable of concealment.

I managed on this first occasion to plead some satisfactory excuse, but, as he continued to ask me from day to day, at length I was obliged to accept, wondering in what manner I should be received by Mrs. Lee, and not without embarrassment at the thought of meeting Mary during this period of my enforced silence.

If, as was apparently the case, Mrs. Lee had not confided in her husband, was it probable that she had spoken to her daughter and told her of the promise she had extracted from me ? If not, what must Mary think of my absence ; of my delay in again seeking her after what I had already said?

But the doubts that perplexed me, as I rung the Captain's door-bell one Wednesday afternoon, just as the town clock was striking the dinner hour, speedily were set at rest by the simplicity of my reception by the family. As for Mrs. Lee, her man-ner could never have been accused of over-effusive-ness, but on this occasion I could not perceive that the atmosphere about her was either more or less chilly than usual.

Our conversation that evening, both during din-ner and afterwards, was general, and although I said little directly to Mary, I was conscious of the fact that we were constantly speaking to each other through our conversation with those about us. Once, as I looked up suddenly, I caught her eyes fixed upon me with an expression that sent the blood coursing to my temples.

She turned instantly away, but I had seen the expression and could not forget it. What did it mean? Was she troubled about the past or anxious for the future? or was it simply coquetry? What would I not have given for the right to demand an explanation on the spot!

During the evening she was asked to sing, but although her father urged her—for he was palpably proud of his daughter's accomplishments—she gently but persistently refused.

This was the first of many dinners that I went to during the next few weeks, at the Captain's invitation, and I was amply repaid for going, for although Mary's face and manner often puzzled me, it was an infinite pleasure to be near her, even if I must not speak my mind.

Often I met other society men there, but most frequently of all Mr. Benjamin, who was both a pronounced admirer of Mary and on terms of peculiar intimacy with the rest of the family; and I must confess to having felt piqued, occasionally, at the easy familiarity with which she treated him, while our own relations were so constrained and unnatural.

I continued also to go as often as ever to Mrs. Jackson's, and was soon satisfied that in this I had done wisely, for she was evidently ignorant of

Madge's and my falling out; or even if, as I sometimes suspected, she saw that all was not right between us, she kept discreetly silent and let matters
take their course.

Major Barnwell, having lately come to town, was
constantly at the house, and his devotion to Madge
rendered my own services unnecessary and their
absence unnoticed. Madge received his attentions
with apparent indifference, but, nevertheless, accepted them, which of itself was sufficient to keep the
ardor of the good Major at fever heat.

Colonel Richard Shorter also called several even-
ings while I was there, and it struck me that he was
obtrusively uncivil to Madge, hardly noticing her
and addressing himself solely to Kate, to whom he
evidently strove hard to make himself agreeable.

His labor, however, was utterly thrown away, for
I remember one evening after he had been talking
to her for an hour or more, she said to me,—

"I do hate that man, I cannot believe one word
he says! All the good in him would not fill this
thimble! I could almost make up my mind to tell
him what I think of him, if it would prevent his
ever coming to the house again."

Soon after this I went one night to a little German given by Mrs. Alvari, where I met Madge
and Colonel Shorter and Major Barnwell. Madge
ostensibly danced with the latter, but, in point of
fact, passed most of the evening on the piazza with
the colonel. This surprised me exceedingly, after
what I had seen at Mrs. Jackson's.

As for poor Barnwell he looked very forlorn at this open desertion of his partner; but a taste of comfort was in store for him, for when the dance was over, they walked home together under the bright starlight ; and then, no doubt, she soothed his ruffled spirits as she could always do by a word or look, for when he dropped in at the Club an hour later, he was fairly beaming with smiles and good nature and as happy as an accepted lover. Kick and abuse your dog to your heart's content, and at the first softening of the voice or patting of the hand, he bounds about you delirious with joy!

But though Shorter's conduct on the evening of the German had surprised me, surprise gave place to anxiety when I discovered that this was not a single instance, a mere whim of the moment, but that he was becoming, week by week, more and more con-spicuously attentive to Madge. Until, at last, where-ever she went he might be found near her, talking to no one unless to her, standing in the doorways watching her when she was with others, or sitting with her by the hour in the dim light of the balco-nies.

She appeared to like his open admiration and evidently encouraged him. He was, as I have said, thought fascinating by many women, and perhaps the mystery that attaches to a man of questionable character added to his attractions. But it aston-ished me beyond measure that Madge, who had heard her sister speak so strongly against him and knew how much he was disliked by Jim, should permit his constant attendance upon her.

Of course such a state of affairs could not long escape remark, especially in a small and gossiping community, and they soon became the common talk of society.

At this time Shorter seldom called at the house, and when he did he prudently continued his old habit of taking little notice of Madge, and, as Mrs. Jackson went rarely into company, it happened for a while, that she neither saw, nor heard anything of it.

But at last, through hints let drop by some lady friend, with mock inadvertency, the news did reach her ears, and one morning when I was calling upon her she broached the subject.

" Harry," she began " I am very much worried about Madge ; but come," she added, getting up and looking out of the window at her victoria, which had that moment drawn up at the door. " I am going to visit one of our old servants, who lives just out of town, and, if you will drive with me, I can talk over my troubles on the way."

I readily assented; and, after she had left me to get her things, Madge opened the door and came into the room.

" Sister ! " she exclaimed gayly, and then seeing me, her whole manner changed, and she continued with almost contemptuous indifference.

" O, I beg your pardon Mr. Strong, I did not know you were here.   Where is sister Kate ? "

"She has just gone to put on her things; she is going out to drive."

"Are you going with her?"

"Yes," I answered, "she asked me, but if you will take my place, I shall be only too happy to have you."

"No," she said in the same indifferent tone, "I have no desire whatever to drive this morning," and then pausing for a moment, and, tapping the table with the fan she carried, she asked, "Where are you going?"

"I believe to visit an old servant of yours on the Springlake road, Martha, I think your sister called her."

"On the Springlake road," she repeated absently, and as if speaking to herself.

"Are you sure, Miss Eustis, there is nothing we can do for you?" I asked.

My voice seemed to recall her to herself, and she answered coldly.

"No. Nothing. Good morning, Mr. Strong," and she closed the door.

In a short time Kate returned and we started out together.

It was a cold, blustering day; the sun shone fitfully through the heavy clouds that came chasing each other in rapid succession up from the northwest. But we were well wrapped up, and, when once out of town and rid of the clouds of dust that swept through the city streets, we found the wind fresh and bracing.

As we drove rapidly along the level country road, Mrs. Jackson returned to the subject that was naturally uppermost in her mind.

"As I was saying, Harry," she began, "I am very much worried about Madge, I have been told of Colonel Shorter's increasing devotion to her. At the same time, she has never spoken to me about it herself, and I am utterly at a loss what to do. I don't like to be the first to speak, for fear it should have just the wrong effect upon her. She has not seemed at all like herself lately. She is preoccupied, indifferent, and when she does speak, is apt to say sharp, severe things, so utterly unlike her. I cannot understand it! But, you know, from a child she has always been rather wayward, and I really do not dare to come to an open issue with her, while she is in this strange frame of mind. If Jim were only here it would be different, for though she is very fond of me, he has always had the strongest influence over her, and I think she would listen to him. He could make her see the folly of allowing her name to be coupled with that of such a man as Colonel Shorter. The insolence of his behaving in this way in Jim's absence, and when they are scarcely on speaking terms, is most aggravating! Besides I really fear something serious may come of it when Jim returns. I know when he hears how far it has gone, and how much it is talked about (as he certainly will if it is not put a stop to), he will be simply furious. What can I do Harry? Can't you help me?"

She seemed to feel it very keenly, and I wished

with all my heart that I could help her as she asked.
Such advice as I could give, she should have ; but
advice to one in actual distress always sounds luke-
warm, no matter how sincere our sympathy.   As it
was, I said, "I think you must speak to Madge,
Kate, whether she likes it or not; for if all that I
hear of Shorter is true, I would never let a sister
of mine marry him.   You must appeal to her good
sense, to her love for you, to her fear of making
trouble between this man and Jim.   Explain to her
the actual danger to Jim, and the scandal that might
follow.   I believe your sisterly love can devise a
thousand ways to move her, that would never occur
to me or to any man.   As for myself, Kate, if any
emergency should arise, do not hesitate to call upon
me at once ; and if there is anything on earth that I
can do for you, I will do it with all my heart.

"Thank you, Harry," she answered, " I believe you
thoroughly and I shall not forget what you have said.
But I see plainly that, for the present, there is nothing—no—nothing that you can do."

As she stopped speaking, we drew up at a little
clearing in the woods, where stood two or three
small log cabins with half tilled plots of ground
behind them, wherein even rows of hillocks told
of coming crops of melons and sweet potatoes.   All
were enclosed by a rude, zigzag, Virginia fence.
Perhaps there were, in all, a couple of acres of
cleared land lying in the sunlight and shadow, and
protected by the tall pine forest that surrounded it.
A few pine stumps peered up here and there

through the rich soil, and on the top of one of them a little fire of fagots, covered with earth, was smouldering; probably an altar of incense to unknown Gods. Swine were grubbing in the underbrush near by, and half a dozen hens sprung up from the middle of the road where they lay half buried in the sand, and scrambled under the fence at our rapid approach.

Negro children were playing about the doorsteps; and one or two old men and women were working in the garden. A large, hulking-looking negro stood leaning against the side of one of the cabins, with his back towards us, but when we stopped before the enclosure, he cast a rapid glance at us, and then slunk behind the house and out of sight. There was something about the man that struck me as familiar even in the momentary glimpse I had of him, though I could not remember where I had seen him.

When old January, who was standing at the gate, came out to the carriage door, I asked him who the man was. He looked up quickly at my question, and then after a moment's hesitation, replied that it was "Cousin Jonah from Cal-lina." But there was an expression of anxiety in his face that aroused my suspicion, and though I saw no reason why he should wish to deceive me, I felt sure that for some cause best known to himself, he had not spoken the truth.

Presently, at Mrs. Jackson's request, he went to one of the cabins to call out his daughter Martha, with whom the old man usually stopped when the

Eustises left The Oaks; and, as she lived near town, this enabled him to come daily to Mrs. Jackson's for orders. In a moment Martha appeared, and came out to us to receive the little package that Kate had brought her.

She was a small woman with jet-black face, and clean, bright turban bound about her head. On her arm she carried a little baby, apparently some few months old, and too busily engaged in securing its midday meal to take any notice of its visitors.

" Well, Martha," asked Mrs. Jackson, " how are you getting on ? "

" Pretty well, Miss, seeing as Andrew's dun bin gone dis las' munf, an' I has de gardin' work to do."

" And the baby ? "

" O, de baby's well nuff, but um's jes' so bad, dey's no doin' nuffin wid um. Ums took arter de old man. I specs I'se dun got my hans full, Miss, to keep um away fum de whiskey bottle ! "

" What have you named it Martha ? "

" Schuyler Colfax, Miss."

" That's very good." said Kate smiling, " but if you wished to be thoroughly patriotic, you should have called him Abraham Lincoln."

" Lor, Miss Kate ! " she exclaimed with an expression of mingled surprise and reproof, " *Ums a girl !* "

" O, of course that alters matters ! Good-by," Kate replied with a perfectly sober face, while I discreetly turned away my head.

"Good-by, Miss Kate," she answered; "please tell Miss Madge huddy for me."

After leaving the settlement, I proposed that we should drive to a little cemetery situated on the outskirts of the town, and somewhat noted for its monuments and trees. It was out of our way but, as I had never seen it and we had an hour to spare before lunch, Kate assented, and gave the necessary directions to the coachman.

It was indeed a picturesque place, with its winding alleys, tall box hedges and shady trees, with here and there a great live-oak, spreading its massive and moss-hung branches above the white-slabbed graves. A month later, spring foliage and blossoming flowers might take something from its gloom, but to-day its appearance was oppressively sombre and sad.

"This is a favorite place for engaged couples," said Kate.

"It seems to me," I answered, "that I would rather take the last, than the first walk here, with the woman I loved!"

"There is a couple now down the side path yonder, who, apparently, are not of your opinion, Harry. How slowly they are walking, and how absorbed they seem to be. See, he is trying to take her hand! Why, good heavens!" she cried, half rising from her seat, "It is Madge and Col. Shorter!"

Yes, she was right. They were at some distance, but coming toward us. They moved slightly apart and stood gazing at us as we passed the end of the path. It was clear that they had recognized us.

"O Harry," exclaimed Kate, fairly crying with vexation and chagrin, "this is, indeed, too bad! What shall I do! What shall I do! I would stop and insist on Madge's coming home with us, but I do so hate scenes, and perhaps she would not come! What will be the end of it all? O why, why will not Jim come home? I will write to him this very day!"

We drove rapidly back to town and on the way I strove, as best I could, to allay Kate's fears; but, after all, there was little to be said, for that there were good grounds for all her sisterly anxiety, seemed evident to me.

Nor was my mind any the less troubled, when, on returning to my room that night, I found a short note from Jim, in which he said, "We have just returned to Palatka for a day, and to-morrow shall take a run up the Ocklawaha. We may be gone ten days or a fortnight, at the outside, and then I shall come directly home. Many things have happened to change my plans since I last wrote, which I will explain when we meet. Your letter reached me safely, my dear Harry; forgive me if I was astonished at what you wrote, but believe me— whatever happens—your devoted friend,

"JAMES EUSTIS."

CHAPTER XXI.

ON THE PORCH.

IT was a warm, summerlike evening towards the
end of March.

One of those scorching waves of heat had passed
over the city during the day, which, occasionally,
in the early spring, burst upon the South, as if the
sun had suddenly thrown open his furnace doors,
to rake down the banked fires and rebuild them for
the summer. The air had fairly quivered in the
noontide heat.

All but the negroes and those whom imperative
duties called abroad, had remained within doors,
with windows shut, close drawn blinds, and in such
light attire as individual ideas of decency admitted,
and had devoted the long day to the hopeless task
of keeping cool.

In the business portion of the city, men, ordinarily
of dignified appearance, might have been seen in
their shirt sleeves and bareheaded, fighting the sun
with umbrellas and taking advantage of every hand
breadth of shade that fell from tree, or post, or
building, upon the blistering pavement.

The dust in the streets seemed deeper than ever,
and the sidewalks harder and more uneven. Shoes

that were too loose in the morning pinched, tight and dry, at noon. Not a cloud was in the sky, not a breath of air stirring, and the fiery sun poured down relentlessly his deluge of unobstructed heat.

For the innumerable bar-rooms this had been, indeed, a gala day. For it would have required nothing short of the cold blood or the virtue of a Joseph Andrews to have withstood the seductive clinking of the ice behind the green baize doors.

Uptown, the streets had been absolutely deserted. Even the pretty parks usually teeming with children, were, for the time, forsaken, and the fountains threw up their feathers of spray, unseen, into the sunlight.

Such a foretaste of approaching summer had been the day.

But toward sunset a breeze came floating in from the sea, soft and delicious and laden with the scent of the salt marsh; and again existence became endurable.

It was a month ago to a day that I had made my promise to Mrs. Lee; and about a week since my drive with Mrs. Jackson.

I supped alone that evening at my hotel and afterwards, in common with the rest of the city's suffering population, went out into the streets for a stroll in the breezy twilight.

Now that the time had come at last when I might speak, I could not determine whether to go at once to Mary, or to wait for some chance meeting. Not that my love had flagged during the past few weeks, but my doubts had more than kept pace with it. If I had spoken a month ago I believed she would have answered " Yes "; but since then what influences might not have been brought to bear, what persuasions, even threats, might not have been used to turn her from me.

Perhaps those strongest arguments of all to a sensitive and loving daughter, the grief and disappointment that the match would bring upon her family; or still worse, a separation forever from a mother to whom she was devotedly attached.

I walked slowly on through the darkening streets until I reached the small park or square on the further side of which Captain Lee's house, with its narrow strip of garden, fronted. The moon had just risen and its light fell full upon the portico and steps.

" Surely some one is sitting there ! " I said to myself as I drew gradually nearer, to see whether or not my eyes had played me false in the uncertain light. No ; I was right ; they had not deceived me ; there was a lady, by herself, upon the steps. I did not for an instant doubt whom it might be, and on the impulse of the moment crossed the park and entered the little garden.

" Good evening, Mr. Strong," she said, smiling brightly and holding out her hand as I advanced to meet her. " Won't you come in? I came out here to get a breath of fresh air after this terrible day. Papa and mamma and Mr. Brown are in the drawing-room. Won't you come in? "

"O no, I thank you!" I replied. "It is pleasanter here. It would be the basest ingratitude to waste such a night as this."

"I quite agree with you, but I thought you might like to see them."

"No," I answered monosyllabically, and somewhat forgetful of the demands of politeness. "Let me arrange that rug for you."

She reseated herself upon the rug, that I had spread near one of the pillars in the moonlight, and I sat down at her feet. She wore a muslin gown, gathered in at the throat and with loose wide sleeves; a soft white shawl was thrown about her shoulders. A little spray of yellow jessamine was fastened in her bosom, and a single rosebud in her hair.

For a few moments, neither of us spoke.

She looked bewitchingly lovely, as she sat there gazing up into the night, with her head resting lightly on her hand; and I longed to tell her of all that had filled my heart during this month of silence, yet dreaded to begin.

At last, I said, looking up into her face.

"Did you expect me, to-night?"

"No, I did not expect you, and yet," she added slowly, "and yet I thought that you might come."

"Why did you think so?" I asked.

"I cannot tell. For no reason. I only felt that you might."

"It is something that you even thought of me," I said in a low voice, and leaning slightly forward to catch her expression. "May I not believe, too, that you wished to have me come?"

While I spoke, her face grew very grave, and turning it away from me, she answered quietly,—

"Yes, I am glad you came."

"Thank you," I said; "you do not know what a struggle it has been to keep away from you these last few weeks, or to be near you, and feel that I could not speak."

"I do not understand you," she answered, glancing up again, and then added with a faint smile, "but, then, as I have often told you, I suppose I never shall."

"Why, surely, you know the reason. Your mother must have told you."

"No, Mr. Strong, mamma has told me nothing. What do you mean?" she asked, looking anxiously into my face.

I was so astonished that for a moment I had not a word to say. Then, after all, her mother had not spoken. Could it be that she had felt too sure of Mary to think it necessary; or, was it possible that her own mind had changed?

However, I would not conceal what had passed between her mother and me, whatever the result might be, and so I answered as steadily as I could, "When your mother interrupted us a month ago, she was very indignant with me. She would scarcely listen to me. She declared she would rather see you dead than married to a Northerner. She was unjust and cruel. She tried to drive me from you without another word, but finding that impossible, she made me promise not to speak to you again till now. And now "—I went on in a low tone, feeling my pulses quicken and my heart beat—" and now, I have come to tell what I have so often longed to say."

"Oh! do not speak so, Mr. Strong, please do not go on; I cannot listen to you!" she cried, in a trembling voice, looking down at me with a face as white as the moonlight itself.

"Yes, my darling, you must listen to me," I answered firmly and quietly. "You must listen to me, though there is little left to say that you do not know already—that my whole heart is yours—that your love alone——"

"O do not say so! do not say so! You must not. It is impossible!" she cried, holding out her hands as if to stop me.

I felt myself trembling from head to foot, but tried to control my voice and answer quietly,—

"What is impossible? Not that I love you, I know. Not that you care a little for me, I believe."

"I do not love you. You are wrong!" she exclaimed. "What do I know about you? I do not understand you. We should never understand each other. We have been brought up so differently. O no! I do not love you. Do not speak of it again. O do not speak of it again!"

She turned her face away to hide her tears. Her hands were clasped across her knees. I disengaged them softly and held them in both of mine.

"Indeed, dearest," I said, "it is true, you do

know very little of me. A little while ago we had
never heard of one another, and yet, I think you
must believe me, when I tell you that I love you,
and shall love you always, whatever happens. Look
in my face and tell me if you do not believe me."

"Oh! I cannot tell," she answered, raising for one
moment her glistening eyes, "I suppose what you
say is true, or that you think it is; but I do not
care for you, at least not in that way. If I loved
you, I should be willing to give up everything for
your sake, but I cannot—I will not—Do not ask
me. It is impossible!"

"I will not worry you any more to-night," I said,
raising her hands to my lips. "But won't you give
me a little hope before I go?"

"I have none to give," she answered slowly and
sadly as she withdrew her hands from mine. "It
would be cruel, if you love me as you say, for I
know I shall never change my mind, and you will
forget about it all when you have gone away."

"You do not yourself believe what you are saying, Mary. If I went North to-morrow and were
never to see you again, I should never forget the
sweetness that has stolen into my life since I first
knew you!" While I was speaking we had both
arisen and I was standing on the step below her.

"Are you going?" she asked, as I held out my
hand, and then added in a hesitating voice, "But—
but—you will not think unkindly of me? We may
still be friends?"

"Friends!" I cried passionately, losing for the

moment all self-control. " Don't speak of friends to
me. I hate the word! I shall never love you less
than I do to-night. You must—you shall love me!
No, my darling, I will never give you up!"

We stood confronting one another. The moon
shone full upon her face, touching with silver the
clusters of her wavy hair.

There was a startled expression on her slightly
parted lips and in her sparkling eyes as they looked
straight into mine.

I seized her in my arms and pressed my lips
passionately to hers.

"O stop, stop this instant! How dare you?"
she cried, struggling to free herself from my close
embrace and, tearing herself away, she fled into the
house.

Half bewildered, I stood and watched her as
she sped like a gleam of moonlight across the
shadows of the hall and vanished at the turning of
the staircase. Then stooping down I picked up
the spray of jessamine that had fallen upon the
steps, and gently kissed it.

I passed through the garden and out into the
street. I was intoxicated with excitement. I still
felt the thrilling touch of her lips and the throbs
of her pliant form as I pressed her for a moment to
my heart. Her very tones of anger rung like sweet
music in my ears!

I passed up the street and into the deserted park,
neither knowing nor caring where I went, so that I
might only be alone. On and on I wandered, now

in this direction, now in that; through the winding paths among the shrubbery, under the tall
pines, or across the open lawns.

What with the exercise and the night air, little
by little I regained composure and drew in the
reins of my excited imagination. Slowly, but clearly,
the words that she had said came back to me,
and with them, in the reaction, misgivings and uncertainty.

At last I sat down upon a bench in the shadow
of a clump of shrubbery. How long I had remained there dreaming, I do not know, when my
attention was suddenly arrested by a woman's voice
close by; one that I could not mistake. Its tones
were excited and low, but I heard the words distinctly.

" You will make me hate you if you say such
things. What has he ever done to you? It is a
cowardly threat, but I think you must have said it
only to frighten me! Come, I have listened to you
too long already."　　　　　.

Then a man's voice answered inaudibly, and the
first voice spoke again,—

" If you loved me as you say you do, you would
never ask it. I tell you I cannot, I will not do it.
Come, I must go at once! " Almost Mary's words
to me and yet how different.

They had evidently paused a moment on the
other side of the thicket behind me.

I had arisen, and as they stopped speaking they
came out into the moonlit path in front of me, face

to face. It was Madge and Colonel Shorter.
Neither of us spoke.

Excepting for one quick glance, Shorter took no
notice of me whatever, and not a muscle of his face
changed. Madge started slightly back, and then,
with a haughty inclination of her head, she took his
arm, and they passed down the path together out
of sight.

I went slowly back to the hotel, absorbed in
thought. What could it mean? I believed in
Madge, in her pride as well as in her purity. But,
alas! what indiscretion, if nothing more!

To what scandal would it not give rise, if it were
known that she had been seen in the Park, at such an
hour of the night, with a man of Richard Shorter's
questionable reputation.

Something should be done, and done quickly, to
bring the poor girl to her senses; but how, and by
whom? Certainly not by me.

CHAPTER XXII.

ADVICE.

I TOOK occasion on the following morning to call on Mrs. Jackson just before lunch, as I knew from experience that she was usually at home, and often alone at that hour.

I found her in her morning-room, writing at her Davenport in some neat little red-covered books (everything about Kate was sweet, fresh and neat) making up her accounts, she said.

I begged her not to let me interrupt her, but she insisted upon putting her books away and coming to the sofa where I had seated myself.

I was still full of last night's meeting, and, in fact, had come to-day to discover how far she was aware of Madge's continued intimacy with Shorter, and, if possible without alarming her, to put her on her guard.

To Jim I should have spoken plainly, as men can, when necessary, speak to one another without fear of being misunderstood. But I felt keenly alive to the difficulty of dealing with a woman, as well as to the delicacy of my own position.

"I suppose you have not heard from Jim lately?" I asked, when she had seated herself beside me.

" No, not a word since you told me he was going

up the Ocklawaha. I do so wish he would come
home. You know what good reason I have to
wish it!" she said with emphasis. "But then, too,
I wish he would come for your sake. It would be
so much pleasanter for you if he were here. There
is little that I can do for you now. You must find
it very dull."

"No! not a bit of it. I have enough to keep
me busy, in one way or another, though I should
rejoice with all my heart to see Jim back again for
both our sakes. Still, with this delicious spring air
to breath and live in, and you to welcome me from
time to time, I have nothing to complain of but the
shortness of the winter, and the fact that my visit
is so rapidly drawing to a close."

"Ah, but surely you will soon come back to us
again, now that you have found the way here."

"I cannot tell," I answered, almost with a sigh.
"As we cannot see a day ahead, I try never to
worry myself over plans for the future. Perhaps
I may come again next winter; perhaps in twenty
years; and just as likely never. Who can tell?"

"Well, at all events, do not talk about it in that
horrid way, Harry. I hate to think beforehand of
my friends leaving me. It is bad enough when the
time comes. Thank fortune, you are not going
to-day nor to-morrow, nor next week, nor the week
after, so we will drop the subject if you please.
In a short time our out of door parties and picnics
will begin, and then, if you do not desert us, I think I
myself shall take up society again for a while."

Here seemed to be an opening not to be lost, and
I asked rather abruptly. "You go nowhere now,
do you? Were you at home last night?"

"Yes. Why do you ask?"

"I thought of coming to see you," I answered,
surprised at my own mendacity.

"Yes, I was at home and alone. I wish you had
come. Why didn't you?"

"Well, it was so long since I had been to the
Lees', I decided to call there instead."

"Why, Madge went there to supper, too, last
evening," she exclaimed, "so you must have seen
her. How strange she should not have mentioned
it!"

"Yes, I did meet her," I said slowly, fairly
staggered by Madge's duplicity; or had she been
there and left before I called? But Kate went on
without noticing me.

"We were both asked; but I have not taken a
meal at the Lees' since Jim's trouble, and could not
make up my mind to go. I bear no ill will to Mary,
for I do not suppose she deliberately went to work
to deceive him; but of all flirts, preserve me from
those innocent girls who are always in earnest!
Don't you agree with me?" and without waiting
for a reply she continued, "However, I persuaded
Madge to go, for I was afraid they might feel hurt
if we both refused. I have an idea that your comical
friend, Mr. Brown, walked home with her."

Before she had done speaking the young lady
herself, in her hat and walking dress, entered the

room. The door had been standing half open, so that she must at least have heard Kate's last words, and how much more I could not tell. She paused a moment on the threshold, and as she looked up from the glove she was drawing on, she blushed crimson.

"Sister," she said, "I am going shopping."

"Shall you be back to lunch?"

"No, don't wait for me. Good-by."

I had risen to speak to her, but she looked straight by me and turning abruptly, left the room without another word.

Fortunately, Kate had crossed the room to ring the bell for lunch, and having her back toward us, lost this little pantomime. Most fortunately, I thought; for otherwise, no doubt, Kate's questions would have brought on a distressing scene.

After Madge had gone, she returned to her seat beside me, and said,—

"I believe I must be a great coward, for, do you know, I have never yet dared to speak to Madge. I have tried a dozen times to approach the subject, but I cannot come to the point. There is something about her that perplexes me—something that I do not understand—an expression in her face sometimes that makes me almost afraid of her; and yet I long to throw my arms about her neck and beseech her to tell me what is the matter. She is very much changed—oh, so much! Do you not see it, Harry?"

"Possibly," I said, indeed not knowing what to answer.

"I feel as if something must have happened to her. What, I cannot tell. However," she continued, with a long drawn breath, "I lay awake thinking about it all last night, and fully made up my mind to have a plain talk with her this evening, whatever comes of it."

Poor Kate! I could not warn her of her sister's deceit and folly. I could not tell her that if Madge went to the Lee's at all, she must have left there very early in the evening; and that I had met her late at night with Shorter, in the park. And yet I felt, more strongly than ever, the necessity of overcoming her weakness and timidity.

"You are right, my dear sister," I said earnestly, "you must not delay another day. In fact, I wish you to give me your word that you will speak to-night, without fail."

"What do you mean?" she asked, looking up quickly and suspiciously into my face. "You know more than you have said. What is it? Tell me, what do you mean?"

"I know nothing," I answered, quietly and decidedly. "But you must remember how you told me long ago, that you should speak, and yet you have not. I know you believe it should be done, and I know, too, it will help you, if you promise me. That is all."

"Well, I will promise, Harry," she answered, with a dreary sigh.

I stayed with her awhile after lunch to smoke my cigar upon her shady balcony. And, at last, I left her in better spirits, and returned to the hotel to get ready for my ride; for every afternoon before dinner, I took a canter through the woods on "Vixen;" sometimes to one of the little hamlets on the "Salts," and sometimes back into the slowly blossoming country.

The day after my talk with Kate, I dined with the Lees. None but the family and Fred Brown were there. Fred had been so busy for the last few weeks, revising and correcting the Captain's "Reminiscences of the Confederate Navy," that I had seldom met him. He was one of those men, who, when once interested in their work, give their undivided energies to its completion, with little rest and no thought of time.

Even if this fixedness of purpose does not in itself insure success, it is, at least, the spade, the pickaxe and the powder that can alone make ready for the culminating spark. But avoid such men when the fit is on them, for, from a social standpoint, they are worse than useless; even their presence is a damper upon society, no matter how agreeable they may be at other times.

And so it was with Brown on the night in question; but soon after dinner, to the relief of all, he retired to the study.

"Where," as the Captain sympathetically remarked, "the poor fellow has passed the greater part of the day. But he has a wonderful power of setting things straight, and bringing out new points in my book—points that I should never have discovered by myself. Why, you would scarcely recognize my manuscript now! He has cut and altered it from its fatigue dress into full regimentals! Really, I had no idea there was so much in it (in fact, between ourselves, there wasn't), but now you may expect to see my name and writings an authority! I don't know what I should have done without him."

After dinner we took our coffee on the verandah. Thus far I had found no opportunity to speak alone with Mary, but at last her father called upon her to sing, and after some hesitation she yielded and arose to go into the house.

"Let me open the piano for you," I said, joining her.

"O no," she answered, stopping hesitatingly at the window; "do not trouble yourself to come. I do not need you."

However, I was not to be stopped by a word, and followed her into the room. The gas was not lighted. She did not wish it. The light from the hall was enough. She should sing without her notes.

As I opened the piano, I said, speaking low and rapidly,—

"Mary, I hope you can answer me to-night."

"You must not call me Mary, Mr. Strong," she said, without raising her eyes from the pile of music over which she was bending. "I thought I answered you plainly before. I shall not change my mind. What more can I say?"

"But I did not believe you. I do not believe you now. I am sure you cannot mean it. Tell me, my——"

"Stop, Mr. Strong," she said, stepping slightly back as I approached her. "Do. not come a step nearer, I command you. I will not have a repetition of the disgraceful scene of the other night! Your pretended respect for me should have restrained you. I tell you plainly, once and for all, that I do not love you, and I never shall. If you value my friendship, you must never, never speak to me in this way again."

· I could not see the expression of her face in the uncertain light, but the sound of her voice was quiet and firm, and I believed that what she said, she meant. If my ear had caught the slightest tremor I would have stayed to fight it out, but as it was, I turned away without a word and retraced my steps to the verandah.

I was completely baffled, for it seemed that, after all, my hopes must have been entirely groundless, and yet I could not wholly believe that I had so deceived myself.

"Isn't Mary going to sing?" asked her father, after I had taken my seat beside him again.

"O yes, I think so," I replied, "I believe she is looking for her music."

The Captain went on chatting in a desultory way, and I did my best to answer him, while every faculty of my being was listening for the sound of her voice. But at last my inattention must have attracted his notice, for he stopped talking, and I was conscious of having made some mistake, and unable to rectify it. So we sat for some time in silence, until he suddenly exclaimed,—

" Why, I wonder what has become of her ! " and stepping to the window, he called,—" Mary ! Mary ! aren't you going to sing to us ? Our patience is almost exhausted ! "

" Yes, papa, in a moment," she answered from within ; and shortly after she struck some stray chords on the piano and then began the plaintive song.

> " Out on the meadows fair,
> Flowers scent the summer, air."

I had often heard her sing it, and sing it well ; but now, when she came to the last verse, which is particularly sad, her voice entirely failed her, and after trying to go on twice in vain, she came to the window and said, with evident embarrassment,—

" I am very sorry, papa, to make such a failure, but my voice has deserted me."

The Captain laughed it off good-naturedly, and made her draw a chair close to his own and sit down beside him.

" I don't care about your singing, my dear, unless you feel like it. The voice, I find, can never be depended upon, except when we stub our toes ! Strong, here, has heard you too often to doubt either your good-nature or ability."

I did not speak to Mary again that night, and I left at an early hour, with a feeing of hopelessness that can be readily imagined.

Oddly enough it happened that, on the morning after this, I received a long and affectionate letter from Alice. She wrote :

" Of course, my dear brother, you would not take the step that you propose without having thought it all over thoroughly. I have no doubt Miss Lee is as lovely as you say she is ; but you should not forget how totally different is the bringing up of these Southern girls from what you have been accustomed to, and how entirely their ideas of every-thing must differ from yours. I know they are said to be attractive and fascinating in society, but that is not all a man wants in a wife, and especially you. So I am only afraid you may live to be dis-appointed, my dear brother ; for although coquetry and flirtation and that sort of thing may be excusable in young girls, they are not, according to my ideas, becoming in married women, no matter what people may say, and I am certain they must lead to un-happiness. Of course, after passing a winter among them you ought to be the best judge, but men are so stupid about such things ! I have often heard, too, that they are lazy and idle, and grow up without any fixed object in life, although possibly this may be exaggerated ; but you must forgive me for putting you on your guard, my dear brother, because I do love you so very much. But I must say that I have met some few of them myself, and have always found their views so diametrically opposed to ours, that I cannot help being surprised that a man of your good judgment should fall in

love with one of them, when there are so many nice
girls left in your own city—ones, too, that we know
all about, and of our own way of thinking. If you
were still a boy it would not strike me as so strange.
However, I do not say all this to influence you, if
you have really taken the step, but simply wish you
to consider everything, and not to decide hastily.
I was dreadfully sorry I was not at home when your
letter first came, so that I could have answered it at
once. Of course, my dearest brother, if you offer
yourself to Miss Lee, I shall do everything in my
power to make her love me as a sister. I am crazy
with excitement about it, so do not fail to let me
know as soon as it is settled, so that I can write and
congratulate her without delay. Perhaps you had
better telegraph me, and remember to send me her
photograph by the very next mail."

Notwithstanding my unhappiness, I could not
help smiling grimly at Alice's letter. Even a suspicion of the possibility of my failure had never entered her mind. To her prejudiced affection there
could be no question of my success ; I had only to
woo to win !

I put her letter in my pocket, feeling in no mood
to write to her, but inclined rather to take flight by
the first northern bound steamer, and answer her in
person.   .

But the next morning found me still undecided.
I could not make up my mind to leave without again
seeing Jim, and before the day was out events took
place that settled the question, and forced me to
remain.

CHAPTER XXIII.

AN ENCOUNTER.

IT was a bright, clear day; and with it dawned upon me the conviction that what I most needed was vigorous exercise. So after breakfast, I started forth and walked through the outlying country to a little village on the "Salts," some eight or ten miles away.

The trees were rapidly pushing out their leaves, and the scent of early flowers was in the air. Birds of gay plumage flashed across my path or twittered their love songs in the neighboring thickets.

The sights and sounds of spring acted upon me, as I had hoped, like a healthful tonic, and my spirits rose and steps grew more elastic, as I left the city with its cares farther and farther behind me; and when at last I reached my destination, my troubles were for the time being scattered to the winds, and my appetite keen for the lunch of fish and fresh boiled crabs, that was served up to me in the shady dining-room of an inn, whose windows overlooked the marshes.

After lunch I took possession of a hammock swung across the end of the broad piazza, and lay there 'sniffing' the cool salt air, that came creeping inland from the sea, until the shadows began to lengthen and I was obliged reluctantly to turn my face again towards the town.

At home, a walk like this would have been nothing to me, but now I began to feel the effects of the enervating climate, and on my way back the road seemed to draw itself out to twice its actual length, and by the time I reached the hotel I was pretty thoroughly 'done up.' However, after a good bath and my dinner the effects passed off and left me all the better for my exercise.

In the evening I went out with the intention of calling upon Mrs. Jackson, whom I had not seen for the last two days, but on the way I bethought myself that Madge would probably be at home, and, therefore, I had better put off my visit until the following morning. So I retraced my steps for a block or two and turned into the broad street that led to the Club.

The night was dark, but the gaslight burning over the entrance to the Club, showed me, as I approached, three men standing on the sidewalk just in front of it, earnestly talking together.

At first I did not recognize them, but, as I was about to enter the open doorway, one of them stepped forward and touching me on the shoulder, said, in a low tone,—

"I have a word to say to you, sir."

Turning back, I saw that it was Colonel Shorter. His whole bearing told me at once that something

serious was "up." Although his manner was cool
and quiet, the intonation of his voice warned me
that his intentions must be other than friendly.

His companions, whom I now recognized as friends
of his, but not of mine, stood some half a dozen
steps off, watching us.

"Well, sir, say what you have to say, I am listening," I answered, provoked at his aggressive manner,
but determined, if possible, to keep my temper.

"I want you to understand, then, sir, once for all,
that I will put up with no interference from you in
my affairs. You have dogged my footsteps too
long already. I have had enough of your insolent——"

"Stop," I said, interrupting him, "if you cannot
speak with decent courtesy you shall not speak at
all. Your affairs are not in themselves of the
slightest consequence to me, but if they involve my
friends, it may be different. As to my time, it has
not yet become worthless enough for me to waste it
in dogging your uncertain footsteps. You are flattering yourself, Mr. Shorter!"

I felt the blood boil within me. I hated the man.
I was in no mood to brook his insulting tone, and
with great difficulty restrained myself.

"How dare you speak so to me! I will hold you
strictly to account for this," he cried, stepping
nearer to me with clenched hands, and hissing the
words into my face.

My first impulse was to strike him, but it flashed
across me that any trouble between us might drag

Madge's name before the public; so that I must, if possible, avoid open hostilities.

"Come, I think, we have had enough of this nonsense," I answered, with forced composure. "It would be a pity to make fools of ourselves for nothing, and I trust you will not compel me to it."

As I spoke, I stepped back a pace or two, but my words and movement seemed only further to exasperate him; for before I had stopped speaking he advanced rapidly upon me with dilated eyes and voice hoarse with fury.

"You miserable Yankee dog! you liar! you coward! you shall—," he cried, and a moment later he was lying on his back in the middle of the street.

"By Heaven, you have killed him!" shouted one of his friends, as they ran to his assistance, for he lay motionless.

"My God! I hope I have! It would serve him right!" I cried, infuriated by Shorter's insults, and ready for hot work, now my hand was in.

They bent over him, unfastened his shirt collar, and raised him slowly to his feet. He was apparently faint or dizzy, and did not speak; in fact, could hardly walk. His friends muttered to one another, but I could not catch their words, and they did not again address me. I stood upon the curbstone and watched them, as they carried him down the street, and disappeared in the darkness.

Notwithstanding my excitement, a smile of gratified pride stole over my face at the very clean sweep I had made, and the appreciation of my success quickly restored my equanimity. It had indeed been a "stinger," and my knuckles still ached! I had cross-countered him, and was altogether too well satisfied at finding my early training still serviceable, to consider, at the time, the probable results of the encounter.

I took a turn up and down the sidewalk to satisfy myself that I was perfectly cool, and then went into the Club.

In the reading-room, I found half a dozen men, and among them Major Barnwell, who arose, and crossed the room to speak to me.

"Have you seen Jim Eustis, Mr. Strong?" he asked.

"Why, no, Major, what do you mean? Jim has not returned, has he?" I exclaimed in surprise.

"Yes, indeed he has. He got back last night. I saw him to-day, and he told me he had been looking everywhere for you."

"I have been out of town, but I did not expect him for a week or two yet. Do you happen to know where he is to-night?"

"I think he said he should pass the evening at home."

"I am much obliged to you Major; I shall hunt him up at once. Good night," and so saying I left the Club and hastened to Mrs. Jackson's.

When I reached the house, Jim was just coming out, and had stopped on the steps to light a cigar.

"Well, old boy," I cried, as he seized me by the hand, "this is a surprise indeed. I am delighted to see you back again. Why didn't you look me up last night?"

"I did not get in till late, and then, I was too busy to leave the house. I have been looking for you, however, all day, and was just now going to inquire for you at your hotel. But come into the library; Kate and Madge have gone to bed, so we shall not be disturbed, and I have much to say to you. You people seem to have kept things pretty lively here since I went away. Where have you been all day? I have hunted for you high and low!"

In the meantime we had entered the library and seated ourselves in the dark, by an open window.

"Well, you must be pretty well tired, after such unusual exertion," he said, when I had told him of my walk to the "Salts." Here, put this chair under your legs, and make yourself comfortable. Take a fresh cigar. There now, this seems quite like old times again," he added, as he reseated himself in an armchair opposite to me. He was evidently in better spirits than when he went away, and I rejoiced to hear something of the old hearty ring in his voice.

"Harry," he began again, "I have so much to say I don't know where to begin."

"Well, then," I replied, "suppose you let me ask you two questions, and perhaps they may lead you to the point. First, why did you stay away so long? and second, why did you come home so unexpectedly?"

"You already know my only answer to your first

question, Harry," he said very gravely; and after a short pause he went on,—"The answer to your second involves a rather unpleasant family matter; perhaps I should not mention it, but I understand from sister Kate, that she has already spoken to you about it."

He stopped a moment as if expecting me to speak, but as I said nothing he went on.

"Just after writing you last, our party was delayed for a couple of days at Palatka, one of the men was taken ill, nothing serious, and on the very morning that we were ready to start again, I got a letter from Kate, telling me about this fellow Shorter. So I gave up my trip and took the next steamer down the river. I missed connections at Jacksonville and had to 'lay over' there another day and so did not arrive here till last night. I was a good deal worked up about this affair, Harry, for Madge had better have never been born than marry such a scoundrel. I have always known him and the profligacy of his life. He has no right to ask any decent woman to marry him. And then the insolence of his paying such attention to her in my absence, and after what had passed between himself and me. When I think of it, I can scarcely contain myself!" he exclaimed with knit brows, jumping up from his seat and starting restlessly up and down the room. "However," he said more quietly, coming back at last and siting·down again. "I have put a stop to it now, I think. But it was most fortunate I came home

before it had gone any farther. I had a long
talk with Madge last night. She was very indignant with me for interfering. I have never seen
her so provoked before. But after a while I managed, I trust, to bring her to her senses and enable
her to see the man in his true colors. I did not
mince matters, for I saw I could not move her
without telling her the whole truth about the fellow.
It was bad work, but there seemed no help for it,
so I laid the case before her without paint or white-
wash. Gad! when I stopped she was livid with
passion! and then burst into a flood of tears.
Poor girl! I cannot tell you how badly I felt. And
do you know," he continued after a pause, " from
first to last she hardly uttered a single word. I
suppose she could not believe it. Well, it did seem
cruel enough to.speak so to her. But, by Jove, sir,
she's a wonderful girl; for although she cut up so
very rough last night, she came down in the morning, after a good night's rest, almost herself again.

She looked as if she had cried her eyes out, but
she was as sweet as she could be. And all day
to-day it has seemed as if she couldn't do enough
to make up for her folly and the anxiety she has
given. After breakfast, I wrote a note to Shorter.
I did not say much, but I flatter myself it was to the
point. I swear, Harry, if that man ever crosses
my path again, I cannot answer for the consequences!" he cried fiercely, and then added more
calmly, " but after what I have written him to-day
I doubt if he ever troubles me again."

I had never known Eustis so thoroughly wrought up and I saw that his feeling towards Shorter was no longer one of simple dislike, but of settled hatred, which, if once roused into action, would hesitate at nothing that is supposed to become a gentleman.

Jim's explanation fully accounted for Shorter's attack upon me that evening. It was natural enough that knowing my intimate relations with the family, and recalling the times when I had interrupted his interviews with Madge, he should have suspected me of acting the spy and informer, and of being, in all probability, the cause of his troubles.

In Jim's present state of mind, I did not think it prudent to tell him of my difficulty with Shorter, fearing lest, on the impulse of the moment, he might do something rash. Of course, sooner or later, he would be sure to hear of it, but in the meantime his own feelings might change, and, at least, the immediate danger of his suspecting that Madge was the cause of our quarrel might be averted. We talked on for an hour longer, chiefly of Jim's experiences in Florida and when at last I rose to go he said,—

"I cannot speak to you to-night, Harry, about your own affairs. We must keep them for another time. But I would like to ask you one question before you go. Of course you must answer it or not as you see fit. You remember what you wrote me—have you prospered?"

As he spoke, he looked earnestly into my face.

"No, Jim, I have not," I answered quietly,

"I might have expected it, if I had not been a fool!"

"What! Has Mary refused you?" he exclaimed with undisguised astonishment, and then seeming to reflect awhile, he added, "I cannot understand it; you surprise me very much. I must take time to think of this."

"Perhaps, after all, my dear fellow," I said puzzled by his manner and laying my hand upon his shoulder, "perhaps, after all, it will prove to be your gain, and if it should, you must believe me when I say I shall still rejoice with you—none more."

"No, no, my boy, that will never be!" he answered almost with a smile. That was a dream never to be realized—a very, very pleasant one—my dream for years, and one that will always be the sweetest of my life, but nothing more. However," he went on more cheerfully, "we will talk this all over to-morrow or next day. If you are to be in your rooms at about twelve to-morrow I will drop in and lunch with you. I have some business to attend to just after breakfast, and, in the afternoon, I must drive out to The Oaks and pass the night there."

So it was arranged that we should lunch together the next day and having bade him good-night I started for home.

As I turned the first street corner, I almost ran into two men coming in the opposite direction, and we stopped short to let each other pass. We happened to be under a gaslight, and I recognized old January as one of them, and spoke a word to him

in passing. The man with him was near the wall
and more in shadow, so that I could not see his face,
but there was something about his gigantic size and
shuffling gait that struck me as familiar, although I
could not remember at the moment where I had come
across him. It flashed across me presently, however,
that it was Armstrong, or one who bore a striking
resemblance both to him and to the man I had seen
the day I drove to Martha's with Mrs. Jackson.

I had never met Armstrong face to face but
once, that time at the polls so long ago. But he
had made too strong an impression upon me to be
easily forgotten, and, I felt convinced that I was
not now mistaken in the man.

But why should he be in company with one of
Jim's servants? Certainly for no good purpose.

I stopped, with the half formed intention of returning to tell Jim and put him on his guard. But,
after all, was it worth while to disturb him again
to-night? I might possibly have been mistaken,
and if not, I reflected, my meeting them would, in
itself, be sufficient to put a stop, for the present, to
any evil scheme they might have been brewing.

So determining to tell Jim what I had seen, when
he should lunch with me on the morrow, I kept on
to my hotel and to bed.

CHAPTER XXIV.

AN EXPLANATION.

IT was the morning of Friday the 27th of March ; and floods of warm sunlight were pouring into my room when I arose. I looked at my watch and, finding it already half-past ten, decided to put off my breakfast until twelve, the hour that Jim was to lunch with me; so I dressed leisurely, and having ordered a cup of coffee, sat down to answer my last letter from Alice.

But Jim proved better than his word, and before I had fairly begun writing, came rushing into my room. I saw at once from his expression and the excitement of his manner, that there was something, "in the wind;" nor did I have to await an explanation any longer than was necessary for him to get his breath, after running up the two flight of stairs to my rooms.

"Why, Harry," he exclaimed, flinging himself into an armchair by the open window, "why the devil didn't you tell me last night about your row with Shorter? When was it? what does it mean? how did it happen?"

"One at a time, young man," I said, smiling at his impetuosity, "keep cool!—Really, you bewilder me. Suppose you try a cup of that coffee to restore your equanimity. Shall I tie a cold-water bandage round your head?"

"No, thank you," he answered, smiling faintly and holding up his hand, as I dipped the end of a towel into the water pitcher. "But really this is no joking matter. The men at the Club tell me, and in fact it is all over town, that you gave Dick Shorter a terrible thrashing last night, and that he challenged you. Why even the girls at home knew of it before I did this morning. When did it happen? After you left me?"

"No, early in the evening."

"Then, as I said before," he burst out again, "why on earth didn't you tell me of it?"

"Well, I thought you had enough on your mind last night, without bothering about my affairs. Besides, you are wrong; no challenge has passed; the thing was not of any great importance."

"Nonsense, Harry, challenge or no challenge, you will find .before long it is of the utmost importance!"

"Well, then, only to me at any rate, you must allow," I said quietly.

"I cannot be so sure of that until you have told me what led up to it."

"A very bad pass on his part led up to it, my boy. One that you as a favorite disciple of our old friend Hercules B. would never have been guilty of" I rattled on. "He just gave himself away at the first 'go off,' or rather 'come on.'"

"Come, Harry," he said gravely, interrupting me, "do talk seriously, I beg of you. This is indeed no time for jesting, and I am quite in earnest when I say I wish to know all about it."

In point of fact, I had been "beating about the bush," to give myself time to consider how much or how little it would be right and necessary for me to say. I could not tell him the whole truth and, I argued to myself, a part would be worse than none. So I logically decided to tell him none, and replied with gravity equal to his own,—

"The fact is, Jim, that Shorter and I were standing by the Club, talking together, when he said something I could not pretend to endorse, and I told him so. Thereupon he took upon himself to speak to me in a tone that I considered simply insulting. You know his manner. It is unnecessary for me to explain it to you. Probably, the same kind of aggressive impertinence led to your first difficulty with him. I gave him to understand that he was a trifle too overbearing, and I was not in the habit of allowing myself to be ridden over, rough shod. He was apparently too obtuse, however, to appreciate the force of my remarks, and grew more insolent than ever. Well I can't remember now exactly what followed, but one thing led to another, until at last he called me a 'damned Yankee,' or words to that effect, and I knocked him down. That is the whole story."

"Are you sure that is all, Harry?" he asked dubiously.

"Isn't that enough? Why, man, what more would you have had me do? Would you have had me beat him after he was down? Or desecrate your native soil by jamming his impudent face into it? Enough?" I went on mockingly, "even you would have thought so, you sanguinary man, if you had seen his condition when his friends picked him out of the gutter, to carry him home!"

I saw he was watching me closely, as if he half doubted my excellent story, and when I stopped speaking, he looked away without a smile, and sat gazing fixedly out of the window, beating the devil's tattoo upon the sill.

Presently, however, he turned to me again and said, still seriously,—

"Well, you know of course what the consequences will be?"

"Really, as yet, I have not dwelt upon them. I am not in the habit of worrying myself about troubles till they actually confront me."

"He will undoubtedly challenge you to-day or to-morrow," he continued, in the same impressive tone.

"Will he really?" I asked, raising my eyebrows and looking down into his sober face.

"Confound it!" he exclaimed, jumping up from his chair, "I do wish you would consider this like a sensible man. You provoke me with your pretended indifference. What will your answer be? You know he is a dead shot."

"I neither know, nor care anything about him,"

I answered seriously at last; "when his challenge comes it will be time enough to decide."

"Shall you accept it ?"

"Probably; if there is no square way out of it. Though it seems hardly worth while to risk one's life for such a miserable hound."

For some minutes he paced up and down the room with his head bent and his hands clasped behind his back, but suddenly he stopped short in front of me, and asked abruptly,—

"Then I am to understand, Harry, you have fully made up your mind to fight him ?"

"As I said before," I answered, "I have thought very little about it. I don't believe in duelling, and I can certainly gain nothing by it in this case. Still, if Shorter demands satisfaction, I am afraid (such is the influence of this semi-civilization of yours) I shall hardly have the moral courage to refuse."

"No, I suppose not, and there is no doubt whatever of his action in the matter," he answered rather to himself, than me; and then continuing his walk, apparently in deep thought, he went on,—

"By the way, Harry, I find I cannot lunch with you this morning; I have more to attend to than I had expected; I must go out to The Oaks and back again to-day; I shall not pass the night there, as I had intended, for you may need me. I will drop in on you some time this evening and see how matters stand. I cannot tell at what hour, but you may depend upon my coming. I do wish you would pass the evening with Kate and Madge," he said, pausing with one hand on the door knob, " but no, I forgot, they are both going to Mrs. King's party to-night. Well, perhaps it is just as well. Good-by, old fellow, God bless you ! " and stepping forward he shook me strongly by both hands and rushed from the room as hastily as he had entered it.

His whole manner throughout the interview struck me afterwards as strange and unnatural, but, at the time, I hardly observed it, attributing any-thing unusual in his conduct to his anxiety about me.

At the beginning of our talk, I had feared that he suspected the true cause of my difficulty with Shorter, but my explanation had seemed to satisfy him. I should have been wretched indeed if he had dis-covered that Madge was at the bottom of it all.

What I had told him was in a great measure true, that I felt very little personal anxiety. I did not realize, nor did I try to realize the dangerous possibilities of the case. I should have enough time for that when the challenge was actually received ; and meanwhile there was nothing but the sudden departure of my friend to interfere with my enjoyment of the excellent luncheon that had been so long delayed.

An hour afterwards I left my room and went to the Club to read the morning papers. Several men, whom I knew but slightly, were sittting in the reading-room chatting together, and, as I entered, I thought I heard my name mentioned. Whatever they were saying, they suddenly stopped when they saw me, and at once arose and came forward to shake hands; a flattering piece of politeness on their parts, and as unusual as it was unnecessary. Nor did their cordiality stop there. They surrounded me. They were effusive. They insisted upon my drinking with them; upon my trying their cigars. Wouldn't I play a game of billiards or a rubber at whist. In fact, they quite overwhelmed me with their attentions, and seeing that what I had in view was utterly out of the question, I beat a retreat as soon as I could do so with decent civility.

I took my usual canter through the woods that afternoon, and as I passed Captain Lee's, on my way home, I saw Mary sitting in her victoria at the gate and pulled up for a moment to speak to her. When I was about to go on again I asked,—

" Shall I see you at Mrs. King's to-night ? "

" No, I am not going. Are you ? " she replied quite unconcernedly.

" No, I am not; though a moment ago I might have answered differently."

As I spoke, a quick blush suffused her face, but she looked up at me out of her serious eyes, and answered earnestly,—

" I am very sorry indeed to hear you say so, Mr. Strong."

At that moment I saw Mrs. Lee coming down the steps to join her, so I merely bade her good-by and cantered on again down the green arched street to my hotel.

How I loved that woman! Her beauty, her voice, her expression; her every movement. They came flitting in and out among my thoughts, at all times and in all places. I could have worshipped the ground she trod on—have kissed the dust beneath her feet.

But how should I win her? If ever she had felt a little liking for me,—perhaps unacknowledged and scarcely realized—had I not destroyed it in a moment of ungoverned passion? If so, how could I regain her confidence and make her believe in me again. Of what value are protestations? *After* distrust has taken root, they are unavailing, *before*, they are unnecessary.

Gifted with insinuating speech or that power of giving weight to sentiment that some possess, I might still have hoped. But one cannot from boyhood repress the expression of emotion and think at my age to deliver himself successfully in rhapsodies. If spoken from the heart, what can sound truer, stronger, sweeter, than the simple words, "I love you?" Does not each syllable added to these weaken them? To me it does; beyond them I cannot go. Yet I have heard of—yes known men—to whom they were but the prelude to lovemaking, the mere beating of time with the foot before the waltz.

How well I recollect that Friday, the 27th of March. Each-little incident is chiselled sharp and clear upon my mind.

I can recall a thousand accessories trifling and unimportant in themselves, having little or no connection with the "grand motif" of the picture and yet as vividly remembered as its central figures. What a relief it would be to deal with them alone, or indeed to stop here altogether! But it is too late to draw back; we must go on; and no matter how warm and pleasant the summer sun upon our shoulders; no matter how cold and deep the water at our feet; we must take the plunge; and the longer we delay, the more difficult our task.

That evening after dinner I lounged about the portico of the hotel, until I had finished my cigar, when, attracted by gay voices above me, I went up stairs and sat for awhile on the open verandah just over the street, where half a dozen young people, tourists on their way home from Florida, were laughing and frolicking together in the cool shadows.

But I was singularly restless and uncomfortable, and instead of being amused, I soon tired of their rather noisy company, and left them to go to my room to write.

I got out my pen, ink and paper to finish the letter to Alice that I had begun in the morning and settled myself deliberately to my work. But it was useless. Even the half congealed ink at the bottom of the bottle flowed more freely than my thoughts.

I was obliged to give it up; and pushing my letter aside and driving the pen hard into the old pine-topped table, where it stood quivering on end, I sprung from my chair and walked nervously up and down the room.

How should I pass the evening? Should I go to the King's? I was expected and should be sure to meet Kate and Madge there. Lent was just over, and this was to be the last ball of the season.

Yes, I would go, if only for an hour. It could not prove less amusing than my own company.

I was in the act of taking out my clothes, but was stopped by the thought of what I had said to Mary, and threw them back into the trunk.

Well, perhaps, after all, I had better give it up and wait in my room for Jim. He would, probably, come in the course of an hour or so.

There was a half-read novel lying on my centre table. I picked it up, drew my armchair to the light, and sat down to read. I mechanically turned the pages, but that was all; they might have been written in Sanscrit for all their meaning to me!

Where was Jim? It was nearly ten o'clock, and still he did not come. Where was the challenge? Jim had seemed to feel so sure I should receive one, that I, too, had at last expected it. Was Shorter ill? or had he decided to let the matter drop? Its non-appearance was almost a disappointment to me in my restlessness. I began to feel curious to see a genuine challenge. How would it be worded? I soon found myself composing one and wondering whether it would conform to the regulations of the code.

I threw my neglected novel on the table and relighting my cigar, went to the open window and with elbows on the sill, looked out into the night.

It was cool and clear. The sky was full of stars, and the moon had just risen above the housetops across the square. The streets were quiet, and deserted, and the gaslights flickered here and there among the trees below me. What a still and peaceful night! Was that a policeman standing in shadow at the nearest corner. Yes, for I heard the thud of his club as he tapped it on the pavement and then walked slowly away.

There! in the hurry of Jim's morning visit I had forgotten to speak of my meeting with January and his suspicious looking companion. I must remember without fail to tell him of it. Where could he be? I looked at my watch for the fiftieth time. It was after eleven, and still no signs of him. Suddenly I heard footsteps hurrying rapidly along the hall, followed by a loud knocking at my door.

CHAPTER XXV.

MIDNIGHT.

"COME in ." I called out, facing about from the window where I had been standing.

One of the negro porters of the hotel entered hastily and handed me a letter.

" Is there any answer, sir ? " he asked, as I glanced at the address and then tore it open.

" Who brought this ? "

" A colored man, sir."

" No, only tell him—tell him, I will come."

" Yes, sir."

He slammed to the door and was gone.

The note was from Kate and evidently written in great haste. It ran thus,—" Dear Harry, come to me at once. Yours, C. J." " At once" was doubly underscored. What could it mean? I read it over and over, seeking in vain for some clue in the simple words. Then I seized my hat and cane and rushed from the hotel through the deserted streets to her house. When I rang at the door, Kate herself, in her ball-dress, opened it for me.

" Come in," she said, in a low voice and without another word, rapidly led the way back through the dark hall into her morning-room. I followed in silence. She closed the door softly and turned towards me, and then, for the first time, I saw her face. Her haggard expression and wild eyes, actually startled me. It seemed as if ten years had been added to her life since I saw her last.

" Madge has gone ! " she whispered, her frightened eyes fixed fast upon mine, and trembling from head to foot as she approached me.

" Gone? Gone where? What do you mean ? " I asked.

" She's gone, gone, gone ! How should I know where? We must find her. I'm all alone. Quick, quick ! Why don't you speak ? " she went on madly, coming close up to me. " We must not lose a moment or we may be too late. Why do you wait? I tell you, you must help me. Why were you so long? O Harry, what shall I do? what shall I do ? " and with a wild cry of anguish she threw herself sobbing upon my breast.

I led her gently to the sofa and made her sit down beside me. She was utterly unnerved and hysterical.

From the little she had said, I saw that there must be necessity for immediate action, but, of course, could do nothing until she had recovered sufficiently to explain what had happened. I did my best to soothe and reassure her, until she gradually became more tranquil and her sobbing ceased.

I felt there was danger of her becoming excited again, if I questioned her, but as fifteen minutes or more had been already wasted, I did not dare to delay any longer, and so ventured to say as gently as I could,—

" Now, my dear sister, you must tell me quietly all about it ; so that we may know just how to act."

To my relief, I found my fears were groundless. She could control herself at last, and when she answered me, although her words came slowly and tremulously, they were coherent ; and her voice gathered strength and steadiness as she went on.

Her story was a simple one. It seemed that Jim had gone to The Oaks in the afternoon, as he had intended, taking with him January and the express wagon, but had not yet returned, according to his promise.

Madge had been urgent to go to Mrs. King's party that night, and, after much persuasion, Kate had finally consented to chaperon her. They were to have gone at half-past nine, but, when the carriage came Madge was not ready; some trouble with her dress or hair. Might not Kate help her? No, if she would go down stairs, she would join her directly. Kate did as she was asked, and after she had been for some time in the drawing-room, Madge, instead of coming down, sent word to her not to wait any longer, but to go on without her and send the carriage back. So Kate went alone to Mrs. King's and ordered the coachman to drive home again for Madge, as she had been requested. At a quarter after ten Madge had not appeared, and still Kate thought little or nothing of it ; but, when it got to be half an hour later, and neither Madge nor any

message from her came, she grew alarmed, fearing
that something had gone wrong—that perhaps she
had been taken suddenly ill; for now she recalled
the fact that Madge had been looking far from well
that afternoon. Fortunately she found a carriage
without delay, and pleading her own indisposition,
left the party abruptly and drove directly home.

It was then eleven o'clock. The house was all
dark excepting a low light in the hall. The servants,
evidently had gone to bed, and she could see from the
street that there was no light in Madge's room. She
opened the front door with her pass-key and with
faltering steps ascended the stairs. The door of
Madge's room was locked and she could hear no
sound within in answer to her knocking. Remembering in a moment that both Madge's and her own
room opened on the same balcony, she passed quickly
out upon it, and half dead with fear entered Madge's
by the open window.

She lighted the gas and looked about her. Madge
was not there. Her room was in a state of great
confusion. Her ball dress was thrown upon the
bed. Some flowers for her hair were lying, already
half faded, upon her dressing-table. The wardrobe
door stood open; the drawers of the bureau had
been pulled half out and left so, and their con
tents scattered here and there about the room.
"What could it all mean?" she asked herself, and
as she stood there gazing vacantly about her, the
truth gradually dawned upon her! She rushed to
the closet where she knew Madge kept her portman-

teau. It was gone ! Now she saw it all ; and though
she hardly needed further confirmation of her fears,
she searched the house from top to bottom, but of
course in vain. What should she do ? Wake
the servants in the outbuildings across the yard.
Ah, no ! she could not do that. They could not
help her, and their prying curious eyes would
drive her mad. They should never know of it from
her ; no one should know of it so long as she had
power to prevent it. Yet how could she act without assistance? To whom should she turn? Suddenly she thought of David, Jim's body-servant.
He had been brought up with them from a child.
He was devoted to Madge. She herself could trust
thoroughly in his fidelity. He lived over the stable,
and there was a bell in his bedroom connected with
the house. She went to her morning-room and
rang for him. In a few minutes he came, and in the
meantime she had run upstairs and put Madge's
room in order (so thoughtful was she even in her
distress).

"Had David seen Miss Madge at any time during
the evening?" No, he had not. But shortly
after Mrs. Jackson went out, he had heard her
coming down the stairs, and just caught a glimpse of
her as she opened and shut the front door. A
few minutes later, Mrs. Jackson's carriage had returned and he told the coachman there must have
been some mistake, for Miss Madge had already gone.
To make sure of it, in fact, he had walked out upon
the pavement and looked up at her window. But,
as he had expected, her room was dark.

Then Kate had sent him for me. We neither of us questioned the cause of Madge's flight. We both knew there could be but one answer. And this, too, explained why I had not heard from Shorter. I took up the evening paper and glanced rapidly over the time tables. No steamboat left the city that night, but I found that a northern bound train would leave at a little past midnight. Kate was still sitting on the sofa eagerly watching me. " Is David at hand?" I asked,—

" Yes, he is in the dining-room waiting."

" Tell him to get out the carriage at once and wait for us at the back gate."

She jumped up and left the room to give the order, while I thought hurriedly over the course we should pursue. When she came back, I said.

" The Northern train leaves at quarter past twelve. No doubt they intend to take it, and we have not a moment to lose. Go up and change your dress, and wrap yourself up warm, for it will be chilly in the woods to-night."

" But shall we not go directly to the station ?"

" No, they would not take the train from here. We must go to the first station out of town."

" Why could we not go to Ocassee by the train ? then we should be sure not to miss them," she asked, still standing at the door.

" No ; we should be recognized at the station here, and, if possible, we must let no one see us. We can still reach Ocassee by the road if no time is lost.

Without another word she left the room, and before I had time to put on a heavy shawl of Jim's, that I found in the hall, she joined me again.

We stole noiselessly from the house to the back gate, where David was already waiting for us with the carriage. I quickly explained to him where we were to go. It was about five miles to Ocassee, and we still had nearly half an hour before the train was due there.

"All right, sir, we can do it if nothing breaks," he said, starting up the horses, while I jumped into the victoria beside Kate, and pulled the rugs about us.

Away we go at a tearing pace, sweeping through the city streets with scarce a sound except that of the wheels as they hiss through the loose sand, or now and again, with the roar and rattle of distant musketry, rush over the uneven pavement of the street crossings.

The moon was high and clear and the night grew cooler, almost cold, when we reached the woods.

In places where the road ran down to the edges of the swamp, a sickly vapor lay upon the stagnant pools among the cypresses on either side—and agues and malaria seemed to be lurking about us in the penetrating air.

We, spoke but little and disconnectedly, as the horses lagged at some slight ascent, or rushed on again in answer to the whip. At one such time Kate said to me. " O Harry, if you had only seen how loving Madge has been to me to-day. Like her own sweet self again. But how could I have known? Now, I see it all, my poor child, my poor child!"

Poor Kate! As she sunk back, relaxed and helpless into the corner of the carriage, with eyes fixed straight before her, she was indeed the very picture of heart-broken misery. Her face was worn and haggard, and the teardrops sparkled in the moonlight as one by one they chased each other down her white cheeks.

We had left the town perhaps a couple of miles behind us, when David suddenly drew up the horses.

"What's the matter?" I asked, leaning out to see why he had stopped.

"Daa's a carriage, sir, jes' ahead, drawed up on de side o' de road, as if dey's waitin' for suffen."

"Stay here, Kate," I said, springing out of the victoria; "don't be alarmed, I must see what it is; it will only take a moment," and I walked rapidly away under the flickering shadows of the trees.

As David said, some fifty yards beyond us, at a crossing of the roads, a carriage was standing.

As I drew near and before I could speak, a lady leaned forward from the door and called to me in a low and agitated voice,—

"O Colonel Shorter! is it you at last? I began to think you would never come!" and then, as I stepped from the shadow into the moonlight at her side, she started back and cried out in bewilderment and anger,—

"What is it? Why have you followed me? what do you want? How dare you come here? Leave me this instant! If he should find you here!"

"Hush, Madge! Listen to me. I am not here alone. I have come with your sister. .She is waiting for you."

"What did you say?" she gasped in a startled whisper and peering into my face.

"Your sister Kate, Madge, is here; she is waiting for you. She has come to take you home," I answered gently.

"O heavens, it is too late! I can never go home again, never! O, I could not stand it!" and then with sudden suspicion, she exclaimed, "You are deceiving me — it is false — my sister is not here! How dare you watch me? How dare you follow me? It is cruel, base, contemptible of you!" She suddenly stopped, and then, as if with great effort controlling herself, she went on in a constrained, defiant tone, "If you have any sense of decency or manhood left, you will leave me this instant, sir. Tell my coachman to drive on."

"Stop!" I said, as she leaned forward to give the order herself, "you do not know what you are saying. Let me call Kate; but here she is herself," I added, for Kate was already by my side, and before either of us could speak, she had opened the carriage door and thrown herself into Madge's arms.

"O Madge! my darling, my darling! what have

you done? what have you done?" she cried in broken accents.

I turned away and walked back to the victoria, with a very dusty feeling in my throat, and an impression that the moon and all the stars had been suddenly merged into one great "milky way."

What passed between the sisters during that next fifteen minutes (among the longest of my life) I never knew; but at last they came slowly down the road, Kate leaning upon Madge's arm as if for support, and without speaking they took their seats in the victoria. Madge's face was cold and rigid; and her bearing calm, erect, and defiant; while Kate was in tears and utterly broken down.

I brought Madge's things from the carriage, took the coachman's name and address, paid his fare, and mounting the box beside David, ordered him to drive as fast as possible back to the city.

David knew the man and assured me that he would see him immediately after his return to town, and that there would be no difficulty in purchasing his secrecy.

So far, then, we had been successful; and now, if only Jim had not returned during our absence, we might hope to keep the unhappy doings of the night unknown; and in this too we were fortunate, for when we reached Mrs. Jackson's there were no signs of Jim. He had evidently concluded to pass the night at The Oaks.

When we stopped, Madge alighted first, and

without a word walked straight across the broad
sidewalk, and into the garden gate.

I helped Kate out, and, as I held her hand, said,
in a low voice,—

"I suppose there is nothing more that I can do
for you to-night. Only remember, Kate, no one on
earth will know of this if you and Madge are silent.
Not even Jim."

" Yes, Harry, I will remember what you say," she
answered, tremulously. "But, oh! I am afraid it is
not all over yet. May God give me strength to
move her! How can I thank you, Harry, for all
that you have done ? "

" Stop! Don't thank me. You do not know "—I
began excitedly, and then, checking myself, said,
"Good-night, my dear sister. Be brave! you have
accomplished much to-night. Depend upon it, your
love will, in the end, set everything right again."

I left her, and sauntered slowly back to the hotel
and to bed; but I could not sleep. Again and
again the exciting scenes of the evening kept passing through my mind. The contemptuous tones of
Madge's voice haunted me. I could see her defiant
bearing and impassive face, as she came down the
moonlit road, with Kate leaning for support upon
her arm. O, how different from her bright coquetry
of a few months ago! What a change from the
light-hearted girl to the stern self-contained woman !

And that expression,— did it spring from defiance or from innocence? Whatever its origin,
how grand she had looked in her proud scorn.

And where was Shorter? Why had he deserted her at the last moment? What could have happened to turn him from his purpose? Had a sudden compunction, or merely some lucky chance, withheld him from the ruin of a young girl's life?

CHAPTER XXVI.

MORNING.

ON Saturday morning, I came down to a very late breakfast, as might have been expected after such a night.

I had not been long in the great barren dining-room of the hotel (which at this hour was entirely deserted), when Fred Brown appeared at the door, and, seeing me, came hurriedly across the room to where I was sitting.

" Well," he exclaimed, taking the seat opposite to me at the table, " so you are still alive, are you? "

" As much as a man ever is before breakfast. It seems to surprise you," I said, observing that his face wore a peculiarly perplexed expression.

" You are right," he continued; "I have heard all sorts of reports about you this morning, and, though I didn't half believe them, this ocular demonstration of their falsity is a great relief, I can assure you."

" Why, what have you heard? " I asked, wondering whether it was possible that rumors of our last night's doings had got abroad.

" I heard that you and Colonel Shorter had fought a duel early this morning, and that you were either killed or mortally wounded."

"That is indeed a terrible piece of news," I answered, laughing and feeling greatly relieved. "Where did you pick up this astounding piece of information?"

"General Houstoun came in this morning while we were at breakfast, and told us about it. His butler told him, and another darkey told the butler, and coming so straight it put us all, or rather the Captain and me (for Miss Mary left the room just after the General began his story), into a state of great excitement. Although we did not entirely credit it, the Captain said there must be something in it; so I thought I'd just run round here and hunt you up, if, indeed, you were still in the land of the living. In point of fact, I myself pooh-poohed the whole thing from the beginning. I maintained that no man from our part of the country would be fool enough to get himself into such a scrape."

"You were quite right, you see, as far as I am concerned; but I am heartily ashamed of myself for depriving the community of such a sweet little morsel of scandal. If they had only given me warning, I might at least have kept out of sight for a day or two."

"Well, I am glad to find you safe, all the same, and now I must leave you," said Fred, taking up his hat, "I promised the Captain I would report at once, and it wouldn't do to let the old gentleman worry any longer about nothing. I shall probably see you later. Good-by," and so he left me.

After I had finished my breakfast, I lighted a cigar and walked up the street towards the Club. I was not surprised at the report of a duel between Shorter and myself, for, no doubt, every one had by this time heard of our difficulty, and like many another false report, it was probably false only in as much as it was premature ; but at the first street crossing I encountered Mr. Benjamin, who at once threw new light on the matter and gave a serious foundation for the rumor.

" Have you heard the news ? " he asked, after an interchange of greetings.

" Well, no, I think not. What is it ? " I replied with a slight smile, speculating in my mind whether it would prove to be simply a revised edition of the old story, or some absolutely fresh scandal.

" As yet, there is nothing definite ; but the air is full of rumors this morning. I thought you might have seen Eustis and learned the truth from him," and as he spoke he looked at me narrowly.

" No, I have not seen him since yesterday at noon. He passed last night at The Oaks ; at least, I think he did."

" If he ever intended to, he must have changed his mind, for there seems little doubt that he fought Dick Shorter early this morning across the river."

" Good God! what do you mean? I have heard nothing of it ! " I exclaimed in astonishment, a cold chill creeping through my veins.

" Well, there are so many stories about, that it is impossible to get at the truth yet," he began

cautiously, and watching me closely as if still uncertain whether or not I knew more than I was
willing to admit. " Some say that Eustis has killed
Shorter, and some that it is just the other way. I
trust with all my heart it is not, for Eustis was one
of the best fellows that ever drew breath. We can't
afford to lose such a man as that. And as for
Shorter, well, he has his points, but,—by the way,
they say you know something of Dick Shorter yourself."

" I do not believe this can be true ! " I exclaimed,
without answering him directly, and feeling less
and less confidence in my assertion as I uttered the
words, for suddenly I recalled Jim's manner when
he left me in the morning, and Shorter's failure to
meet Madge last night. " Where did you hear
this ?   Who are said to have been the seconds ?
Have any of the men returned ? "

"I don't know," he replied, " every one is talking
about it, though no one seems to have any authentic
information. It must have been kept very close, for
it is not even known who the seconds were ; although
as Barnwell was in town yesterday and cannot be
found to-day, I suspect he went with Eustis. The
only thing that seems certain is that something has
happened and somebody been hurt, though which of
the two, Heaven only knows.   But such men as
Eustis and Shorter don't go out unless they mean
work, and, as you know, they have not been on
speaking terms since last autumn."

    As Mr. Benjamin apparently, could, throw no

further light upon the subject, I left him rather abruptly and hastened up the street to Mrs. Jackson's.

David came to the door and in answer to my inquiries, stated that "Massa Jim" had not yet returned from The Oaks.

What should I do, or where should I go next? In my present state of anxiety and excitement I could not merely remain passive and await developments. I must find some clue to the affair. I knew where Barnwell lived when in the city, and went at once to the house. The people had not seen him since yesterday, and knew nothing of his movements; but just as I was turning away discouraged, a carriage drove up to the door and Barnwell himself alighted. His face was grim and distressed. His black slouched hat was drawn down over his eyes, and his clothes, unbrushed and creased, bore unmistakeable evidence of having been worn all night. A heavy blanket shawl was slung across his arm, and among its folds I caught sight of a pistol butt.

" Where's Jim? " I asked, as he met me on the steps.

" I left him at home five minutes ago. He's all right," he added, looking quickly up at me.

" Thank God ! " I exclaimed, " I was afraid he had been——"

" No, he's all right ! " he repeated solemnly. " He's as sound as I am, but he had a narrow escape this morning. Come to my room, if you will, while I dress ; I'll tell you about it. We've had a bad time of it to-day."

·Accordingly I followed him into his room, which apparently had been shut up for a day or two and smelt musty and strong of stale tobacco smoke. He threw up the window sashes and, bidding me be seated, slowly recounted the adventures of the night.

According to Barnwell, Jim had come to his room at about two o'clock on Friday afternoon, within a couple of hours of the time he had left me at the hotel, and asked him to act as his second. He was greatly excited and said he had just had a serious difficulty with Shorter, which must be settled the next morning at daybreak. He refused to give any explanation of the affair further than that it was a matter of life and death. Barnwell had said what he could, in ignorance of the facts, to quiet him and to dissuade him from fighting, but he was thoroughly determined, and the only effect of Barnwell's words was to make him threaten to look elsewhere for a friend. So Barnwell, finding expostulation useless, had taken the matter promptly in hand. He found no difficulty in arranging a meeting at the time proposed, for Shorter, whatever else might be said against him, was not the man to hang back, or temporize. In fact, he seemed almost more anxious than Jim that they should meet at once. It was not the first time that he had been in the field. Either as principal or second he had taken part in half-a-dozen duels, and report said that on one occasion, at least, he had killed his man. Barnwell had felt very anxious about it, for it was evident from the bearing of both men that this was to be no play at duelling; and Jim, though as brave as a lion and a good shot, had never fought before.

It was agreed that the parties should meet at a ferry some few miles above the city, at half-past four in the morning, cross the river to the next State, and fight at five o'clock. The surgeon was to go with Shorter and his second.

Jim, in his light wagon, called for Barnwell during the afternoon, ostensibly to drive out to The Oaks, but they stopped about five miles from the city, and within a couple of miles of the ferry, at a small inn where they put up for the night. Jim had ordered January to meet them there with the express wagon. No doubt, the shrewd old darkey had his suspicions, for he came fully prepared for a night in the woods if necessary, and had put a bundle of hay in the wagon, either to sleep on himself, or to use in case of some more serious contingency.

" I don't exactly know why," said Barnwell, " but it struck me as an evil omen, to see that old man with his cart and bundle of hay. It reminded me, I suppose, of the evening we carried Jim back to The Oaks, from the 'Ten Acre' drive in that very identical wagon."

They passed a most uncomfortable night at the inn, with plenty of mosquitoes and sand-flies to keep them awake, and fully alive to their own serious reflections. Their breakfast was of cold hoe cake and chicory coffee, and by four o'clock in the morning, they were again on their way to the ferry.

Jim had been talkative and excited the evening before, but this morning he seemed much altered. He looked pale and worn. He scarcely uttered a word unless spoken to, and then answered only in monosyllables, but there was a quiet, determined look in his eyes, and his lips were firmly set.

They found Shorter, his second and the surgeon waiting for them at the ferry. They had already roused the negro ferryman from his shanty near by. It was very dark, for the moon had set, but a faint light in the east heralded the day. The ferry-boat, a "dugout," hollowed from the trunk of a single gum-tree, was not large enough to carry the entire party at once; so they were forced to cross the river in detachments.

Eustis and Barnwell went first, and, as the river here was nearly half a mile wide, they were obliged to wait for the others for some time after reaching the shore.

Eustis had not spoken since they arrived at the ferry, but as they two stood there waiting on the oozy river bank, in the glimmering light, he turned to Barnwell and said,—

"Major, if I don't go back to-day, I wish you to take a message to Strong. My last request, my last word to him is, not to take this matter up. He must not follow in my footsteps. I know the man well, and how hard it will be for him to resist the impulse. But this is no affair of his, though he would surely try to make it so. Beg him, for my sake, and that of others, to let it end here."

" I expect you to carry your own messages, Jim," said Barnwell, " but I will remember what you say ; and, if the worst comes to the worst, is there nothing else I can do for you ? "

Then Jim sent some messages to his sisters and others, that Barnwell forebore to repeat.

Presently the boat arrived on its second trip, the men got out upon the bank, and the whole party started forward.

By the time they reached the little path under the trees that led to an open field beyond, where the duel was to be fought, the light in the east had strengthened, and threw a dusky haze across the woods. It was very cold on that low land, level with the river, and most of the party wore overcoats to protect them from the unwholesome air. Barnwell was wrapped in the folds of a heavy shawl. Eustis and Shorter both wore army cloaks reaching below the knee, and in the dim morning light they did not look unlike one another, being of nearly the same height and build ; although, perhaps, Eustis was somewhat the heavier man.

The party walked slowly up the path, two by two, Shorter and Barnwell in front, Eustis and Ames (Shorter's second) a few paces behind, and the surgeon bringing up the rear.

They were just emerging from the woods into the " open," when Shorter stopped for a moment, apparently with the intention of saying something to his second, and thus separated himself from Barnwell, with whom he had been walking. He had turned half round, and was on the point of speaking, when suddenly the loud report of a gun, followed by a fiendish yell, rang out from the thicket near by, and echoed through the woods. Without a word or a cry, Shorter sprang high into the air, and fell, a shapeless, quivering heap in the middle of the path.

For an instant the others stood back speechless with horror, and then rushed to his side.

How strange for men who have deliberately made up their minds to encounter death, to be horrified at its appearance in an unexpected form. But such has often been the case, as upon this occasion. Even the would-be suicide by drowning has been frightened from his purpose by the threat to blow his brains out, if he should advance another step toward the water.

There was no necessity for the surgeon to give his verdict, for when they reached him, it was evident to all that Shorter had already passed to his accounting. The heavy charge of buckshot had bored its way straight through him just below the shoulder blade.

The men were all armed, and without an instant's delay, and scarce a word having passed between them, started in hot pursuit of the unknown murderer.

The thicket from which the shot had been fired, was on the edge of a narrow belt of woods full of underbrush, running down to the river bank, and skirted by the path on one side, and an open field on the other.

Ames and the surgeon took the field. Barnwell ran back along the path, and Jim sprung through the thicket and into the woods.

They had given the man or men fifteen or twenty second's start, but as Jim dashed impetuously on, nearing the river at every spring, he soon heard the twigs and underbrush snapping and crackling ahead of him, and a moment later distinguished, in the uncertain light, the figure of a large man running at full speed across an opening in the woods, some fifty paces in advance.

He shouted to him to stop and then fired, more in the hope of checking than of actually hitting him at such a distance ; but the man rushed precipitately on, and in an instant disappeared behind the undergrowth on the river bank.

When Jim reached the spot a few seconds later, he saw, just below him on the river, a small canoe bottom up, with its oars floating lazily away upon the tide, and some fifty feet beyond it a man in the water striking out desperately for the other shore.

Again he shouted to him to come back, but it only had the effect of making the swimmer put more strength into his long powerful strokes.

Again he aimed and fired at the black head above the water, but it was out of range and he could see the splash as the ball struck the water in his wake and ricochetted over and beyond him. For an instant the swimmer turned to face his pursuer and in that instant Jim recognized Tom Armstrong.

Meanwhile the rest of the party, hearing Jim's shouts and shots, came running through the woods to join him.

"It's that scoundrel Armstrong!" cried Jim, "Barnwell,—you and Ames run down to the ferry and follow him with the boat. The doctor and I will wait here in case the rascal should turn back."

They followed his directions at once and in five minutes were rowing lustily out across the river.

Armstrong was by this time a quarter of a mile or more away, but of course they gained upon him rapidly. He was swimming more slowly and laboriously now. He was evidently losing strength or courage, and kept looking wildly back at his pursuers.

Suddenly, as they drew near to him, he threw up his hands with a cry of despair, or fright, and sunk at once out of sight. Barnwell and his companion rowed into the centre of the widening circles where he had disappeared, but he did not again rise to the surface. They waited and watched about the spot until satisfied that further delay was useless, and then pulled slowly back to the landing, where Jim and the surgeon were waiting for them.

"I think he must have been seized with cramp," said Barnwell, "or it is just possible that Jim's first shot in the woods struck him; but I would not suggest this to him, for he seems to be enough cut up by the whole affair as it is, without making it worse."

"But why did Armstrong kill Shorter. Had there been any trouble between them?" I asked.

"None whatever, that I can find out," he replied.

"Nevertheless, he appears to have been fully acquainted with your movements, and to have laid his plans well, except that I should hardly think he could have hoped to escape."

"Well, I don't know about that," said Barnwell. "If he had not capsized his canoe in jumping in, I very much doubt whether we should ever have caught him."

"And do I understand you to say that Jim is at home now?" I asked.

"Yes, he has just gone home. We waited to bring Shorter's body back to the city. Jim is completely used up, poor fellow! He feels it almost as much as if he had shot Shorter himself. I hope, with all my heart, I shall never have to go through such a day's work again. As for Shorter, no doubt he had his faults, but he was the soul of honor and plucky to the last degree. He will be a great loss to me in a business way, for he has always been my factor. More than that, he has been my friend and helped me through many a hard pinch. Well, poor fellow, he is gone now," he ended with a deep sigh, "and I, for one, shall never have a word to say against him."

CHAPTER XXVII.

LEAVE-TAKING.

A FEW days after Colonel Shorter's death, the Eustises moved out from their town-house to The Oaks.

Madge was ill. The excitement of that last week and its fatal termination had proved too much for her. Strong as she was both in health and will, she had given way at last.

Jim could not stand the gossip with which the city was fairly bubbling over, and to give society a chance to talk itself out in his absence, decided to return to the country for the remainder of the season, and until the rice-field malaria should drive him away for the summer.

I stayed on in the city, but saw nothing of the Eustises for several weeks, except an occasional glimpse of Jim when he happened to come to town on business.

From time to time, I dined or supped with the Lees, and often met Mary at home, or at the little picnics and boating parties that followed up the spring.

As I did not urge my suit, our intercourse again became friendly and unconstrained. If by chance I did overstep the bounds of commonplace, I knew by her expression, or her silence, that I was on dangerous ground, and drew back, however reluctantly.

It was evident, (I argued,) that the prejudices of birth and education could not be abandoned; they had grown too deep before we met for me to uproot them now; and why should I render us both wretched by a hopeless struggle against them. If I must appeal to her once more it should not be until the very end. So, meanwhile, I kept back the words that often rose to my lips, determined that no folly on my part should mar the pleasure of our last meetings.

Colonel Richard Shorter had been buried with such ceremonies as became an officer of one of the popular military companies of the place, and a man of social position. But one may doubt if much honest sorrow was felt at his death; unless among his creditors, of whom there were a goodly number; for it turned out, to the surprise of all, that his estate was utterly insolvent, and many of his most intimate friends were the heaviest losers. His books showed that for several years he had been a wild speculator, and had not scrupled, when pushed to the wall, to meet his private losses with securities belonging to others and placed in his hands for sale or safekeeping.

Greatly to my regret, I learned that poor Barnwell was among the unfortunates, and that the savings of years of hard labor and economy were lost, and that he was reduced again to the position in which the war had left him.

After the state of the Colonel's affairs became
known, he retired at once to his plantation, and
Jim, who often saw him, told me that he bore his
misfortune like a man, and could not be induced to
say a word in censure of his dead friend.

It was towards the end of April and within a
week of the time set for my going North, when
Jim came to town for me one morning, and, in the
warm summer-like afternoon, drove me out to the
Oaks to pass the night and bid the family good-by.
How natural seemed the long, level, pine-shadowed
road and the broad sunlit stretches of marsh
where we crossed the rivers! How it carried me
back to the time when first I took this drive with
Jim; when this same scenery, now so familiar, and
so full of associations, had seemed strikingly un-
interesting.

As we drove along through the forest, I asked
Jim about Kate's plans for the summer and his own
movements. I advised him to take some house at
the North, near us by the seashore, where he and
I could boat and fish together and Kate and Alice
renew the friendship of their youth.

"Well, Harry," he replied, "I wish with all my
heart we could, but I am afraid we shall have to
weather it out at the South this summer. However, I won't absolutely say no. You must talk it
over with Kate and see what she says. At one
time I thought we should have to send Madge away,
but, thank goodness, she will pull through now.
One could hardly believe her to have been so dan-

gerously ill, for she looks almost as well as ever again. It seems strange she should have broken down so completely. I always thought her as strong as an ox. But society and late hours proved too much for her, poor girl. And Shorter's death, too, must have greatly shocked her. Not that I believe she ever really cared for that man, but as their names had been connected, she must naturally have felt it. Barnwell was telling me this morning—and that reminds me I shall be only too glad to take charge of that loan; with average luck he will pay back the entire amount in the course of a few years."

" By the way," I asked, interrupting him, " What has become of old January ? "

" O, he is still with us. Why, haven't I told you about him ? " he answered with surprise. " Well, some weeks ago, the old man was taken ill. He thought his time had surely come to climb up ' Jacob's Ladder '; so, one day in great distress he sent for me. I went to his cabin and he told me, very mysteriously, that he had a secret he could keep no longer. I expected some confession of the whiskey bottle or old Isaac's store, but found it concerned me more nearly than I had imagined. It seemed, Armstrong had scared him so, that he hardly dared call his soul his own. It was really extraordinary how old January stood in dread of him ; for although he knew the brute was dead and gone, he would not utter his name above a whisper, and as he told me his story lying on his mattrass, his wild, frightened little eyes went dancing about from door to window and window to chimney-piece as if at any moment he might see the grim visage of his tormentor. From the time of our trouble at the polls Armstrong had constantly haunted and threatened the old man; from him he learned about our hunting party, and fired the shot that I laid at your door, young man. He met him immediately after at Isaac's store, and told him he had killed me, and from that time on, January was in fear of his life, and kept Armstrong informed of all my movements. No doubt, but for my trip to Florida, the scoundrel would have shot me long ago. It is strange how vindictive these brutes can be! After our baffling him that day, his sole thought and aim seems to have been to avenge the insult, as he considered it. How little I dreamt I was taking my life in my hand every time I went into the woods or into the streets at night! And then to think that poor Shorter——"

" Why didn't you deliver January up to the authorities? " I asked, as he stopped short.

"I don't know. I never thought of such a thing. What good would it have done? No, as soon as he had sifted his conscience he 'picked up' again, and now he is going about as lively as a cricket. "

" But isn't he afraid of being arrested ? "

" Of course not. Why should he be? Such an idea would never enter his head. Besides, there is no danger, for no one knows of his part in the affair but myself and you."

Presently we entered the driveway to The Oaks. The dark green leaves of the famous old trees were falling fast, to make room for a brighter foliage, and a mere suspicion of green in the long tendrils of the Spanish moss showed that it too had felt the vitalizing breath of spring.

Kate was on the piazza waiting to receive me, and it so chanced that soon after my arrival she and I were left together for a while.

Madge had gone to ride with Major Barnwell, and Jim was called off by his overseer to examine a new dyke that he was building. I made good my opportunity to urge upon Kate what I had already proposed to Jim, and sketched in glowing colors the summer we might all spend together near some picturesque New-England fishing village.

" Well, Harry, you certainly make it sound very tempting," she said, after I had fairly exhausted my powers of imagination. " But I cannot decide yet. Perhaps we really may come, but (to tell you a secret that you must not breathe to a living soul), Major Barnwell has proposed to Madge, so you see it must depend upon her. She has not accepted him. She was to give him her answer to-day. I do hope she will take him. He would make her such a steady husband. He has been devoted to her all through her sickness, and is as gentle and forbearing as a woman with her. He puts up so sweetly with her variableness,—and you know, she is just a little uncertain at times ! I think they are exactly suited to each other. Don't you ?" she asked, looking up at me.

" Well, I can hardly go so far as that," I answered

with hesitation ; for although I had expected this to take place eventually, it was a surprise to me at this time, coming so soon after Madge's affair with Shorter, and in the midst of Barnwell's money troubles.

" They are certainly very unlike in character ; still, as you say, I have always thought he would make a good husband,—but, is he in a position to marry ? "

" Perhaps not from your standpoint ; but from a Southerner's he is," she answered with a little asperity. " He has his place, and has made a loan, I hear, that will enable him to pay off his mortgages. It does not cost so very much to live in this part of the country, and at all events," she added emphatically, " he is desperately in love with her."

" And she with him ? " I asked.

" Yes, of course she is," she answered, without looking at me, " or, at least, I think she likes him. I wish you would not be so disagreeable, Harry. You are utterly unsympathetic. I thought you would feel as I do about it."

I protested that I did ; and to the extent of gaining an honest and faithful protector, the match would undoubtedly prove a good one for Madge. But yet it did seem a thousand pities that such a brilliant girl should be thrown away upon such a very commonplace fellow as this, and allowed to rust out—to go gradually to pieces with his fences, and finally be lost amidst the general dilapidation of his farm. How often had I chaffed her about him and how often had she declared she would not marry him, if he were the only man on earth !

I had not seen her since I left her and Kate at the garden gate of their town house after our midnight drive, and I asked Kate whether she thought her much changed.

"Yes," she answered quietly, "very, very much, not in her face, for she looks as well as ever, but her light-heartedness has all gone. O Harry!" she went on impulsively, "how could it be otherwise with the poor child? How can she ever forget the past? She must have been sorely tried, poor girl, I know she must have been! Why, have I not watched her day by day for years? Have I not known her through and through, marked every change and phase of her character from childhood. She was as pure and high-minded as any girl that ever lived. O no! this has been all, all wrong," she cried, "and I shall never understand it. I will not believe even the evidence of my own eyes and ears. There is some mistake, that, I would lay my life, she could explain."

"I wish, then, with all my heart she would!" I answered earnestly, and with the words upon my lips, I turned and saw Madge standing at the parlor window near us. I could not tell from her expression whether she had heard what we had been saying, though it seemed hardly possible that the last few sentences could have escaped her.

She had ridden home through the woods with Barnwell, and he had left her at the gate behind the house. She was in her riding-habit, always so becoming to her shapely figure. I could discern no

outward change except that perhaps she had grown
a shade more slender than when I saw her last, but
her fair complexion, slightly flushed with exercise,
her bright, clear eyes and elastic step, bore not a
trace of invalidism. However, as Kate had truly
said, her manner was subdued and softened. Her
old vivacity, rising at times to the verge of boister-
ousness in her excess of spirits, had vanished, and
there was something almost touching in the gentle
dignity that had replaced it.

She received me so simply and naturally that
I could scarcely realize all that had passed between
us.

I did not speak with her alone until the next
morning, half an hour or so before I left The Oaks ;
Then we happened to be standing together on the
front piazza looking down into the rose garden, as
we had done so often in the early days of our acquaintance.

"Do you remember how indignant you were with
Jim when you found he had stolen all the roses
from your favorite bush?" I asked, smiling to recall the scene in the breakfast room, on the morning after my arrival; "if it were not for the profusion of flowers in the garden now, I might, as I
stand here, almost imagine that I came last night."

"Could you? It seems a long time ago to me,"
she replied.

"And to me, too, unless by a slight effort, I shut
out what has gone between."

"That I cannot do," she answered simply. For

a few moments we were silent, and then she began speaking with hesitation and embarrassment.

"There is something I wish you to do for me. Will you take this and promise me faithfully not to open it until you are at sea? I never expected to ask a favor of you again, but this shall indeed be the last. Will you promise me?"

"Of course I will, Madge," I answered frankly and earnestly as I took a sealed letter from her hand. "Is that all?"

"Yes, that is all," she said, at the same time turning quietly away.

These were our last words together, or, at least, the last that we spoke alone.

She left my side and went down into the rose garden. I did not follow, but stood with arms upon the balustrade watching her from above.

The sun lay bright and warm upon the rose-bushes, broad beds of violets, and the white paths below me, and glittered among the dark, glossy leaves of the camelias as upon rippling water.

The tall, fair girl with golden hair went in and out among the shrubs and bushes and gathered flowers into the skirt held up before her to receive them, now bending low to the violets and again on tiptoe for some sprig almost beyond her reach. It was a scene to be remembered,—this bright patch of parti-colored garden, encircled by the tall, dark oaks and pines.

Jim was to drive me back to town, and presently the horse and wagon were brought to the gate.

I said my last few words to Kate and Madge upon the piazza, and as I bade the former good-by she whispered in my ear,—

" Perhaps, after all, if Jim will consent, you may see us at the North this summer. Are you glad to hear it ? "

" I am truly delighted, Kate," I answered, heartily, " it is the best news I have heard for many a day. I shall set to work at once on my return, to hunt up that little New England paradise that I described to you yesterday. Believe me, I shall find the spot if you will only come and people it."

And thus I bade my friends good-by—friends who, in a few short months, had worked themselves into the very centre of my life ; whose kind faces and good cheer were never to be forgotten. Nor shall I forget the old white house, standing there in a deluge of spring sunshine, and the two figures waving their handkerchiefs from the balcony as I saw them last through the moss-hung vista of the old oaks.

CHAPTER XXVIII.

DOWN THE RIVER—BEACHGROVE—EPILOGUE.

SOON after my return from The Oaks I - was asked to a picnic that was to take place on the last Thursday in April, two days before the sailing of the steamer by which I had engaged my passage for the North.

The excursion was to Beachgrove, a fine old country seat on one of the sea islands within an hour's sail from the city.

Beachgrove had for many generations belonged to the same family, and in old slavery times, when the great planters of the South had inexhaustible bank accounts and balances in the hands of their factors from year's end to year's end, money had been lavished upon its walks and its drives, its fruit and flower gardens.

Nor was this little principality, with its forty miles or more of beach and bluff, its groves of cypress and palmetto, and pine, and oak, and nut trees, without many natural advantages to the horticulturist and landscape-gardener. The land rose gradually from the lagoons and salt marshes, that bounded it on the west, to the centre of the island and then fell away again towards bluffs and beach that faced the Atlantic. And what a beach was that! Broad, white, and level, except when furrowed and ploughed up by the storms. The sand so fine and hard that carriage tracks could not be traced along its shining surface. Not a stone, nor a pebble, nor even a bunch of seaweed upon it as far as the eye could reach; nothing to arrest the sight unless where the ribs of some old wreck cropped up. A grand parade that, with its fence of blue pines on the one side and curbstone of foam on the other.

During the war and the few years that followed it Beachgrove had not been kept up; and although the hedges were still well trimmed and the gardens around the house still full of flower beds and flowering shrubs, the outlying lands had fallen into disuse with the exception of a few acres that supplied the family with vegetables.

It was, no doubt, out of consideration for the purse and larder of its present owner, Mr. Fleming, that the excursion took the form of a picnic. Jim had come to town for the occasion. Captain Lee and Mary were there with Fred Brown, too, who was to sail with me on the coming Saturday.

He had finished his work for the Captain and was . to arrange for its publication at the North. For the rest, they were principally the set of people, that I had met most frequently in society during the past winter.

It was a perfect morning when we boarded the "Arrow" and steamed down the yellow river, winding in and out for many a mile among the marshes. At last we left the river's mouth, and with a short reach across the shallow bay or sound that lay between the island and the mainland, made Beachgrove at noonday.

The steamboat was run so close to the shore that we landed from her guards upon the beach, where Mr. Fleming was waiting to receive us; and we followed him at once through the shady gravel paths up to the house to pay our respects to the hostess and her daughters.

On such a day as this, people could not be kept within doors, and soon the drawing-rooms, though cool, and teeming with flowers, were deserted for the piazzas and gardens below them, where bright dresses glanced in and out among the trees and shrubbery like butterflies in a rose bed. We had brought musicians with us, and under the trees there was a platform for dancing, but in the noonday heat few of the young people were energetic enough to use it.

In the morning, on the boat, Mary had agreed to walk with me in the afternoon; perhaps it would be our last walk together, and I could think of nothing else. I was restless and unsettled in mind, and for a long time strolled about the place alone. I examined the endless varieties of roses in the gardens. I watched the dancers. I wandered through the groves and alleys and took a peep at the white beach and sea beyond, to whose care I was so soon to commit myself, and at the sounding of a gong returned to the house to lunch. I was nervous and excited. I could eat but little, and was very glad when at last the long luncheon was over, and the time that I had been waiting for so impatiently arrived.

I joined her on the piazza and we passed together through the gardens, along an avenue overarched with the dark foliage of the orange, and out on to the beach. The sun was hot, but a cool easterly wind was blowing in from the sea and tossing the little blue ripples into diamonds at our feet. We walked for awhile along the margin of the water, just out of reach of the waves, and then took a path that led to the top of the bluff, where, under the shadow of the pines, we found a pleasant resting place.

The Atlantic, blue as the Mediterranean, lay spread before us to the horizon with here and there a sail upon it, and below us the beach stretched away in either direction, a long, white pathway between the green and blue.

Our intercourse of late had been unusually free and pleasant, and at times I believed I could not be mistaken in thinking there was a touch of more than friendliness in her tone and manner; but yet again she would seem to guard herself with a reserve that prevented any advances on my part.

I had intended to offer myself again before I left, and wanted no better time than this, when I might have her to myself for an hour without danger of interruption. But now that I was actually about to speak, my mind was filled with misgivings. I could think only of the little encouragement she had given, and the prejudices ready to battle against me. I dreaded the encounter and, though determined to speak, felt that my fate was sealed.

Why, at the critical moment, I should have given such weight to my doubts, I cannot understand, for I am usually hopeful, and regard him who goes into action with hesitation as already at heart a deserter. But how often, from some strange perversity of nature, does the one great chance of a lifetime escape us! An influence that we do not recognize, but before which we are powerless, puts on the brakes and either reverses the wheels or blocks them altogether. We are driven to speak and act as we should not, or neither to speak nor act at all. Sacrificed, perhaps, to an eternal order, we still regard ourselves as the victims only of our own stupidity and folly, and, with an example in itself based upon the very point in question, think that we hold our own fate as firmly as the die between the fingers, which we can place upon the table with its one or its six uppermost. Well, let us believe it, if we can, for, if only a conceit, it will add somewhat to the pleasure and contentment of our lives.

She had taken off her hat and was arranging some wild flowers among its ribbons. I lay at her side pushing the pine cones over the edge of the bluff with my cane. Presently, she said,—

" So you are going on Saturday ?"

" Yes," I answered, without looking up. "I am going on Saturday, unless you will ask me to stay."

I stopped a moment to listen, but she did not speak and I continued : " Will you send me away without a word? Ask me to come back to you in a month, in a year, in ten years, and I will come, but do not tell me it must all end now."

" Ah, please do not speak in that way ! " she said, looking pleadingly into my face. " Why can we not remain simple friends? I have been so happy lately, thinking that it might be so, and now—and now you will make me very miserable. I would like, so much, to be your friend always. Will you not take my friendship ? " she continued, with a tremor in her voice, and timidly holding out her hand toward me. " Indeed, indeed, you will not ask me to give you more."

How sadly and sweetly her words rang in my ears. I heard them and yet I heard them not! Heaven only knows how it could have happened, unless because I so fully expected her refusal, but I only heard her words and not the feelings that their tone betrayed. I took no notice of her outstretched hand, and as it dropped again listlessly at her side, I answered coldly : " That is not enough. As I have said before, I must have all or nothing. If you had said you cared for some one else, bitter as it would have been, I would have left you without a word——"

" Indeed I do not," she cried, interrupting me, " but——"

"Then listen to me while I speak for the last time," I continued in the same hard tone. " What

I shall say will not be flattering nor pleasant; but it
is the truth and shall be said before I go. Perhaps
you will withdraw the friendship you have offered
me just now; but what difference can it make? We
shall probably never meet again. I could almost
say I hope we may not, even though you have been
so much to me. You were the first woman I ever
cared for. For a long time I did not tell you of it
because—well—I could not speak in honor until the
night your mother interrupted us. Then I knew
you cared for me. Do you think I could have been
mistaken?" I cried. "Not a bit of it. I knew it,
and nothing in the world can make me disbelieve it
now. But, fool that I was, I could not and would
not believe that love could remain the slave of prejudice. I thought that I could win you against
the teachings of a lifetime. That your affection
must in the end conquer your false pride. But I
was wrong, utterly wrong. With some women love
knows no obstacles, no barriers, no bounds, opposition only strengthens it. With you, well, you were
sorry—you are sorry to have me go—you care for me
enough for that. But you dare not stretch out your
hand to stop me. You dare not face the criticisms
of your people."

I had become more and more excited, stung to the
quick by the picture I had drawn. I was hopeless,
and reckless, and forgetful of everything but my own
grief and disappointment.

She had arisen to her feet. Her face was as
white as the muslin about her throat. Her gray

eyes shone like diamonds as they looked straight into mine.

"Now, I believe, I do understand you," she said in a low voice, with trembling lips. "Indeed, indeed, how little have we ever known each other. Thank Heaven, it is not too late!"

"Stop!" I cried, but she turned quickly from me and walked rapidly down the path. I sprung to my feet and followed her. Suddenly she paused for a moment as if in doubt ; and looking along the beach I saw some people wave their handkerchiefs at us and hurry away towards the house.

Then for the first time I noticed that half the sky was already overspread with massive clouds, that came rolling up from the north and west. We neither of us spoke, but hastened side by side along the narrow path, following the top of the bluff, that we might not lose the shelter of the pines.

I was too excited to speak. I believed, at the moment, I had said nothing but the full, plain truth. I knew that all was over, and yet knew not why it was so, nor how I had happened to give way to such bitter feelings. I tried to recall and weigh my words, but I could not. I could remember only that I had spoken the truth strongly and harshly, but still the truth ; and that all was over between us ; that the end had come.

We had just gained the broad piazza when the great drops began to spatter up the dust on the dry gravel walks, and a moment later down came the rain in a flood; as if it would sweep everything before it.

The musicians had been brought indoors, and the dismantled parlors were already full of dancers, and without delay the tireless round began. Waltz, galop and polka succeeded each other, hour after hour in rapid succession, to the accompaniment of intermittent thunder and lightning, and ceaseless torrents of rain. But the storm without did not dampen the ardor of the gay party, and the dancing grew faster and faster, and the talking and laughing louder and gayer as the day drew to a close.

I, myself, remained on the piazza smoking, and chatting with, or rather being chatted to by my host, who was a talkative man, and relieved me without apparent effort of the burden of the conversation. But, at last, to my relief, the time came to leave Beachgrove, if we would reach the city before nightfall; and the elders of the party stopped the music at its height, and ordered the young people to get ready to start at once, lest an ugly night should overtake us on the river.

Very soon all was reported in readiness, and our party, having declined the hospitable entreaties of our hosts to pass the night with them, started for the beach with the scanty protection of such shawls and overcoats as they had brought with them in the sunny morning. There was much huddling together under umbrellas, and joking and laughing as they left the house. All were in the best of humor, and ready to accept, if necessary, a good ducking as a joke.

When I returned to the piazza, after bidding good-by to the ladies of the house, I found Mary waiting near the steps for Jim, who was trying to single out his own from a stack of umbrellas that stood in the corner near by.

We came face to face, and the color mounting to her cheeks as she turned away and looked out into the rain. For a moment I was undecided whether to speak or not. It was only for a moment, and then I stepped to her side and said in a tone that could not be overheard,—

"Before I go, I must say one word. I owe it to us both, though, no doubt, you think I have said too much already. I suppose I had no right to speak as I did to-day. I forgot myself. I beg you to forgive me. I shall not forgive myself."

My voice sounded constrained and uncertain. I stopped, for I felt I could not trust myself to speak.

"Do not think of it again," she answered earnestly, without raising her eyes. "Who knows, perhaps we have both been unjust. And, as we must part, it would be very foolish,—would it not—" she said hesitating, and looking up with a tremulous smile about her lips; "it would be very foolish not to part as friends."

"Well, here we are at last!" cried Jim, suddenly interrupting us. "Now, Miss Mary, is your skirt up, so it won't get wet? I wish this umbrella were big enough for three, Harry; but stop, hold it yourself, my boy, I can get along without it; come, do take it."

"No, thank you, this coat of mine is waterproof, I like the rain," I said, leaving them abruptly and starting down the steps and along the path alone.

What a change had come over the face of nature since we landed on the Island! How black the heavens overhead! How dark and gloomy the path under the arching trees, where the sunlight had flickered and shimmered in the morning! The rain had cut it into furrows and rills to feed the red torrents that coursed along it on either side. The wind wrestled fiercely with the trees, now and again flinging their twigs and branches with a snap and a crash to the ground.

When I reached the beach, the scene there was still more wild and dismal. The steamer was lying at anchor a hundred yards off shore, tossing about in the heavy chop made by cross wind and tide. There was not above a mile of shallow open reach on this side of the island, so the waves rose short, and high, and sharp; foaming and sputtering in the furious wind, and whipping themselves upon the hard beach with the rattle of musketry. It was ugly looking water; and the clouds rushed wildly over it, black, threatening and low.

Umbrellas were useless, and fortunate indeed were the few who had provided themselves with waterproofs; for those who had not, found shawls and overcoats of little avail against the driving rain, and stood drenched, bedraggled, and shivering in groups upon the sands, utterly forlorn and miserable.

For myself, I was in no pleasant mood, and savagely enjoyed the scene. I caught the evil spirit of the storm as it swept by me, and rejoiced in its fury. It exhilarated, it excited me. I welcomed the fierce rain as it beat upon my face. I could have shouted defiance at the loud blasts of wind as I bent forward to meet them. I stood alone, well back, upon the high crest of the beach, and watched the manœuvres of the people below me.

Barelegged negroes, wading waist deep into the water, carried out the people one by one to a heavy row boat that was plunging in the surf and attached by ropes to the steamer directly to windward of us. When the boat was loaded, those on the steamer drew her slowly out alongside, and took the passengers abroad. It was a slow process, and, self-absorbed though I was, its dangers did not escape my notice. If the rope had slackened enough to let the heavy laden boat swing round into the trough, she would have filled at once. Many of the women were frightened, as well they might have been ; and and I heard their little hysterical screams and cries as the negroes carried them through the water and placed them in the tossing boat.

Presently there was a slight lull in the storm. Already half a dozen loads had been hauled out to the steamer in safety, and another, which I had been watching with especial interest, was just approaching her side, when to my horror, and from some unseen cause,—the slackening of the hawsers or a cross chop,—the boat suddenly swerved round into the trough of the sea, and a great wave broke completely over her!

She was close to the steamer, and I saw Jim, who was standing in the bow, lay hold of a rope that was hanging from her side and swing himself up on deck. Then a quick, piercing cry arose, followed by men's shouts and women's screams. The boat was bottom up, and the people struggling in the water.

Some seized the rudder chains, and rudders of the steamer. Some clung to the bottom of the upturned boat, which floated luckily close under the steamer's guards. The men on deck set vigorously to work, and by means of ropes and boards and oars, and whatever they could lay their hands on, began to haul the men and women one by one aboard, to the embraces of their friends.

All at once to the left of the steamer, and at some little distance from her, I caught sight of a woman struggling with the waves. The tide was bearing her swiftly out, and the short seas sweeping over her.

"She's trying to swim, and making a bravefight too, but without help a hopeless one!" I muttered between my teeth. At the same instant a man—yes, it was Jim Eustis—sprang from the steamer's deck into the water, and struck out manfully towards her. I saw instantly, that, in that rough sea, there was not a chance for them. Even if he should reach her, they could never swim ashore against the tide. I glanced rapidly about me for help, and to my joy espied, drawn up into the long grass close at hand, a large flat-bottomed skiff with oars and thole-pins in her. I sprung to her side, and seizing her by the bow, with more than ordinary strength, dragged her swiftly out of the marsh grass and down the sands.

Before I reached the water's edge, a big muscular looking negro, who also had taken in the situation, came running down the beach to join me. We quickly pushed the boat out through the surf, jumped into her together, and without a word began pulling for dear life. How the gale blew against us! How the mad waves flew up and struck our oars almost wrenching them from our grasp! How my heart grew sick as I looked over the rough water between us and felt the tempest hold us back! But one of us was armed with the strength of desperation, and the other of long training, and we did not fight in vain. Through the wind and the rain and the rushing sea we reached them and still in time.

I did not have to look into the unconscious face that Jim held above the water to know that it was Mary's. My God! How white and drawn it looked. How firmly the blue lips were clenched together! How cold the hands that afterwards I laid upon her breast!

When at last we came ashore a small crowd had collected to receive us, and drew in our boat. Mary was taken gently out and laid upon the beach. Two physicians of the party and her father bent over her and applied the remedies at their command.

The rest of us, in deep anxiety, kept back to give them room. Jim, with a dazed expression on his face, and trembling in every limb from excitement and exhaustion, stood by me resting his arm upon my shoulder for support. The breathless suspense was terrible.

At last the Captain looked up from his work with a quick reassuring smile.

"Thank God!" gasped Jim. His hand slipped from my shoulder, and he fell unconscious at my side!

In the meanwhile the steamer remained at her anchor, for those who had come ashore to await the result of the accident. Captain Lee decided that he and his daughter and Jim must accept the hospitalities of the Flemings for the night; and both he and Mr. Fleming begged me to remain with them. I declined, however, and after seeing the invalids removed in safety to the house, took leave of my host for a second time.

Captain Lee insisted upon walking down to the boat with me, and with tears in his eyes thanked me for the service I had done him. "I am sorry you should have to put up with me to-night, Harry, in place of Jim and Mary," he said as he shook me by the hand for the last time. "They will no doubt envy me this parting word. I am sorry from the bottom of my heart to have you go. But now you will always know the point of the compass to steer by when you are in search of friends. You have made some warm ones here, and will not be forgotten. Come early or late, my boy, we shall be ready to receive you. Good-by, good-by! God speed you and bring you a quick return!"

I can see, as if to-day, the sturdy old man standing there in the twilight under his umbrella on the wet beach, waving his handkerchief to me as we pulled out from shore. Good-by, my kindly friend. Never have I met a more warm-hearted, generous nature. Frank and simple, yet vigorous and strong.

As Fred Brown also concluded to remained at Beachgrove overnight, the Captain asked me to call on Mrs. Lee and explain to her why they had not returned home. So, as soon as I landed, I plodded up to their house through the wet, and gave her an account of the accident, but without referring to my own part in the affair.

When I had set her mind at rest, she thanked me civilly for the trouble I had taken, and, as I bade her good night, even went so far as to wish me a comfortable passage North. But did she ask me to return? Did she express the hope that we might meet again? No, not she; for she was as truthful as she was unforgiving. She could not unbend even with the full consciousness of victory. She received me in the drawing-room where I had had my only battle with her, and there we parted with civility but little kindly feeling between us. Heaven forgive me; if at such a time I was uncharitable in my judgment of her!

How long and dreary the next day seemed to be.

In the morning I took a walk, and in the afternoon I dawdled about my room, and chafed at the delay! Alternately I packed and did nothing. With tiresome pertinacity my thoughts returned again and again to the scenes of yesterday, until at last, giving myself up to them, I dropped into an armchair by the window and gazed vacantly into the street.

I wished I had gone a week ago. Why had I not? For what had I stayed? A last word and last hope. The last word had indeed been said; and there was no longer hope. Could I lay my defeat altogether at her mother's door? How had I striven to win her in the last half hour? What had my own part been? Simple, earnest and honest. Had I gone forward like a man, stood frankly before her, and offered her my confidence and love? O no; how different had been my tone; earnest enough, perhaps too earnest, but suspicious and complaining. Telling her she loved me, and in the same breath doubting her. How could she in her pride have stooped to prove her affection for a man who already questioned it—who taunted her? How for one moment could I have dishonored with ungenerous doubt the woman I professed to love? Fool that I had been, could I ever undo my folly?

I thought I saw it all plainly now, and believed I had dealt the blow with my own hand. I would not go to-morrow; I would stay a week longer. I must, yes, I must see her again!

I sprung from my chair and peered out into the gathering twilight, when suddenly the door of my room opened and Brown entered.

"Halloa Strong!" he exclaimed, apparently in high spirits, "caught you mooning, did I? I didn't suppose you were given to that sort of thing. I've just arrived from the Island, had a fine row up this afternoon, with the sun in my eyes, dead calm, and a million sand-flies; I came alone, Jim and Miss Lee were neither of them very well" (he gave me a knowing wink) "so the Captain thought best to stay down there with them over Sunday. I suppose you are all ready to start to-morrow? I must say I think I'm about prepared to go now. I guess, on the whole, I shall look upon my native shores again with equanimity, not to say pride, don't you?"

"Well, yes, Brown," I answered, striving to make up my mind as I spoke. "I shall be glad to see New England again, but, to tell you the truth, I am not sure that I shall go at once. I am thinking of remaining here for another week, I want very much to see Jim about——"

"Oh! that reminds me," said Brown, thrusting his hand into his coat pocket—"I have a letter for you from Jim; but I hope you don't seriously think of leaving me in the lurch. I depended upon you —O, here it is," he added, handing me the note. "Come! you must go to-morrow—I insist upon it—I can't possibly get along without you," and on he talked, but I did not hear him.

"MY DEAREST OLD FELLOW—" the letter read— "I believe you love me well enough to rejoice with me when I tell you that I am engaged. I am almost as surprised as you will be, but it is true, my own dear boy, and I am the happiest man on earth. I am hardly strong enough to come up to-day to see you off, but I cannot let you go without telling you the news. God bless you, my old friend! Believe me, if you stood in my shoes to-day, I should not love you less than I do now. I shall never forget what you did for us yesterday, and the happiness you placed within my reach. It is a debt that can never be repaid. The Captain especially desires me to send his love. You shall hear from me again very soon. With heaps of love,

"I am ever your devoted friend,

"EUSTIS.

" BEACHGROVE,
"Friday afternoon."

I stood looking out of the window, with the open letter in my hand.

"Well, Strong, you haven't answered me. Shall you go, or not? What are you looking at so intently?"

Fred's voice startled me. "O yes; no, I beg your pardon! I—yes, I shall sail with you to-morrow."

The sea had been like molten glass all day, and in it the reflection of the hot sun a ball of fire. But at last the tardy wind came puffing from the west, with a fragrance suggestive of land not far below the crimson horizon. The red disk that had shimmered and glared near the vessel's side for so many hours was shaken to pieces and sprinkled over the myriad little waves that came chasing the evening breeze over the water. The white awning stretched above the hurricane deck, where I was sitting alone, glowed in the light, and the few sails in sight towards the east shone bright and strong out of a purple sky.

The voyage had been hot and uncomfortable, cloudless, and without a breath of wind, until this of to-night, which, in its cool spring odor, seemed like a message from home. And in four and twenty hours at home again I should be, with Alice and the children ; and then soon, perhaps very soon, the last six months would have dropped out of my life, to be placed on the retired list of completed episodes; thereafter, perhaps, to be run across from time to time and recognized, but not remembered over well, and with no part nor place in the present.

"Ah, no! " I thought to myself with a sigh, unconsciously playing with a little confederate coin that hung from my watch-chain. "Absurd! impossible! What has passed is indeed no episode. It is the fulness of life itself ; and the future, however long or short it may be, however much or little it may bring, must be the sequel."

I looked idly down upon our wake, that, with a ready moral, grew whiter and whiter as the shadows deepened about it, and then at the still radiant west.

It was as beautiful as that sunset at sea so long ago.

I turned away and taking an unopened letter from my pocket, broke the seal and read as follows:

"Friday Morning, *March* 27.
"My dearest Angel:

"For, thank Heaven, I may call you so at last. I have just received the answer for which I have fought so hard and long. You know better than any one how little I could have expected it. Brief as it is—and cold to a man at fever heat,—it is very sweet to me, even sweeter for the delay.

"At the very moment when there is nothing in life to which I dare look forward but the satisfaction of silencing our common enemy, your dear note comes, and under its influence my private wrongs and troubles, and they are many, are set aside, if not forgotten. I can think only of the unspeakable happiness that awaits me, and the devotion that shall in time atone for your sacrifice. For, believe me, dearest, I am not blind to what you must give up, nor shall I ever be. Thus, although the time which you have set must debar me from what yesterday I held dearer than life, I shall not question it.

"I too am capable of sacrifice, and can lay what fools call honor at your feet, as I would life itself.

"The world may censure us, while he whose interference has driven us to flight must go unpunished. The world itself will soon forget, but I shall not.

"However, this is no time for such thoughts as these.

"I shall be at the appointed place punctually at

twelve.   Have courage, and do not fail me.   Have no fears. Trust everything to me, my dearest, and, as I live, not a cloud shall dim the full sunshine of our happiness.

  " Until we meet to-night and forever,
   " Your humble and devoted servant,
     " RICHARD SHORTER."

 As I finished reading, a gust of wind blew the open letter from my hand.   I tried in vain to catch it.   For a moment it followed the ship, whirling slowly round and round in the eddy of air as it fell, until touching our wake it sped swiftly down the white pathway towards the South.

www.ingramcontent.com/pod-product-compliance
Lightning Source LLC
Chambersburg PA
CBHW021106270326

41929CB00009B/748